YEMEN

المال قاموس شعبنا [وهو] هذه الأرض التي لبى نامت عليها

قبور الأجداد ورقصت عليها مواكب الأبناء وأحفاد

عبد الله البردوني

'Our land is the dictionary of our people – this land of far
horizons where the graves of our ancestors sleep, this earth
trodden by processions of sons and sons of sons.'
  Abdullah al-Baradduni, *Funun al-adab al-sha'bi fi 'l-yaman,*
1995

'One's ideas as to the nature of Arabia are entirely upset.'
  Walter Harris, *A Journey through the Yemen,* 1893

YEMEN

Travels in Dictionary Land

Tim Mackintosh-Smith

with etchings by

Martin Yeoman

JOHN MURRAY
Albemarle Street, London

For my parents
and in memory of
Hajj Muhammad ibn Ali ibn Ali al-Sayrafi, of San'a

Contents

Illustrations

Acknowledgements

I should like to thank: Venetia Porter, Allestree Fisher and Peter Clark, for enabling me to come to Yemen in the first place; Edna O'Brien, for telling me it was a crime to be in Yemen and not write about it; Jay Butler, for getting me started; Eric Hansen, who has encouraged me all along; all those who have commented on the text, especially Claudia Cooper, Debbie Dorman, Roger Hudson, Kevin Rushby, Hasan al-Shamahi and Iain Stevenson; John Cleaver, Mike Gowman, Muhammad Ali al-Hasani, Malcolm Johnson, Wendy Lee and Brendan MacSharry, for 'logistical' support in one form or another; my agent, Carolyn Whitaker, for all her wisdom and enthusiasm; Gail Pirkis and Caroline Knox at John Murray, for indulging a book which is perhaps unfashionably digressive; Martin Yeoman, who has coped with dust, sun and melting etching plates to draw Yemen from the life as no one has before; all those who helped him come back – Dr Abdullah Basodan, the British-Yemeni Society, Heather Bull, Stephen Day, J.N. Ellis, Alan Richards, and, in particular, Francine Stone; Ali Zayd al-Ashwal and the staff of Yemen Airways, for supporting Martin so generously, and for turning a blind eye to his excess baggage; and, of course, the countless Yemenis – friends, acquaintances and strangers – whose kindness and hospitality has often been overwhelming, in particular Abdulwahhab al-Sayrafi, Hasan al-Shamahi (again), Abdulsalam al-Amri, and their families. If this book conveys something of the gratitude, respect and affection I feel for them, and for the others I have not named, it will have achieved its purpose. The Prophet Muhammad said of the Yemenis: 'They have the kindest and gentlest hearts of all. Faith is Yemeni, wisdom is Yemeni.' His words still hold true.

Bayt Qadi, San'a
April 1996

Prefatory Note

Yemeni history is at times bewilderingly complex. Although in Chapter 2 I have tried to sketch in the general lines of pre-Islamic history, I have avoided doing so for later periods so as not to overload the reader with dates and dynasties. To compensate, the Glossary includes brief notes on some of the more important rulers of Yemen; also, the Bibliography is fuller than is usual in a book of this nature. It is a book which, I admit, treads the thin line between seriousness and frivolity. If at times it veers towards the latter – as it does, for example, when I relate the more questionable anecdotes of the medieval traveller Ibn al-Mujawir – I can only repeat his near contemporary Yaqut's apologia concerning the edible monopod poets of Hadramawt: 'I have merely quoted from the books of learned men.'

In transliterating Arabic words, I have followed the most commonly accepted system but minus the macrons and subscript dots; I have omitted initial *ayns* and *hamzahs* but have retained final *ayns*; the two letters are not distinguished when they occur within a word. A few readers may find this annoying, but it makes for clearer typography. Thus, the capital city of Yemen, Ṣanʿāʾ (otherwise Sana, Sanaa and Sana'a), appears in this book as San'a. As for my rendering of Suqutri words, I apologize in advance to the half dozen or so scholars of that language for any deficiencies they may find.

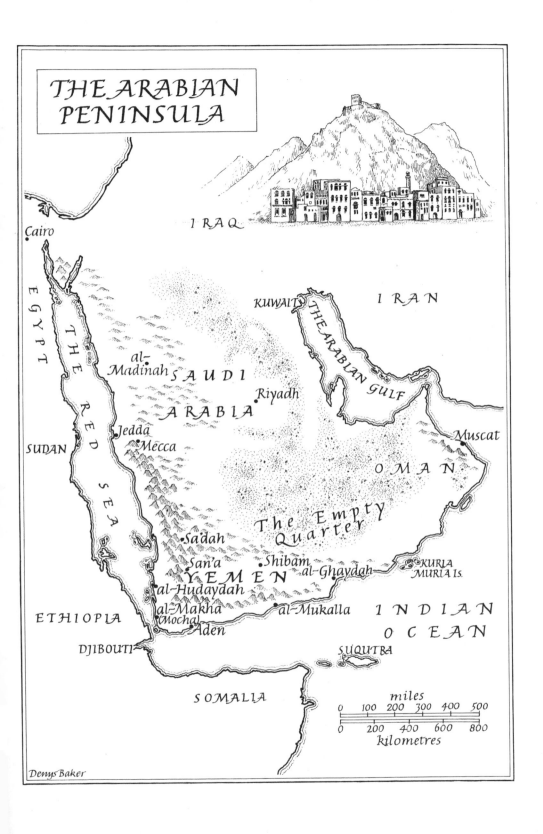

THE ARABIAN PENINSULA

Cairo

IRAQ

EGYPT

KUWAIT

IRAN

THE ARABIAN GULF

THE RED SEA

al-Madinah

SAUDI

ARABIA

Riyadh

Jedda

Mecca

SUDAN

Muscat

OMAN

The Empty Quarter

Sadah

San'a

Shibam

al-Ghaydah

KURIA MURIA Is.

YEMEN

al-Hudaydah

al-Makha (Mocha)

Aden

al-Mukalla

INDIAN

OCEAN

ETHIOPIA

DJIBOUTI

SUQUTRA

SOMALIA

miles
0   100   200   300   400   500

0   200   400   600   800
kilometres

Denys Baker

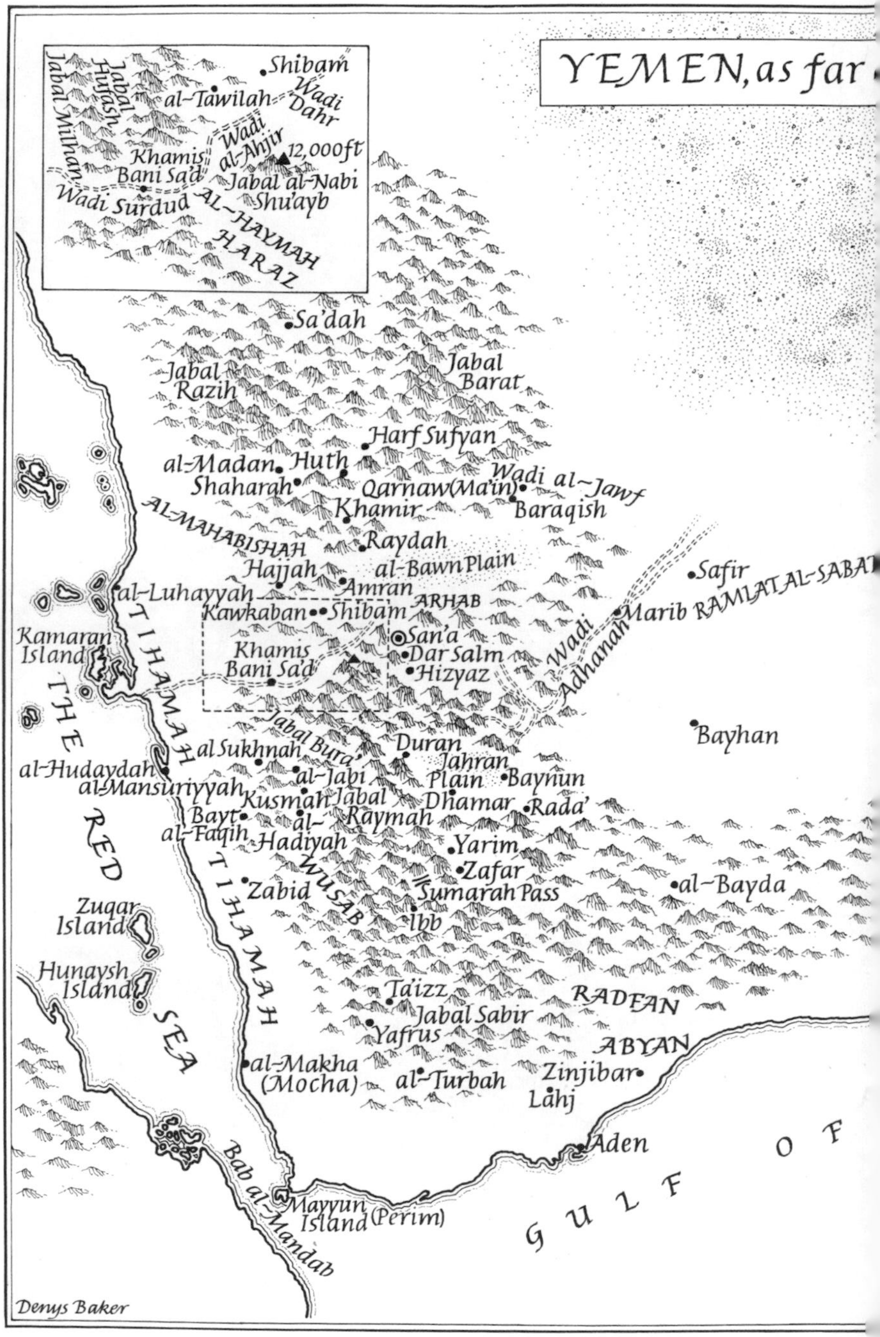
YEMEN, as far
Shibam
Wadi Dahr
al-Tawilah
Jabal Hufash
Jabal Milhan
Wadi al-Ahjir
12,000ft
Khamis Bani Sa'd
Jabal al-Nabi Shu'ayb
Wadi Surdud
AL-HAYMAH
HARAZ
Sa'dah
Jabal Razih
Jabal Barat
Harf Sufyan
al-Madan
Huth
Shaharah
Qarnaw (Ma'in)
Wadi al-Jawf
Baraqish
Khamir
AL-MAHABISHAH
Raydah
al-Bawn Plain
Hajjah
Amran
Safir
al-Luhayyah
ARHAB
Marib
RAMLAT AL-SABA
Kawkaban
Shibam
Kamaran Island
San'a
Dar Salm
Hizyaz
Wadi Adhanah
Khamis Bani Sa'd
TIHAMAH
THE RED SEA
Bayhan
Jabal Bura'
Duran
al-Sukhnah
al-Hudaydah
al-Jabi
Jahran Plain
Baynun
al-Mansuriyyah
Kusmah
Jabal Raymah
Dhamar
Rada'
Bayt al-Faqih
al-Hadiyah
Yarim
WUSAB
Zafar
Zabid
Sumarah Pass
al-Bayda
Ibb
Zuqar Island
Hunaysh Island
Ta'izz
Jabal Sabir
RADFAN
Yafrus
ABYAN
al-Makha (Mocha)
al-Turbah
Zinjibar
Lahj
Aden
Bab al-Mandab
Mayyun Island (Perim)
GULF OF
Denys Baker

Western Mahrah

THE EMPTY

QUARTER

AL-MAHRAH

Bir Barhut
Wadi Hadramawt • Hisn al-Urr
Tarim •Qabr al-Nabi Hud
Shibam •Aynat
Sayun • Wadi al-Masilah
Qishn
Huraydah Mawla al-Ayn• •Itab
habwah al-Hajarayn AL-JAWL Sayhut
Wadi Rakhyah

al-Hami
Shuhayr• •al-Shihr
•al-Mukalla

Bir Ali/Qana

ADEN
and
environs

al-Shaykh Uthman

Balhaf

Madinat al-Shab
(People's City)

Khur
Maksar
Sawayih Wall
(Slave/Workers) Jabal
Island Hadid
Back
Bay Hujuf al-Maalla
Steamer al-Tawwahi Sirah
DEN Little Point
Aden Aden Crater
Tanks Jabal Ra's
Elephant's Shamsan Marshaq
Back

| 0 | 50 | 100 | 150 | 200 miles |

| 0 | 50 | 100 | 150 | 300 kilometres |

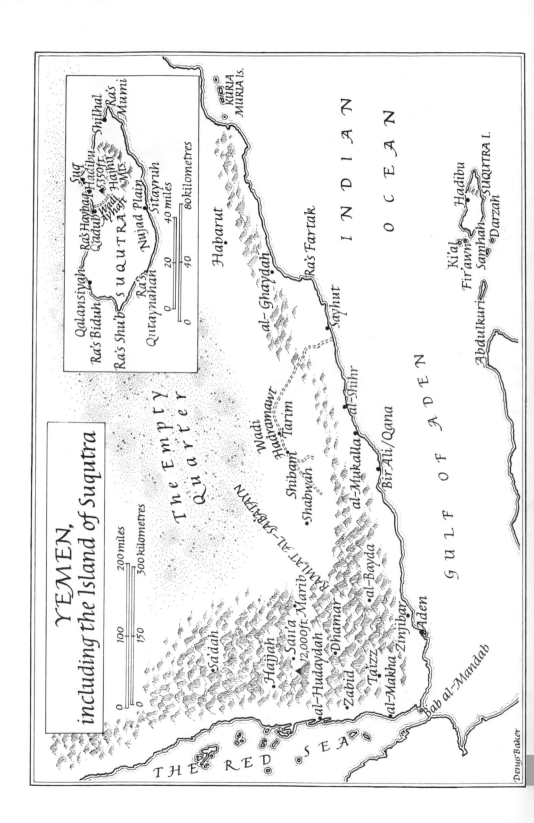

YEMEN,
including the Island of Suqutra

THE RED SEA

THE EMPTY QUARTER

Sa'dah
Hajjah
Sau'a
12,000ft. Marib
al-Hudaydah
Dhamar
Zabid
al-Bayda
Ta'izz
al-Makha
Zinjibar
Aden
Bab al-Mandab

GULF OF ADEN

Wadi Hadramawt
Tarim
Shibam
Shabwah
RAMLAT AL-SAB'ATAYN
al-Mukalla
al-Shihr
Bir Ali/Qana

Habarut
al-Ghaydah
Ras Fartak
Sayhut

INDIAN OCEAN

KIRIA MURIA Is.

Ki'al
Fir'awn
Abdulkuri
Hadibu
Samhah
Darzah
SUQUTRA I.

100   200 miles
150   300 kilometres
0

Denys Baker

Inset map (Suqutra):

Qalansiyah
Ras Bidah
Ras Shub
Ras Qutaynahan
Ras Hayban
Qadub
Suq
Hadibu
Wadi Ayhaft
1,550 ft.
Hajhir Mts.
Shihal
Ras Mumi
SUQUTRA
Nujad Plain
Sitayruh

0   20   40 miles
0   40   80 kilometres

Introduction

'A definition is the enclosing of a wilderness of idea within a wall of words.'

Samuel Butler, *Notebooks*

THE RAIN BEAT DOWN. Horns rasped against the door: a sheep trying to get in. I didn't blame it – spring was late in the Isle of Harris and it was cosy inside, all peat smoke and roll-ups. An easterly gale was whistling across the Sound from Skye and flinging sackfuls of hail at the tin roof of the croft house. The noise was deafening.

You have to be somewhere quiet like Harris in the early stages of learning Arabic, somewhere you can walk around unheard, muttering strange, strangulated syllables, limbering up minute and never-used muscles of tongue and glottis. I got up to make tea. '*Hhha*'!' I said to the matches when I found them; '*Ghghgha*'!' when they refused to light. ' '' I mouthed to the hooded crow on the fence outside the window; that innocent-looking sign represented the trickiest letter of all, 'a guttural stop pronounced with constriction of the larynx', my grammar said. The hoodie croaked back and flapped off to peck out lambs' eyes.

The fire let out a rich belch of smoke. I threw on another sod of peat and drew up a chair. Cowan's *Modern Literary Arabic* lay open at 'The Dual' (not content with mere singulars and plurals, Arabic also has a form for pairs): 'The two beautiful queens', it said, 'are ignorant.' The odds against ever uttering the sentence were high: grammars, like theatre, call for a suspension of disbelief. Under Cowan was an Arabic reader produced for British officers in the Palestine Mandate. At the bottom of the pile, as yet untouched,

I

was a dictionary. I reached for it and looked at the title page. The dictionary had been compiled for the use of students and published *Ad Majorem Dei Gloriam* by the Catholic Press, Beirut, in 1915. As I turned its foxed pages, I broke through the wall of words into a wilderness of idea. It was another world, a surreal lexical landscape whose inhabitants lived in a state of relentless metamorphosis.

Over there was a *zabab*, 'a messenger' or possibly 'a huge deaf rat', while in the distance grazed a *na'amah*, 'an ostrich', although it might have been 'a signpost', 'a pavilion on a mountain' or even 'a membrane of the brain'. Nearer to hand someone was *maljan*, 'sucking his she-camels out of avarice'; he'd be in for a shock if he had *istanwaq* them, 'mistaken male camels for she-camels'. He could just be suffering from *sada*, 'thirst', also 'a voice', 'an echo', 'a corpse', 'a brain' or 'an owl'. Maybe his well was *makul*, 'holding little water and much slime'. He was in a bad mood so I passed on quickly, worried that he might *tarqa* me, 'strike me upon the clavicle'.

In Dictionary Land you could come across a *malit*, 'a featherless arrow' or 'a hairless abortive foetus'. That, at least, showed a clear semantic link. So did *firash*, 'a mat/wife', and *siffarah*, 'an anus/whistle/fife'. But other entries defied rational explanation, seeming no more than the word-associations of a hopeless headcase: you could take your *qutrub*, your 'puppy/demon/restless insect/melancholia', for a walk; *qarurah* could be 'the apple of one's eye', also 'a urinal'. With a single verb, *nakha'*, you could both 'slay someone' and 'bear them sincere friendship'; with another, *istawsham*, you could 'look for a tattooist'; and if you were a calligrapher, you could be adept at *yayyaya*, 'forming a beautiful letter *ya*' – perhaps thus: ‿ّ. On the culinary side, you might be *akra'*, 'fond of trotters' or 'thin in the shank', while with the verb *karrash* you could 'contract your face' or 'prepare a haggis'; the latter could be accompanied by a helping of *wahisah*, 'a dish made of locusts and grease', and washed down by *adasiyah*, an 'aromatized soup of lentils' or 'bat-dung used as a medicine'. *Alkhan* doubled for 'a rotten walnut' and 'a stinking uncircumcised person'. The sounds of Dictionary Land included *inqad*, 'the squeaking of eagles/the noise of fingers being cracked/the smacking of lips to call goats' or even 'the noise made by truffles being extracted'. The truffles might be of a species called *faswat al-dab'*, also the name for a kind of poppy and, rendered literally, 'the noiseless flatulence of a male hyena'.

Somebody once said that every Arabic word means itself, its opposite or a camel.* But to me the world of the *qamus*, the dictionary (or 'ocean'), was even more bizarre. To do it justice called for the descriptive faculties of the pre-Islamic poet Ta'abbata Sharra, whose name means He Who Carried An Evil Under His Armpit. And this dictionary was a shadow of Lane's, which in ten folio volumes over a period of thirty-four years only got as far as the letter *qaf*. Lane's was based on works like *The Bridal Tiara* of al-Zabidi, the great Yemeni-educated lexicographer and a contemporary of Dr Johnson. As a small boy I used to stare for hours at the fanciful oriental watercolours on my grandmother's walls; dreamed recurrently of flying over desert encampments in a telephone box; was shown, by my father, a strange, misshapen red globule which he produced from his bureau and said was the blood of an Arabian dragon. Now, out of these pages, the exotic beckoned once more, and I was hooked.

The door opened. I turned round, expecting to see a black woolly face, or a Person from Porlock; but it was Roddy, the person from next door. He had been out gathering his flock and was soaked. A bottle stuck out of his poacher's pocket.

'Och, you've let the fire burn out.' He looked briefly at the dictionary, sighed and snapped it shut. 'Let's have a drop of the Grouse.'

★

The vision was not shattered – just temporarily blurred. Time and again in the years that followed, some verbal curiosity or weirdness of phrase would sidetrack me out of the corridors of the Oxford Oriental Institute and back into Dictionary Land.

'I didn't get the drift of lines 66–7. Could you, er . . . ?'

'"Verily I have seen upon your mandibles the belly- and tail-fat of a lizard./ Your words reveal the buttocks of your meanings."'

'I'm sorry?'

---

* For example, *rash*, 'to eat much/to eat little/a camel hairy behind the ears'.

'"*Your words reveal the buttocks of your meanings.*"'
'Oh.'
They taught us abstruse and arcane mysteries, how to compound the base elements of syntax into glittering and highly wrought prose. We were apprentices in a linguistic alchemy. And, like alchemy, Arabic seemed to be half science and two-thirds magic. The Arabs themselves are spellbound by their language. Look at the effect on them of the Qur'an: the Word – divinely beautiful, terrifying, tear-inducing, spine-tingling, mesmerizing, inimitable – was sufficient in itself. It did not need to become flesh. But Qur'anic Arabic is only one manifestation of the language. You can be preacher, poet, raconteur and fishwife in a single sentence. You can, with the Arabic of official reports, say next to nothing in a great many words and with enormous elegance. You can compose a work of literature on the two lateral extremities of the wrist-bone. You can even be cured of certain ailments by procuring a magic chit, infusing the ink out of it, and drinking the water: word-power at its most literal. They taught us all this, but they didn't teach us how to speak it. After two years of Arabic I couldn't even have asked the way to the lavatory.

★

My tutor spun round from his computer screen. '*Yemen?* Why do you want to go *there?*'

It must have been a shock. Usually only a truly major disaster, a wrong case-ending or a misplaced definite article, would unstick him from his corpus of Andalusian erotic verse.

'I . . . I met a Yemeni who said Yemeni Arabic was the closest dialect to Classical.'

He smiled a painfully long smile like the rictus on a ventriloquist's dummy. 'They all say that, you stupid boy. *Yemen.*' His mouth puckered around the word as if it were some disagreeably bitter fruit. *Lemon.* 'Why don't you go somewhere *respectable* . . . Cairo, Amman, Tunis?'

Cairo was out, a bedlam of smog, smugness and touts where the last Wonder of the World was disintegrating under acid rain and tourists' feet. Amman, I had been told, was the most boring city in the Arab world. Tunis was, well, *complexée*.

In fact I'd lied. I'd never knowingly set eyes on a real live Yemeni. But I felt that my tutor would find the true reason for my demanding a sabbatical in Yemen even less palatable. Some years before, the Museum of Mankind in London had recreated a corner of the market of San'a, the Yemeni capital, as part of Britain's World of Islam Festival. Yards from Piccadilly was a secret, labyrinthine microcosm of the *suq*. Even its sounds and smells were reproduced. The swiftness of transposition was unreal, although little more so than the ten-hour flight from London to San'a. The exhibition wasn't Yemen, but over the years it became a Yemen of the imagination which I peopled with faces seen in books: faces which were proud but not arrogant, grave but not severe, delicate but not weak, their eyes intensified by kohl and calligraphic eyebrows.

My reading revealed that others, too, had been bewitched by Yemen. 'Never', wrote one medieval visitor, 'have I seen glances more penetrating than those of the Yemenis. When they look at you, they dive into you . . . ' Many references, however, were hardly complimentary. Yemen was seen as at best a backwater, more usually as backward. For example, a Yemeni who had been extolling his country at court in eighth-century Baghdad was attacked thus: 'What are you Yemenis? I'll tell you. You're nothing but tanners of hides, weavers of striped shirting, trainers of monkeys and riders of nags. You were drowned by a rat and ruled by a woman, and people had never even heard of Yemen until a hoopoe told them about it!'* I was not put off. My first glimpse of Yemen had been at far too impressionable an age.

Besides, Yemen – the Yemen I was seeing at second hand – had something of Dictionary Land about it: as well as the talking hoopoes and dambusting rodents, men chewed leaves and camels lived on fish; they (the men) wore pinstriped lounge-suit jackets on top, skirts below, and wicked curved daggers in the middle; the cities seemed to have been baked, not built, of iced gingerbread;

---

* The jibe refers to two of Yemen's traditional crafts, and to the baboons which live in its mountains. The remark about nags is unfair – Yemeni horses were held in high esteem. The rat was the one said to have gnawed away at the great Marib Dam and caused its collapse. The woman was the biblical Queen of Sheba/Saba, who the Qur'an says was brought to Solomon's attention by a talking hoopoe.

Yemen was part of Arabia but the landscape looked like . . . well, nowhere else on Earth, and definitely not Arabia.

In the end my tutor relented, even gave me his blessing – though he warned me not to be away too long. So I set out to explore Dictionary Land on the ground; and perhaps, eventually, to understand the people who lived in it.

I've been there ever since.

I

Hard by Heaven

'Thou coveredst it with the deep like as with a garment: the waters stand in the hills.'

Psalm 104, v.3

Long ago, shortly after the waters of the Flood had begun to recede and the Himalayas, the Andes and the Alps were still islands on the face of the deep, some two-thirds of the way along a line from Everest to Kilimanjaro and just inside the Tropic of Cancer, a few eddies marked Arabia's re-entry into the world.

It was not a dramatic rebirth – the Mountain of the Prophet Shu'ayb is an unremarkable hump. Shu'ayb himself was still seventeen generations off; by his time mankind would be back to its wicked old ways. But for the moment it was a clean start, the world an empty stage.

Enter Sam. Sam ibn Nuh, or Shem the son of Noah, knew that the future of humanity lay in his loins and in those of his brothers Ham and Yafith. He was to beget and give his name to the entire Semitic race: perhaps it was the weight of this awesome responsibility which, the medieval traveller Ibn al-Mujawir says, he wished to alleviate by finding a place 'with light water and a temperate healthy climate'. This stony and windswept mountain would not do, but 4,500 feet below and half a day's journey to the south-east was a plain ringed by rocky peaks, where the flood had left a rich layer of silt.

This was the spot. Sam bounded down the mountain and

7

pegged out a foundation trench, only to have his guideline stolen by a bird. The bird flew off with the line and dropped it on the east side of the plain. To Sam, this was a clear sign. So it was there, on the future site of the Palace of Ghumdan, under the rising of Taurus with Venus and Mars in conjunction, that he came to build the world's first city: San'a.

Elsewhere, the receding floodwater had revealed a chain of mountains running from north to south, broken by occasional hollows and plateaux where, as in the plain of San'a, alluvial deposits would attract settlers. To the west and south the mountains ended abruptly in jagged escarpments overlooking plains; the plains lay just above sea-level and were hot and sticky but more fertile still. Eastwards, the mountains shelved into a desert which, even when Sam's progeny had multiplied, would remain empty except for outlaws and oilmen. Far to the south-east and close to the desert's fringe was a deep scar of a valley, hemmed in by barren steppes, where one of Sam's descendants would settle, giving it his nickname Hadramawt – Death Has Come.

So the veil was drawn back from the rucked-up corner of Arabia called Yemen, being on the right side, *yamin*, of the Ka'bah of Mecca; or because it is blessed with *yumn*, felicity; or after Yamin the brother of Hadramawt.

All this, some say, is nonsense. Around the beginning of the Christian era San'a grew from an outpost where the road from Marib, capital of the ancient kingdom of Saba, meets the watershed; Hadramawt is just another pre-Arabic name, the traditional etymology a fanciful back-projection; Yemen, *al-yaman*, simply means 'the south'.

The truth is that Yemen's distant past is still obscure. Archaeology has hardly begun to come up with solid facts. Early Yemeni historians, though, produced their own interpretation using genealogy. At the base of the family tree comes Sam. Higher up is Sam's great-grandson, the Prophet Hud. Hud's son Qahtan is at the top of the trunk, and from him spring all the South Arabian tribes, branching across the map of Yemen and beyond. In the process, the names of people and places have become inextricably intertwined: the family tree has grown luxuriantly, fed by the genealogists on a rich mulch of eponyms and toponyms. To get to know Yemen as the Yemenis see it means clambering around this tree, one which spreads vertically through time and horizontally through space. History and geography, people and land, are inseparable.

The new school of historians are doing a hatchet-job on the family tree, questioning the very existence of the traditional ancestors. But in the end it hardly matters who is right. Whether Qahtan – the central figure, the South Arabian progenitor – was an actual person or not, he represents a people who share a distinctive culture, one which has lasted for at least three thousand years.

As for the story of Sam, even if it is a legend, it is the South Arabians' Genesis.

★

My landfall in San'a was more prosaic than Sam's. The Ethiopian Boeing lurched and creaked its way down through layers of turbulence. For the last couple of minutes before landing, the plane circled over the city. It was not as I had expected.

Like those desert plants which grow suddenly after decades of suspended animation, San'a had shot out suckers, tentacles of development. In the past, arrival had always been through its gates; the principal entrance, Bab al-Yaman, had come to be seen as an architectural statement of the city's famed introversion, emphasized perhaps by a row of severed traitors' heads along the parapet, its gates shut at night, putting a stop to all movement. Now you arrived along roads of half-finished buildings. The statement of entry had been upstaged by a preamble of petrol stations.

I was afraid that San'a, with the dissipation of its dramatic presence, might have lost something of its soul. But, just as Ingres had conjured up the East in his Paris studio – and sanitized it, giving us the odalisques but not the odours, the eunuchs but not the screams of castration – so I had invented San'a in Oxford. The mistake had been to think of it as a museum.

Today, the ribbons of building have joined into an all-but seamless urban weave. San'a is busy, at times frenetic. It suffers from traffic jams and lack of planning. But it is lively, diverse and – even with the country's current economic difficulties – still prosperous. What I had imagined to be the timeless calm of an ancient walled city was stagnation, a comatose sleep ended by the brute kiss of revolution.

In the Old City the heart still beats. The noise of al-Zumur, the quarter named after a mosque founded in 1547 by Uzdimir Pasha, the Ottoman conqueror of San'a, pulsates outside the front door: car horns, motor-cycle taxis, two egg-sellers competing with loudhailers, the cassette shop across the road, the crackle and pop of roasting black peas. Yesterday there was a man with wild hair and a drum extemporizing songs, lays of old Baghdad (not about Harun al-Rashid, but Saddam Husayn and his adversary, George Bush: 'O would that I were a bird,' says Saddam. 'For I would land on Bush's head and . . .' – the crowd is in suspense – '. . . *and shit on it!*'). And last Ramadan, every day before the sunset prayer, a fettered man would call for alms beneath my window; a taxi driver who had crashed, he was in gaol until he could collect the blood-money for his dead passengers. His insurance policy had been with God; now, coin by coin, the Faithful were paying out his claim. The sounds all float up from four floors below, a distraction to writing. So, San'ani houses being tall, I'll move up another couple.

From here the ring of mountains surrounding the San'a plain can be seen in full; a tradition says they flew from Sinai to Yemen in shock when Moses asked to see the face of God. Over there is the place where Sam first began building, and through the other window is Jabal Nuqum, near the base of which the bird dropped his guideline. Even this is hardly the best place to be writing, this belvedere on the roof; it is too easy to get carried away by the skyline of which you are a part. But up here, among the birds and the occasional flying plastic bag, street noises are far away, and you could be sitting in a jewelled casket – the room is tiny, eight feet by five, and lit by coloured glass windows. It is sometimes called a *zahrah* – in the dictionary, 'a flower/beauty/brightness'. My house is a few centuries old but the changeless style of San'ani architecture makes it hard to date. Only yards away a man is putting the final cursive plaster frieze on to a similar room, hanging on a swing above the chasm of the street. Behind him the dust is beginning to obscure Jabal Ayban and the road to the sea. A west wind is blowing up, banging the shutters. And with it comes the call to prayer – not the effete recorded invitation of other lands but a live,

human roar: COME AND PRAY! – gusting across Yemen from Zabid to Zinjibar, from Hizyaz to Habarut and all the way to Suqutra, the Island of Dragon's Blood off the Horn of Africa.

I must go down and pick up some more cigarettes, down the seventy-seven (I think) steps into the dark entrance hall. I slide back the bolt of the massive door and light and noise and piles of alfalfa tumble in – my neighbour sells the plant for fodder, along-side jars of marigolds, roses, basil and rue. She is veiled and wrapped in a *sitarah*, a large blue and red cloak like a tablecloth. Next to her a man from the Red Sea coast has tobacco from the other side of al-Mukalla on the Indian Ocean; then a boy with a headscarf full of walnuts from Hajjah, in the mountains north-west of San'a. In front of them is a line of barrows, some with oranges, some with plastic shoes, some with knives, razors, nailclippers, torches and mechanical drumming monkeys. Across the street are the secondhand clothes sellers. All the synthetic textile wealth of the Far East is here in a mêlée of colours and patterns. Behind the clothes is a row of gold shops, tarts' parlours of 22-carat glitter set off by pink and peach velvet walls and more mirrors than a hair-dresser's. The *sharshaf* maker, who runs up a ladies' all-enveloping outer garment of Ottoman origin (any colour as long as it's black, any number of pleats as long as they froufrou), adds a sober note, a crow among peacocks.

The secondhand clothes sellers are a long way from the subfusc mustiness of an Oxfam shop. They are lost in a maelstrom of flying cloth and brown forearms thrusting from under *sitarahs*, glinting with gold bangles. Only the man selling platform shoes is alone. Menswear is often startling, with lots of fake fur and checks that shriek, but I've picked up a dove-grey jacket lined in scarlet which could have been from Huntsman of Savile Row, except for the stitching. Another find was a smart barathea tailcoat. I tried it on but it was tiny, shrunk by the sea and cast up on a beach from a 1930s P&O liner gone down in the Gulf of Aden, the dance band playing 'Eternal Father, Strong to Save' as the sharks of al-Shihr scented the supper of their lives . . . Well, maybe.

One day I saw on the street something that stopped me dead. It was a piece of clothing as familiar to me as my own body, but translated into another sartorial idiom. A boy was wearing it over a *zannah*, an ankle-length shirt, and a miniature *jambiyah*, a curved dagger. He was scuffing a deflated football along. I called him to stop. There it was, grey flannel with navy piping and a fleur-de-lis on the breast pocket: my prep-school blazer.

I looked inside. 'Steer & Geary Gentlemen's Outfitters'. There was the ghost of an inkstain on the pocket, where my birthday

Parker had sprung a leak in 1972. The space for the name-tape was empty.

As he kicked the ball away a wave of nostalgia flooded over me. It passed, leaving behind a strange, deep stillness of spirit. It was the calm of completeness, of the wheel turning full circle, of being in the right place at the right time.

★

If that had been an intimation of spiritual completion, a later experience, in San'a Airport customs shed, provided a fair simulacrum of Limbo. The place is a vast metal box, echoing with cries of supplication – owners begging for the redemption of their goods. To get to it I had to cross a great Stygian lake where the city's sewage had bubbled up.

Inside the shed I found the crate containing my motor cycle. It had come here via Addis Ababa and appeared to be in one piece. I gave it a pat and made for the low buildings which house the Customs *mas'ulin*, the responsibles – literally, those who are asked questions. To get in I waved a piece of paper, the central portion of which was a typewritten request to import the machine into Yemen, addressed to the Director of Customs. Over the weeks it had sprouted marginalia, each ending with the enigmatic squiggle which in Arabic passes for a signature.

On my first visit to the Customs Authority I had buttonholed the Director as he was getting out of his car. Using the wing as a writing-desk and with a flourish of his costly pen, he wrote what I eventually deciphered as: 'No objection. For the attention of the Secretariat.' Beginner's luck. The Head of the Secretariat had no objection either and with a second marginalium – written with a less costly but still desirable pen – passed the matter on to the Head of External Affairs. In External Affairs it was the same story: no objection, refer to another department. I noticed that the lower the position in the hierarchy, the more complex the signature became. At the same time the pens decreased in quality until, in a nameless department where bottom-drawer bureaucrats sat reading the newspaper or practising their signatures, someone was persuaded to write something with a chewed and leaking biro. By now, time was beginning to distort: I had been in Customs for a good part of each working day for a fortnight. Where could they refer the case to now? Only the tea boy hadn't been consulted. I looked at the latest addition to the document. 'No objection. For the attention of Director of Customs.' The buck, it seemed, was in perpetual – and slow – motion. Like the Buddhist soul, it had described a complete circle while the officials were reincarnated in ever lowlier forms. As I left the office my eye caught the main front-page headline of a newspaper: 'Minister of Civil Service and Administrative Reform Calls for Immediate Shake-Up.' The paper was a month old.

As a last, desperate ploy, I returned in a suit and tie, the letter in a smart imitation leather attaché case, and headed for the Director's office. Over the past two weeks, a bond of camaraderie had grown between us co-petitioners, but now the disconsolate men squatting by doorways didn't recognize me. The soldier on the door of the Director's antechamber cleared a way through the crowd. I entered the sanctum sanctorum, the eye of the storm. The few people in the room addressed the Director in hushed voices. The costly pen glided.

My turn came. 'You may remember me . . .'

'Ah,' he interrupted, smiling. 'The man with the fiery bicycle.'

Everyone else called it a *mutur*, even if fiery bicycle was what you used in written Arabic. The Director leaned back and stroked his moustache. 'Their importation into Yemen is prohibited.'

I recited to myself the mantra of a British Resident Adviser to one of the sultans of Hadramawt in colonial days: Never get angry, be quiet, very quiet, speak and act softly. 'I may be mistaken, but you have already written "No objection". I beg to be allowed the honour of contributing to the exchequer by paying duty. Besides, there are thousands of fiery bicycles in San'a. Indeed, I came here today on a fiery bicycle taxi.' I paused. No sign of softening. I went on: 'But perhaps that was an illusion. Perhaps I, who appeared to be moving so swiftly and noisily through the traffic, was in reality riding on air and', I looked out of the window, 'farting.'

The Director snorted. I looked at him and saw he was laughing. He wrote in the last empty bit of margin, 'No objection. Refer to Airport Customs Department. Calculate sum due.' I had broken out of the circle, achieved a minor nirvana.

At Airport Customs, I watched the responsible concerned make his calculations. The process seemed to be based not on simple addition but on logarithms and exponentiality. The sum due was thirty thousand *riyals*.

He saw my dumbstruck look, crossed out the three and wrote a two. 'Is that better?'

I said I was most grateful, but it still seemed a lot for two wheels. He scrubbed out the whole figure and wrote fifteen thousand. 'Happy now?' Such transactions are like painting in watercolour or cutting hair: go too far and the thing is ruined. I said I was delighted and left, clutching the papers.

★

If the customs shed is Limbo, then Ali's Restaurant is a foretaste of Hell. 'The San'anis possess culinary skills unsurpassed in any other land,' wrote the great tenth-century historian and geographer al-Hamdani. Measured against the rest of the Arabian Peninsula, the comment is true: San'a has an old and indigenous cuisine. My lunch was the same as that described by Ibn al-Mujawir in the thirteenth century: wheat bread, *hulbah* – fenugreek flour whisked to a froth with water – and meat. Ali himself stands in a cloud of smoke on a platform high above the ground, ladling beef broth, eggs, rice and peppers into a row of stone bowls. In front of him is a rank of cauldrons, each one big enough to boil a missionary. Below him minions tend gas cylinders that send great blasts of flame shooting up. Conversations are impossible in the roar; explosions are not unknown. The bowl of *saltah*, as they call the mixture, is brought to you red-hot, carried with a pair of pliers and topped with a seething yellowish-green dollop of *hulbah*. Lumps of meat are flambéed in a wok-like vessel, and ten feet above this the ceiling is black from years of fireballs. Men squat on the floor, on benches, on tables (the ones in suits and ties are from the Foreign Ministry across the road). Those who have not yet been served wail and shriek for attention – '*Ya Ali! Ya Alayyy!*' – while Ali stands, erect and unhearing, his body immobile within a parabola of arms – all his own, like those of a Hindu idol. The lucky ones who have been served eat with the *saltah* spitting in their faces, sweat pouring from their brows. The walls are covered with a huge photographic

mural of the gardens at Versailles: parterres, statues of nymphs, cooling fountains.

Lunch at Ali's is not merely a matter of eating. It is the first step on the way to *kayf*. The meaning of the term has been discussed by Sir Richard Burton. One might call it, he wrote, 'The savouring of animal existence . . . the result of a lively, impressible, excitable nature, and exquisite sensibility of nerve; it argues a facility for voluptuousness unknown to northern regions . . .'; but in the end the translator of *The Arabian Nights* admitted defeat: *kayf* is 'a word untranslatable in our mother tongue'. Lexicographers, who cannot be so realistic, have described it as a mood, humour or frame of mind. I, who chew the leaf of the *qat* tree, shall attempt a definition.

Ali's Restaurant is all to do with the humours. Blood, phlegm, yellow and black bile must be in balance to ensure perfect health and to enable the *qat* chewer to attain his goal of *kayf*; since *qat* excites the cold and dry black bile, prophylaxis against its ill effects means that the blood, which is hot and wet, must be stimulated. Hence the heat, the sweat, the bubbling *saltah*. Hence also the visits to the public baths before chewing *qat*, the insistence on keeping windows and doors shut during chewing, the elaborate precautions to avoid the dreaded *shanini* – a piercing and potentially fatal draught of cold air.

An old joke illustrates this obsession with heat. The angels, it is said, periodically visit Hell to make sure the fires are turned up. One day a group of them are detailed to check on the really wicked sinners, who spend eternity in individual ovens. Inside the first oven is a Saudi. He screams to be let out. Roasting nicely, they think, and slam the door on him. In the next oven is an Englishman; then come an American, an Egyptian and so on. All beg to be let out, but the angels show them no mercy. Eventually they open the last door. Inside sits a Yemeni, chewing *qat* and apparently oblivious of the flames around him. He draws languidly on his water-pipe, turns to the angels, and says: 'Hey, could you shut that door? I'll catch my death of cold.'

The other day – it might, in fact, have been almost any day – I had lunch at Ali's then bought my *qat* from blue-eyed Muhammad across the road. He swore I wasn't giving him what he'd paid for it (the oaths of *qat* sellers are notoriously unbinding). I argued. 'All right,' he said, 'take it for nothing. A present.' I folded some more notes, stuck them behind his dagger, and walked off with my purchase. Wrangling over the price is part of the business of working up a sweat. (Real *mawla'is* – that is, those 'inflamed with passion' for *qat* – used to run half way up Jabal Nuqum, singing, before they chewed.) It was half past two and I was ready to start. My molar, as they say, was hot.

In a house in the centre of San'a, I climbed the stairs to another room on a roof, grander than my own. On the way up, I called 'Allah, Allah,' to warn women of my presence. Perhaps I should make the point here, if it needs to be made, that this is a very male book. As a man I am excluded from the society of women, as they are from that of men. Outsiders tend to see this dual, parallel system as a form of repression. The idea never occurs to most Yemeni women. They know that they wield power in many spheres, notably in the choice of marriage partners which, given an endogamous system, is a major influence on the distribution of wealth. Women play only a small role in the public domain, as they did in the West until quite recently; at least in Yemen, in contrast to Saudi Arabia, women are able to drive cars, enter Parliament, become top-ranking civil servants. But it is in the private realm of the home that the woman dominates, in practice if not in theory; men often gather to chew *qat* together because their homes have been taken over by visiting women.

The veil, so overlaid with symbolic meaning for Westerners, is for Yemeni women just another item of dress. If it is not essential as protection against the cold, then neither are stockings, bras or neckties. Casual Western observers, for whom the black *sharshaf* is a dehumanizer and who equate the veil with a gag, are allowing an obsession with symbolism to pull the wool over their own eyes. Underlying the use of hair- or face-coverings there are, of course, Arab-Islamic concepts of honour and modesty which the West does not share or has lost. The question of *what* to conceal – face, breasts, ankles, the legs of a grand piano – is not a question of sense but of sensibilities. The Turkey merchant Sir Henry Blount wrote in the seventeenth century of the Turks that they live 'by another kind of civilitie, different from ours, but no less pretending'. His message has yet to get across. The veil is indeed a potent symbol, but a symbol of the unwillingness or inability of the West to understand the Arab world. The Iron Curtain has been and gone; the muslin curtain still hangs, and probably always will.

Panting from the ascent, I slipped off my shoes and entered the room. It was rectangular, with windows on all sides which began a foot above the floor. Above them were semicircular fanlights of coloured glass. Into the tracery of the fanlights, and in the plaster of the walls and shelf-brackets, were worked the names of God and the Prophet, and verses of a pious nature – it was a very legible room. Polished brass gleamed everywhere: rosewater sprinklers, incense-burners, spittoons with little crocheted covers, the great circular tray with its three water-pipes. Low mattresses covered with Afghan runners lined the walls. About a dozen men were sitting on them, leaning on armrests topped with little cloth-of-gold cushions.

I greeted the chewers, interrupting their *zabj*, the rapid banter, the swordplay of insults that starts all the best *qat* sessions. I'd scarcely sat down when an old man opposite turned on me.

'I was in Sa'wan this morning, and I saw this Jew. And, do you know, he looked just like you. You could have been twins!'

'But . . . but I haven't got any side-locks,' I parried feebly. Jewish Yemenis are required to advertise their religion by cultivating a pair of long corkscrew ringlets.

'Ah,' he went on, 'you know what they say: "Jewishness is in the heart, not in the length of the side-locks."'

I made a feint to gain time: 'Tell me: exactly how many side-locks did this Jew of Sa'wan have?'

'What do you mean? Two, of course.'

'Well, it's a funny thing, but I saw a Jew in the *qat* market today and he looked exactly like you. You could have been twins. But he had four side-locks . . .'

After half an hour of this verbal fencing, the *zabj* lost its momentum and devolved into solo joke telling.

'Once', someone said, 'there was a blind girl. She was twenty-five years old and longing for a husband; but whenever she brought the subject up with her father he'd say, "My daughter, you are blind. No one wants you. But don't worry – you'll find a husband in Paradise." Well, one day she was up on the roof hanging out the washing when she tripped and fell, down and down, six storeys. By chance she fell into a lorry carrying bananas and was knocked unconscious. The lorry drove on. Ten minutes later she came to. Ah, she thought, I am dead. Then, as she felt the bananas, she remembered what her father had told her and gave a little shriek: "Slowly, slowly, men of Paradise! Please, take your turn!"'

And many more in the same vein. Yemenis, and particularly San'anis, are a mixture of earth and polish, in contrast to their dour Saudi cousins of Najd and the unspeakably polite Levantine. Their contradictory nature was explained by al-Hamdani as the result of the conjunction of Venus and Mars when Sam founded their city: the Venusian aspects, he says, are 'religiosity, faithfulness, upright living, breadth of character, soundness in body, knowledge, poetry and dress, ease of living, and many other such qualities'; the in-fluence of Mars imparts 'a surfeit of passion, adultery, frivolity, fondness for music, singing and unseemly jokes, quarrelsomeness, and a tendency to mess about with knives and allow themselves to be henpecked'. As for the women of San'a, while they are 'incomparably beautiful, swift and graceful', they are also 'prone to jealousy, coquettish and forward'.

Weightier matters are discussed at *qat* chews, and they are a major forum for the transaction of business and for religious and political debate. Many people also chew to aid concentration on study or work, and *qat* is the inevitable accompaniment to all important occasions from weddings to funerals. A funeral chew is known as *mujabarah*, a word which also means 'the setting of broken bones'. But at the classic San'ani chew, it is 'lightness of blood' – charm, amiability – that is admired, not gravitas. At a *qat* chew, one walks what a ninth-century poet called 'the sword-edge that separates the serious from the frivolous'.

My *qat* was good, a Hamdani from Tuzan. *Qat* is a dicotyledon known to science as *Catha edulis*. Unremarkable though it appears, chewers recognize a huge variety of types and are fascinated by its origin: when one buys *qat* one first establishes its pedigree. Quality is judged by region, by the district within a region, even by the field where the individual tree is grown and by the position of the leaf on it. The product of a tree planted inadvertently on a grave is to be avoided – it brings sorrow. *Qat* can be any colour from lettuce-green to bruise-purple. It comes long or short, bound into bundles or loose, packed in plastic, alfalfa or banana leaves. In San'a, as a rule of thumb, the longer the branch, the more prestigious it is: less image-conscious chewers – and I am one of them – buy *qatal*, the pickings from the lower branches.

Just as in the West there are wine snobs, in Yemen there are *qat* snobs. I once found myself opposite one. Fastidiously, he broke the heads off his yard-long branches and wrapped them in a dampened towel. It was almost an act of consecration. When he had finished, he drew on his water-pipe and appraised my bag of *qatal* with a look that threatened to wither it. 'Everything', he said in an audible whisper, 'has pubic hair. *Qatal* is the pubic hair of *qat*. Besides, dogs cock their legs over it.' He tossed me one of the tips from inside his towel. It was as thick as asparagus, its leaves edged with a delicate russet, and it tasted nutty, with the patrician bitter-sweetness of an almond. There was a tactile pleasure too, like that of eating pomegranates – a slight resistance between the teeth followed by a burst of juice. I chased it with a slurp of water infused with the smoke of incense made from sandalwood, eagle-wood, mastic and cloves.

Qat does not alter your perception. It simply enhances it by rooting you in one place. There is a story in *The Arabian Nights* about a prince who sat and sat in his palace. Sentient from the waist up, his lower half had been turned to porphyry. 'I used to wish the Arabian Tales were true,' said Cardinal Newman. They usually are, to some extent.

After the *zabj* and the jokes, conversations took place in smaller groups, then pairs, then, towards the end of the afternoon, ceased. I looked out of the windows at the city.

'There are three earthly paradises,' said the Prophet. 'Merv of Khurasan, Damascus of Syria, and San'a of Yemen. And San'a is the paradise of these paradises.'

Many have looked on San'a and seen a divine aesthetic at work in its setting. An Iraqi visitor earlier this century eulogized the city in verse:

San'a, home of lofty civilization,
Dwelling of every brave and generous lord,
Paris, London, and all the great cities
Of the Romans and Americans do not match you in beauty.
The beauty of those other places is but embellishment and
    artifice;
Your beauty is unaffected, the gift of your Creator.

The mountains, says the historian al-Shamahi, are perfectly placed, 'neither so far away as to tire the eye when it focuses on the edge of the plain; nor so close as to stifle refreshing morning breezes or constrict the views that, just before sunset, take on such wonderful colours'. They are mountains to be contemplated, like Fuji, if never so geometrical (although I once saw Nuqum, just after dawn, with a circle of cloud hovering over it, so precise that it might have been drawn by a compass).

The climate, too, is perfect, if a bit dusty. And a little too cold in winter, added Ibn al-Mujawir, 'when ducks get frozen alive in ponds, with their heads sticking out of the ice. Foxes come and bite the heads off.' But San'a is not as cold as the village of Bayt Ma'din on the slopes of Jabal al-Nabi Shu'ayb, where in winter the mosque ablution pool freezes over and a *qadi* is said to have excused the villagers from the dawn prayer, 'even if their bollocks are made of iron'. Very occasionally, it snows on the Prophet Shu'ayb. The event causes a certain linguistic complication, as Yemenis have no word for snow. You have to say, 'Ice that falls from the sky . . . No, not hail. The stuff that falls slowly and looks like cotton.'

San'a at street-level is crowded and labyrinthine; but from this room on the roof you can see the green of gardens hiding behind walls of dun mud. The house façades themselves are never sombre, because of the plaster friezes that zigzag round each floor, increasing in complexity with every successive storey.

The San'a house has its prototype in the Palace of Ghumdan. Probably built early in the second century AD and first mentioned in an inscription of the third-century Sabaean King Sha'ar Awtar, the palace has been celebrated by poets and historians ever since. Exaggeration is to be expected: its shadow reached the lip of Wadi Dahr, ten miles to the north-west; its lights could be seen in the holy city of al-Madinah, 750 miles away. Ghumdan, to judge by more sober descriptions, rose ten storeys, to a height of around 120 feet – miraculously tall for its period. Built of variegated stone, it had hollow bronze lions and eagles on its parapet that roared and screeched when the wind blew. But the crowning glory of Ghumdan was its alabaster belvedere, so translucent that if you lay on your back and looked through the ceiling you could tell kites from crows as they flew overhead; the experience, according to al-Hamdani, was 'physic for a care-worn heart' and the nearest thing to heaven in this world:

> If Paradise's garden is above the skies,
> Then hard by heaven the roof of Ghumdan lies.
> And if God made on Earth a heaven for our eyes,
> Then Ghumdan's place is by that earthly paradise.

All that is left of the palace now is a hillock to the east of the Great Mosque, covered with later building. Yet its spirit survives in the tower-house of San'a. Since the city burst its walls after the Revolution of 1962, space has not been at a premium. But people still build upwards, subconsciously imitating the Sabaean builders of Ghumdan. Every upper room is a memory of that alabaster belvedere, a place of luxury and refinement implicit in the word *mafraj*.

The *mafraj* is not always on the roof. There are ground-floor versions with pools and fountains, and a proverb goes: 'If your heart is at ease, even a donkey's arsehole can be a *mafraj*.' But the classic type is like the one in which we are sitting, watching the kites and crows, looking at the view (*tafarraj*, from the verbal root of *mafraj*), having our cares dispelled (again, *tafarraj*). In today's roofscape, however, the bronze lions of Ghumdan have been replaced by water tanks, some fashioned as globes or Scud missiles, or by satellite dishes. CNN offers even more distant prospects than Ghumdan.

I find myself looking towards the place where the sun must have just disappeared. This high above sea-level we are spared the more vulgar sort of sunset. The afterglow is dusty, the sky above the city like the inside of a shell. But I'm looking towards it, not at it – there's a distortion in the window pane, interesting and annoying at the same time. *A man that looks on glass, on it may stay his eye.*

It is six o'clock, or five to twelve in the Islamic day that starts with the sunset prayer. But, for a time, it is neither: the Hour of Solomon has begun, *al-Sa'ah al-Sulaymaniyyah*. *Sa'ah* has among its root meanings in the dictionary 'to be lost, to procrastinate'. At the Hour of Solomon time refracts, as if bent by a prism.

No one speaks. Introspection has replaced conviviality. Somewhere, my fingers are working at the *qat*, polishing, plucking. When it was still light I found a fat horned caterpillar. A good sign – no DDT – but you don't want to chew one.

Were there a singer here, this would be his time. But the songs of the Hour of Solomon are as perilous as they are beautiful. Earlier this century in the days of Imam Yahya, singers could only perform in locked rooms, their windows stuffed with cushions. They had to hide their instruments for fear of imprisonment (fortunately, the old lute of San'a was small enough to be carried in the voluminous sleeves then worn). The Imam had banned singing

with good reason: the songs are siren songs that tell of the flash of teeth beneath a veil like a silver coin in a well, of the saliva of lovers' kisses intoxicating like wine, of beauty that is cruelly ephemeral. *Lasting we thought it, yet it did not last.*

It is now quite dark. The coloured windows of neighbouring houses are lighting up, like Advent calendars.

We *qat* chewers, if we are to believe everything that is said about us, are at best profligates, at worst irretrievable sinners. We are in the thrall of 'the curse of Yemen' and 'the greatest corrupting influence on the country' (two British ambassadors to San'a); we are in danger of 'loss of memory, irritability, general weakness and constipation', and from our water-pipes 'there is certainly a danger of getting a chancre on the lips' (*Handbook of Arabia*, 1917); worse, we are prone to 'anorexia' and to becoming 'emotionally unstable, irritable, hyperactive and easily provoked to anger, eventually becoming violent' (*Journal of Substance Abuse*, 1988), while in Somalia, *qat* has 'starved the country's children' and 'exacerbates a culture of guns and violence' (*San Francisco Chronicle*, 1993); even if we don't turn nasty, we 'doze and dribble green saliva like cretinous infants with a packet of bulls-eyes' (the English writer David Holden). In Saudi Arabia we would be punished more severely than alcohol drinkers; in Syria blue-eyed Muhammad would be swinging on the end of a rope.

In contrast to the above quasi-scientific poppycock, the only full and serious study of the effects of *qat* (Kennedy's – funded, it should be noted, by the US National Institute of Drug Abuse) concludes that the practice appears to have no serious physical or psychological effects. Yemenis themselves, while admitting that their habit is expensive, defend it on the grounds that it stimulates mental activity and concentration; they point out that at least the money spent on it remains within the national economy.

Qat has inspired a substantial body of literature. Compare, for example, Holden's dribbling infants with a description of a handsome chewer by the seventeenth-century poet Ibrahim al-Hindi:

Hearts melted at his slenderness. And as he chewed, his mouth resembled
Pearls which have formed on carnelian and, between them, an emerald, melting.

As well as poetry, there is a weighty corpus of scholarly literature on the legality of *qat* in Islam. It has been unable to find any analogy between the effects of the leaf and those of the prohibited narcotics. In the end, though, the question of its desirability and permissibility revolves around matters of politics, taste, ethnocentrism and sectarian prejudice.

I can just make out my watch. Half past seven. Time, which had melted, is resolidifying. It is now that I sometimes wonder why I am sitting here in the dark with a huge green bolus in my cheek;

why I, and millions of others, spend as much time buying and chewing *qat* as sleeping, and more money on it than on food.

If we are to believe another major Western study of *qat*, we are 'making symbolic statements about the social order' and engaging in an activity that is 'individual, hierarchical, competitive'.* Where you chew, and with whom, is certainly important. But to reduce it all to a neat theory – *rumino ergo sum* – is to over-simplify. It ignores the importance of the *qat* effect – something almost impossibly difficult to pin down, for it is as subtle and as hard to analyse as the alkaloids that cause it. It takes long practice to be able to recognize the effect consciously, and even then it sidesteps definition except in terms of metaphor, and by that untranslatable word, *kayf*.

Kayf – if you achieve it, and you will do if you choose the *qat* and the setting carefully – enables you to think, work and study. It enables you to be still. *Kayf* stretches the attention span, so that you can watch the same view for hours, the only change being the movement of the sun. A journey ceases to be motion through changing scenery – it is you who are stationary while the world is moved past, like a travelling-flat in an old film. Even if briefly, the chewer who reaches this *kayf* feels he is in the right place at the right time – at the pivot of a revolving pre-Copernican universe, the still point of the turning world.

One day I was buying *qat* when a group of tourists walked past. Blue-eyed Muhammad said to me, 'Why do people spend thousands of dollars rushing round the world, when they can chew *qat*?' *There is Africa and all her prodigies in us.*

I've chewed in taxis, on buses, on my motor cycle, on a truck-load of firewood, in a military transport plane, in an overturning jeep, on the 5.30 from Victoria to Sutton. In retrospect, the movement was incidental. Back in the Oriental Institute, they didn't teach us the meaning of *kayf* – they couldn't have. Now, I would venture to call it a form of untravel.

★

In the room on the roof, sounds began to impinge: the rasp of a match; the noisy slurping of water; caged doves cooing; the snap

---

* Shelagh Weir, *Qat in Yemen*.

of a twig to make a toothpick; someone buckling on his dagger. Then there was the click of the light switch. Everyone screwed up their eyes, blessed the Prophet, and went home.

There are a number of things you can do after chewing *qat*. You might start digging up the paving stones in your entrance hall to look for Solomon's Seal, as a neighbour of mine used to do. Or, like the Turk early this century who had not seen his wife for sixteen years and was noted for his abstemiousness, you might involuntarily ejaculate. I tend to go home, have a glass of milky tea, and do some writing. Out of the corner of my eye I used to see my pencil sharpener move very slightly, around midnight, until I stopped buying that sort of *qat*.

2

A People Far Off

'When we are dead, seek for our resting-place
Not in the earth, but in the hearts of men.'
Jalal al-Din al-Rumi (d. AD 1273)

IN THE WILDERNESS of Abyan, somewhere between San'a and Hadramawt, lies Iram of the Columns, the great city built by the people of Ad. The Adites, a race of giants, have disappeared, obliterated in a burning hurricane because of their refusal to heed the Prophet Hud and acknowledge God. 'Have you not seen', the Qur'an says, 'what your Lord did to Ad?' Iram awaits archaeological investigation. The problem is that no one knows where it is. In the seventh century, a nomad stumbled across it while looking for some lost camels but never found the way again. For the moment, Iram remains veiled from sight, an Arabian Atlantis.

An extant Iram of the Columns may be a legend, a city-dwellers' desert mirage; but Yemen is littered with more tangible remains of its early history. Some were already ancient when the Palace of Ghumdan was built. North of the Wilderness of Abyan and across the dunes of Ramlat al-Sab'atayn, a finger of sand thrusting south-west from the Empty Quarter, is the most famous of them all, in fact the most famous archaeological site in Arabia, the Marib Dam. The barrage wall is gone, but on either side of Wadi Adhanah, near the ancient Sabaean capital of Marib, the great masonry sluices are still in pristine condition more than 2,500 years after they were built.* Channels leading away from them

---

* For brief accounts of the Sabaeans and other rulers of Yemen, see the Glossary.

once supplied the two gardens of Saba, the vast area of fields and orchards on either side of the *wadi* which is mentioned in the Qur'an.

Upstream from the Sabaean construction is a new dam. With a capacity seven times that of its predecessor, it was finished in 1986 at a cost of $70 million, paid for by Shaykh Zayid of Abu Dhabi. Irrigation works have yet to be completed, but silt deposited before the foundation of Rome is now once more covered with crops.

Shaykh Zayid's reasons for parting with such a hefty sum were not purely philanthropic. The old dam is important not only as an archaeological site but also as a symbol of unity. For it represents the common source of those Arabs who trace their ancestry back beyond the time when nationalities were invented, to Qahtan, the son of the Prophet Hud, great-great-grandson of Sam and progenitor of all the southern tribes.

Until a little over a hundred years ago, the divisions of Arabia were expressed in loosely defined geographical terms – al-Sham, 'the North', al-Yaman, 'the South', Najd, 'the Uplands', and so on – and in terms of ancestral origin. A particular region might develop a cohesive cultural identity, as Yemen did early on, but there were no fixed borders. 'Territory' equalled 'sphere of influence'; boundaries were as mobile as people.

This was not good enough for the expanding imperialist powers of the nineteenth century. While political officers on the ground knew where things stood, or didn't stand, the bureaucrats of the British and Ottoman empires thought along more rigid lines. Gradually, borders were superimposed on the Arabian map, at first lightly, then with a heavier hand as oil came on to the scene. The need to decide who owned what began to arrest the old fluidity. As the Iraqi invasion of Kuwait in 1990 showed, the process is not yet over.

The British, who grabbed the port of Aden in 1839, and the Ottomans, who from mid-century onwards pushed into Yemen and entered San'a in 1872 (with the help of reinforcements shipped through the new Suez Canal), were eventually forced into drawing a border between themselves. They took a long time to do it. The Anglo-Ottoman Boundary Commission only started work in 1902, and its results were not ratified until 1913. The historical basis for the border was shaky, to say the least. Except for a brief period in the twelfth century, Aden had been politically part of the rest of Yemen until the al-Abdali family seceded from San'a in about 1730. The al-Abdalis, originally appointed as military governors of the Aden region by the Imam – the temporal ruler of Yemen and spiritual leader of the Zaydi sect – declared themselves Sultans of Lahj, and it was from them that the British took Aden. From 1839 onwards, the government in Bombay cultivated an Arabian mini-North West Frontier, raising other would-be potentates of this microcosmic Raj to the rank of Sultan and Amir. With the titles came treaties of protection and, more important, stipends: it was a border built on rupees.

To the north, the Turks were implementing a similar policy. When they left after the First World War, Imam Yahya announced his intention to reunify the country. Border clashes during the 1920s led the British in Aden first to demonize him, then bomb him. The Yemeni reaction came in a famous verse:

> Go gently, Britain, gently,
> For the power of God is mighty:
> The power that long ago destroyed
> Pharaoh, and Thamud, and Ad . . .

However, the two sides arrived at a status quo of sorts, which wobbled along until the British left in 1967. But the border remained for another two decades, shored up by ideological differences between the post-Imamic Yemen Arab Republic (YAR) and the post-Independence People's Democratic Republic of Yemen (PDRY). Only with Yemen's reunification on 22 May 1990 did it seem that the imperial ghost had been exorcized, and this most artificial of Arabia's borders effaced for ever.

Shaykh Zayid, then, by bankrolling the new dam, was reminding the Yemenis and his own people that Marib was the land of his forebears, that ancestral roots still run beneath the lines of political demarcation. The chain of events that led his ancestors to settle in what was, until recently, an insignificant spot in the lower Gulf, is traditionally presented as starting with a big bang, a single massive damburst that deprived the wealthy farmers of Marib of their live-lihood and forced them to emigrate to all corners of Arabia and beyond. One version says that the ruler who owned the dam had been forewarned of its collapse by a soothsayer. One day the king's son returned from the hunt with news that he had seen a rat with iron teeth gnawing at the dam's foundations. (A subplot records that the rat had come from Syria by jumping from hump to hump along an immensely long caravan of camels.) Knowing that the soothsayer's prophecy would be fulfilled, the king ordered his son to strike him in the face publicly; the boy, perplexed but dutiful, carried out his father's orders. 'How', the king then asked his sub-jects, 'can I remain among you now that I have lost my honour?' He packed his bags and sold the dam to a consortium of buyers for a heap of gold, which he measured by sticking his sword in the ground and waiting until the pile of coins had reached the top of the blade. Cheap at the price, the buyers thought; they hadn't made a structural survey. The rat completed its task and the dam broke, drowning, among others, one thousand beardless youths upon one thousand skewbald horses.

Recent archaeological research and a pocket calculator have produced a more credible but less entertaining account. It has been estimated that Wadi Adhanah brought some 3.2 million cubic yards of silt down from the mountains every year. This necessitated periodic dredging by vast labour gangs. If left unattended, the silt building up would endanger the structure of the barrage. Inscriptions record emergency repairs, one in about AD 450 and the next by the Ethiopian ruler Abrahah a century later; but the routine maintenance and rebuilding that were necessary to keep the dam in one piece had long been neglected, probably since the focus of power had shifted to the highlands with the emergence of the Himyari state there several centuries before. The dam's final collapse later in the sixth century was a recent event for the early Muslims. Referring to it, the Qur'an says, 'We have given them, instead of their two gardens, a harvest of camel thorn, tamarisk, and a few *ilb* trees.' Until recently, this was still an accurate descrip-tion of the flora of Marib.

Just as it is dramatically neater to present the long process of the dam's decay as one cataclysmic event, so the diaspora it caused is usually seen as a single happening. 'They dispersed like Saba' is still proverbial for any sudden and irreversible break-up. But the history of emigration from Yemen began long before the sixth century, and continued long after.

The Yemenis who left their homeland, Sabaeans or others, were not going into the unknown: communications with the rest of Arabia and further north, as well as with East Africa, dated back to the beginning of the first millennium BC. Colonies of Yemenis sprang up along the East African coast, in Ethiopia and in Syria and Iraq, and long-distance raiding parties are often mentioned by the early historians.

Some accounts are impressively imaginative. The twelfth-century encyclopaedist Nashwan ibn Sa'id claims that there was an independent Yemeni state in Tibet, 'the land whence musk is brought', founded by men left behind when the Himyari King Shammar Yuhar'ish mounted an expedition to China. Nashwan also says that the king named Dhu al-Adh'ar, He of the Frights, was so called because he brought back as captives from the Land of the North some *nisnas*, 'a race of men whose faces are upon their chests'. Here we are in a no man's land of confusion and invention, first described in the accounts of Alexander the Great's expeditions, and explored intrepidly by the monkish cartographers of Hereford's *Mappa Mundi* and later by Sir John Mandeville. The *nisnas* seem, in fact, to be the same as the Blemmyes of European accounts, who are in turn identified with the Bejas of the African Red Sea coast. Fact and fiction had got mixed up in a geographer's version of Chinese whispers.

There was an upsurge of migration in the early Islamic period, with Yemenis in the vanguard of Islam's conquering armies. The populations of the new cities in Syria and Iraq were largely Yemeni. Some Yemenis went as far as Dongola in Sudan; others settled in Tunisia, intermarrying with the local Berber population. Yemenis also founded colonies in Spain and briefly occupied Bordeaux.

Yemeni blood flows across the Arab world. Some Arabs have forgotten their Yemeni origins; many have not. A taxi driver in Muscat who had identified my adoptive home from my speech refused payment, 'because you live in the land of my grandfather.

He was from Marib.' The Omani was talking about an ancestor of perhaps fifty generations ago.

★

Turning off the San'a–Marib road, I headed northwards. On the left was the escarpment of the highlands, skirted by the old incense road; on the right a shimmering gravel plain extended beyond Marib until the sand crept up on it. A few depressions dotted with tamarisks marked dry watercourses; when the rain came they would feed into the great *wadi* of al-Jawf, where the remains of the Ma'inian capital Qarnaw lie and where the main interest of the people is, and always has been, fighting.

Tracks crossed and recrossed, all heading the same way. The borrowed jeep lurched and bounced, and a cloud of powdery dust streamed through its tattered canvas sides. I stopped for air and scanned the horizon: it shuddered perceptibly in the dead quiet of noon. Ahead, there was a smudge, slightly darker than its surroundings. For the next twenty minutes of driving I kept my eyes on it until it began to resolve itself into something more solid, a sight familiar from photographs but infinitely more impressive, crouched in isolation on a slight hump in the featureless plain. The sun was moving west and the sharp lines of bastions were beginning to emerge from the blank expanse of the walls of Baraqish.

I left the jeep outside the fence erected by the Department of Antiquities and walked in, the only sound dust squeaking under my feet. Suddenly a shout from the left made me jump, and a slight figure with long wild hair and an assault rifle bounded down over a hummock of silt.

He was grinning. 'Did I frighten you?'

'A bit.' The blood was draining back into my face. 'I didn't expect to see anyone.'

'I'm the guard,' he said. He took my hand and led me towards the walls of the city.

At the foot of one of the bastions he stopped and squatted, unshouldering his rifle and laying it across his lap. 'Look . . . look at the stones.' He caressed the fine ashlar. 'What machines did they have to cut them like this?'

'They had no machines. Only hand tools,' I replied.

34

The guard shook his head. I shrugged. The quality of the stone-work was superb – it looked as if it had been cut from butter. (A belief used to be current among the country people that in ancient times stone would spontaneously soften in the month of August.) Inscriptions dotted the walls, recording the names of those who had paid for their construction over two millennia before, when for some three centuries the wealthy merchants of Ma'in formed a state independent of Saba. The inscriptions might have been carved yesterday. The masons of Baraqish put their successors to shame, and if evidence were needed of the high level of sophistica-tion they had achieved, here it was: as building, it was not just defensive, but conspicuously, consciously beautiful; as craft, it was perfect. The epitaph on the Himyaris attributed to the poet-king As'ad al-Kamil applies equally to the people of Ma'in:

> These are our works which prove what we have done;
> Look, therefore, at our works when we are gone.

Si monumentum requiris, circumspice.
   The guard seized my hand again and pulled me up a collapsed section of wall. Inside were the remains of later buildings, includ-ing a circular tower or *nawbah*. Potsherds and fragments of glass, mostly multicoloured bangles, littered the ground; many scraps of faded indigo cloth were embedded in the dust. Baraqish has had a series of occupants. Aelius Gallus, the Roman governor of Egypt, garrisoned it before his unsuccessful attack on Marib in 24 BC; twelve hundred years later Imam Abdullah ibn Hamzah, whose descendants still live in the villages nearby, used it as a base against the Ayyubid invaders. Both of them must have been overawed by the architectural achievement of their predecessors.
   The temple at Baraqish has now been excavated to floor level by an Italian team, but at the time of my visit you had to crawl between the columns with the ceiling a few inches above your back. The building is rectangular and of simple construction, with monolithic square-sectioned columns morticed into the beams which carry the ceiling slabs. Again, the quality of workmanship is outstanding and the limestone joinery executed so faultlessly as to suggest an origin, like that of Classical Greek architecture, in

timber building. It pleases the eye in the same way as, say, Shaker furniture.

I went and sat in the shade cast by the *nawbah*. The guard chucked stones into an empty well while I read an article I had brought, 'Baraqish According to the Historians'. The old name of Baraqish, Yathill, appears in Strabo's account of the Roman expedition as 'Athrula'. Al-Hamdani's story of the renaming of Yathill runs as follows: the people of Yathill were subjected to a long siege. Their only source of water was a well outside the city walls, connected to the city by a tunnel.* One day the besiegers saw a dog emerging from the tunnel, which they had not noticed before: by following it back, they were able to take control of the city. They renamed it Baraqish, 'Spotty', after its betrayer.

By the time I had finished the article, the guard had disappeared and the sun was heading for the escarpment. To the north lay the broad depression of al-Jawf. The ruins of Qarnaw glinted distantly. Then the scene slipped into monochrome, except for a few patches of green in the *wadi*'s far side that seemed to radiate the last remains of the sunlight.

Ten minutes out of Baraqish on the way back to the Marib road, I stopped the jeep and looked back. The lines of the bastions had disappeared and the city looked like a work of nature – something not built, but dropped on to the plain.

---

* Until the 1960s, San'a was supplied by water in the same way, by a system of wells and underground tunnels known as *ghayls*.

Baraqish, of course, has lost its context. Like Marib, it is sur-
rounded by banks of silt, the remains of ancient field systems. The
area covered is tiny compared with the land watered by the old
Marib Dam, but it must have provided much of the city's food.
More important is the wider context of the trade routes on which
Baraqish, Qarnaw and all the other cities of the ancient South
Arabian states were staging posts. These routes were the arteries of
Saba, Ma'in, Qataban and Hadramawt, channels for their enor-
mous wealth – wealth generated by tight control of their major
commodity: frankincense, the product of the unprepossessing tree
Boswellia sacra.

At a very early date, these South Arabian states had become aware
of the demand for aromatic gums, as the Pharaonic Egyptians were
great burners of incense and consumers of another Arabian
product, myrrh, used medicinally and in the mummification
process. By the tenth century BC, the Yemenis had been able to
develop the overland camel trade with the north, as the visit of the
Queen of Sheba/Saba to Solomon shows. The appearance of
civilizations in the Fertile Crescent had opened up more markets for
aromatics, and in the time of Herodotus no Assyrian lady would
make love without first censing herself. Incense-burners from this
period, remarkably similar in form to Arabian examples, are found
over the whole of the Eastern Mediterranean. But it was the growth
of Rome that provided the biggest boost to ancient Yemen's
prosperity. As their empire expanded, the Romans developed a
fascination for the Orient and things oriental that became
entrenched in society.

Frankincense and myrrh were not the only commodities traded.
Cinnamon, for example, was brought from India although the
South Arabians managed to keep its source a secret in order to
retain their monopoly on its carriage. But frankincense was their
principal export, and by leaking selected information or disin-
formation on production methods, they added to its mystique and
its desirability. The Romans were led to believe that the incense
groves were guarded by vicious flying serpents which could only
be subdued by the smoke of rare plants. It was an early case of
advertising hype.

Thus the Mediterranean world viewed the people who produced

the fuel for its prayers with the same mixture of awe, envy and incomprehension that the West reserves today for the oil *shaykhs* who produce the fuel for its motor cars. South Arabia exported an estimated 3,000 tons of incense and 600 tons of myrrh annually. Given that the people of Rome alone spent 85 tons of coined silver a year on incense, that myrrh was vastly more expensive, and that the spices and other luxury goods which passed in transit through South Arabia fetched similarly high prices, the income for the Sabaeans and their neighbours would have compared favourably with the present-day revenues of an oil-exporting state.*

Rome continued to consume the gum of *Boswellia sacra* until it embraced Christianity and Pauline disapproval blew away the smallest whiff of heathenism. From the end of the second century onwards, the early Church fathers campaigned successfully against the use of incense. A certain amount of backsliding was to occur and incense later found a place in Christian rites, but never at the obsessive level it had reached under the pagans. Besides, the Romans had developed the navigational skills needed to sail down the Red Sea and beyond, bypassing Southern Arabia, and so land routes turned to carrying more prosaic and far less profitable commodities like hides.

In its heyday, most of the incense was brought by boat and raft to Qana – the modern Bir Ali on the Hadramawt coast – from the eastern Hadrami domains where it was grown. The rafts, we are told by the anonymous Graeco-Egyptian author of the first-century navigational guide, *The Periplus of the Erythrean Sea*, were 'held up on inflated skins after the manner of the country'. (Such rafts were still to be found off the southern coast of Arabia early last century, when the British Indian naval officer Wellsted noticed fishermen using them in the Kuria Muria Islands.) From Qana the incense was taken inland to the Hadrami capital, Shabwah. Rules governing carriage were stringent, and a reminder of this can be seen in the 180-yard-long wall which blocks the Shabwah route as it passes up a narrow valley, forcing caravans to pass through a single gate. Other checkpoints lined the way for, Pliny says, 'the laws have made it a

---

* By a quirk of history, oil is now being extracted from just those areas where the ancient trade in incense was centred: Marib, Shabwah and Hadramawt.

capital offence to deviate from the highroad'. At Shabwah, Pliny goes on, a tithe of the incense was taken in honour of the Hadrami god and used for defraying expenses such as the entertainment of strangers. Civil servants and taxes had to be paid, and money found for water and fodder, so that 'the expense for each camel before it arrives at the shore of our sea [the Mediterranean] is 688 *denarii*'.

The way to the Romans' *mare nostrum* was long – according to Pliny, 2,437,500 paces – and each territory the caravans passed through extracted duty. From Shabwah the caravans, thousands strong and miles long, went via Marib and al-Jawf to Najran. Here the route split, one branch cutting across the peninsula to the head of the Gulf, the other going through al-Madinah and on to Petra for shipment at Gaza or onward carriage to Damascus.

The vital position of Gaza in the incense trade is illustrated by an anecdote in Plutarch's life of Alexander the Great. Alexander, as a young man, had been ticked off by his tutor Leonidas for burning too much incense in the temple. Years later, when he captured Gaza, he sent Leonidas a message: 'No longer need you be so stingy towards the gods.' With the message were thirteen tons of incense and two tons of myrrh.

Trade was two-way. Money, ideas, goods and gods also came to South Arabia from the Eastern Mediterranean. People were imported, too: an inscription of the third century BC in the temple of Athtar (also the name of a Phoenician deity) at Qarnaw, which mentions Gaza no fewer than twenty-eight times, lists details of naturalization requirements for foreign women. Some of the women were Phoenician, others Egyptian or Arab; most came as wives or concubines of Ma'inian men. The God of the Old Testament used the prospect of transportation to Yemen as a threat: 'I will sell your sons and daughters into the hand of the children of Judah, and they shall sell them to the Sabaeans, to a people far off.'

Individual ancient South Arabians are hard to picture; but disparate clues and a dash of imagination can help sketch the outlines of, say, the life of a well-to-do trader of Baraqish like Zayd Il ibn Zayd, a merchant who exported myrrh and frankincense to Egypt in the mid-third century BC. At this time the Greeks controlled merchant shipping in the Mediterranean, and it was one of their vessels that he boarded in Alexandria to make a tour of the eastern end of the sea. The journey took him to cosmopolitan Delos, where one of his countrymen was later to dedicate an altar with a bilingual South Arabian-Greek inscription to the Ma'inian national god, Wadd. Zayd Il would naturally have looked into frankincense futures before leaving Delos for Gaza, where he picked up a Phoenician concubine to take back to his home town. On a later trip to Egypt he succumbed to the rigours of an international businessman's life. He was embalmed with his own myrrh and buried in a sarcophagus inscribed with his name and occupation in Ma'inian.

Contemporary Classical writers transmit a fair amount of information on the ancient Arabian peoples, some fabulous but much with a factual basis. Herodotus is the earliest and, as usual, the most entertaining. He wrote that cinnamon was collected from birds' nests and the gum *ladanum* from the beards of billy goats; Arabian sheep had such fat tails that they had to trundle them along on little wooden trailers.* Herodotus's successors are more credible. For example, most of the place-names on Ptolemy's map of Arabia can be identified at least tentatively and, except for sites far inland like Mara (Marib) and Nagara (Najran), latitudes are little more than fifteen per cent out. The map was not substantially updated until the Niebuhr expedition of the 1760s.

A strange story linking South Arabia, Byzantium and Northern Europe perhaps demonstrates that the Mediterranean world knew something of the celestial nature of early Yemeni religion: the Empress Helena, famous for her search for the True Cross, also sent envoys to Hadramawt. There, in 'Sessania Adrumetorum', they discovered the bones of one of the Magi which, after travelling via Constantinople and Milan, finally came to rest in Cologne in 1164.†

---

* This fancy – if that is what it is – recurs in later works. On the *doombur*, the Indian fat-tailed sheep, the compiler of *Hobson–Jobson* quotes a contributor to the *Journal of the Asiatic Society of Bengal*: 'I was informed by a person who possessed large flocks, and who had no reason to deceive me, that sometimes the tail of the Tymunnee *doombas* increased to such a size, that a cart or small truck on wheels was necessary to support the weight, and that without it the animal could not wander about; he declared also that he had produced tails in his flock which weighted 12 *Tabreezi munds*, or 48 *seers puckah*, equal to about 96 *lbs*.'

† The French archaeologist Christian Robin has pointed out that among the Sabaean names for incense are two terms for unknown varieties, 'gold' and 'divine gold'. Perhaps, then, the first gift of the Magi to the infant Christ was another aromatic.

The Mediterranean peoples saw the ancient Yemenis only as traders in aromatics and other luxury goods. But to the Yemenis themselves, the cultivation of essential crops was the basis of life. The two gardens at Marib stretched for at least fifteen miles and were clearly a masterpiece of irrigation. Elsewhere, too, enormous effort was put into getting the best out of limited water supplies. Around the Hadrami capital Shabwah, now a barren place on the edge of the desert, some 12,000 acres were under cultivation, while after the Marib Dam the most impressive irrigation works are to be found at Baynun in the central highlands. Here, floodwater was channelled out of its natural course, through tunnels cut in the solid rock of two small mountains, and into a dam. One of the tunnels is still intact, 150 yards long and big enough to drive a car through. Today, many villages of highland Yemen still rely on rainwater collecting tanks that were built two thousand years ago.

As Yemen opened itself increasingly to outsiders over the first few centuries of the Christian era, Arabia Felix was demystified. Sailors from Ptolemaic Egypt had learned to navigate the dangerous shoals of the Red Sea, and the overland trade went into recession. The nomads saw their earnings as guards and camel men plummet, and turned on their former employers by raiding the settled lands of Yemen. The rulers of Himyar – a people whom the genealogists, with their rationalizing minds, traced back to 'Himyar ibn Saba' – were now able to use their position in the central highlands, safe from the nomads, to increase their authority; they claimed the title 'Kings of Saba and Dhu Raydan', Raydan being the area around their capital, Zafar. Towards the end of the third century AD the Himyari leader Shammar Yuhar'ish had most of present-day Yemen under his control and assumed the title 'King of Saba, Dhu Raydan, Hadramawt and Yamanat' – the latter probably the southern coast. But Yemen was to fall prey to the rivalry of superpowers who, acting through satellites, concealed imperialism in ideology.

From the third century onwards, Ethiopian Axumite influence had grown in Yemen; later, there were many converts to Christianity. The backlash was extreme: a Judaized noble, Yusuf As'ar, seized the Himyari throne and began an anti-Christian campaign, resulting in his burning the Christians of Najran. The Axumites thus had their pretext to mount a full-scale expedition to South Arabia. So, in AD 525, began the final eclipse of Yemen's pre-Islamic civilizations.

Yusuf As'ar (whom the historians call Dhu Nuwas, He of the Ponytail) had ascended the throne by unorthodox means. Nashwan tells us that his predecessor had been warned that he would be killed by the most beautiful youth of Himyar: the king was scornful of the prophecy but took the precaution of having his many handsome young visitors frisked. The power-hungry and good-looking Yusuf, on whom the royal eye inevitably fell, overcame the problem by designing a double-soled sandal. When he was admitted to the royal chambers he got the old king drunk and, like James Bond's adversary Rosa Klebb, whipped out a stiletto concealed in the sole. He killed his would-be seducer, and proclaimed himself king.

Whatever the truth of Nashwan's account, other evidence seems to confirm that Yusuf As'ar grabbed the throne in a coup. His come-uppance, following the Najran incident and years of resistance to the Ethiopians, was bathetic. After his final defeat on the shores of the Red Sea he spurred his horse into the waves and was never seen again. So ended the Kingdom of Saba, Dhu Raydan, Hadramawt, Yamanat and – as it had lately been styled – the Arabs of the Highlands and the Lowlands. The most plangent laments on its passing were composed by the blind poet Alqamah ibn Dhi Jadan, known as the Mourner of Himyar. His verse on Duran, a great Himyari castle ravaged by the Axumites, recalls the apocalyptic vision of Babylon:

> Himyar and its kings are dead, destroyed by Time;
> Duran by the Great Leveller laid waste.
> Around its courts the wolves and foxes howl,
> And owls dwell there as though it never was.

The Great Leveller had a bizarre end in store for the most famous Axumite ruler of Yemen, Abrahah. At some time after the middle of the sixth century, Abrahah declared himself independent from Axum and assumed the title of the old Himyari kings. He then began trying to divert lucrative pilgrim traffic from Mecca – the major centre of pilgrimage even before Islam – to San'a. When, in AD 570, one of the Meccan family in charge of the Ka'bah passed comment on this policy by defecating in the San'a *ecclesia*,* Abrahah set off to capture the northern city. He took with him a secret weapon which gave the final battle its name: the Day of the Elephant. Destruction would have been certain for the city of the Ka'bah had events not taken a Hitchcockian twist. Flocks of partridge suddenly appeared and bombarded the Ethiopians with stones, killing all but a few of them. The defeat is commemorated in the Qur'an, and in folklore; the route from San'a to Mecca is still known as the Way of the People of the Elephant, and al-Hasabah, now a suburb of San'a, is said to have been named after the pebbles, *hasab*, that finished off the remnants of the fleeing Axumite army. Villagers around Amran, north of San'a, say that the small fossilized shells found in the area are the actual projectiles. It is claimed that they fell with such force that they entered through the victims' skulls and left by their anuses.

Yemeni resistance to Abrahah's successors coalesced under the Himyari prince Sayf ibn Dhi Yazan. Sayf, however, was too weak to pursue a policy of non-alignment and summoned Persian military assistance. The call resulted in Yemen becoming a Sasanian satrapy. But the rule of these new incomers was short-lived: a new power was rising, inexorably, to the north.

The Prophet Muhammad, born in Mecca in the year of the Day of the Elephant, was dispatching delegates to all corners of Arabia from the new Muslim state in al-Madinah. To San'a he sent Farwah ibn Musayk, a Yemeni who had embraced Islam at the Prophet's own hand. Muhammad commanded Farwah to spread the new religion, killing those who did not accept it. However, a timely visit by the angel Gabriel, who enjoined Muhammad to 'show kindness to the children of Saba', prevented a slaughter. In the event the Yemenis accepted Islam willingly. The Prophet developed a soft spot for them: 'The people of Yemen', he said,

---

* The great church built by the Ethiopians, now a hole in the ground near the *suq* but still known as 'al-Qalis' after its Greek name.

43

'have the kindest and gentlest hearts of all. Faith is Yemeni, wisdom is Yemeni.'

Nonetheless, there was opposition. In the following year, AH 11, a soothsayer named al-Aswad al-Ansi declared himself a prophet and mustered a force of tribesmen whom he led on San'a and Najran. He was defeated and killed by Farwah. Reviled by the Islamic historians, who record that he had a pair of demonic familiars in the form of swine, al-Aswad was later hailed by the PDRY Marxists as a revolutionary. A later false prophet claimed to the tribes of Hamdan that the Archangel Gabriel had also revealed a *qur'an* to him. As an ecumenical measure he had, too, an Ark of the Covenant, which followed him around on the back of a mule.

Islam swept away the most obvious signs of paganism. The spirit of iconoclasm was at large, and all over Arabia the idols were toppling. As a poet said, 'Can we call it "Lord" if foxes piss upon its head?' And as Islam spread, Yemen became politically marginalized. Yemenis had been the spearhead of Islamic expansion; but during the century of Umayyad rule up to AD 750, and then under the Abbasid caliphs, they felt themselves increasingly eclipsed by Arabs of northern origin who came to have more in common with the Byzantines and Persians they had conquered than with their Arabian roots. Yemen's intellectual counter-attack produced a great treasure of history and poetry. More important, it created for the Yemenis powerful concepts of their own past. In the tenth century, al-Hamdani, known as the Tongue of Yemen, drew on the works of his predecessors and supplemented them with his own research to produce the massive ten-part genealogical and historical compendium *al-Iklil*. A pioneering antiquary who recorded inscriptions from Baraqish and elsewhere, al-Hamdani was also at heart a romantic who dwelt on the melancholy of ruins and faded glory.

A large section of *Iklil VIII* is devoted to tombs and their occupants. The most notable feature of al-Hamdani's deceased ancients, 'old men dried out upon their beds', is that they were often buried with an inscription bearing the first half – and sometimes, prophetically, both halves – of the Muslim creed: There is no god but Allah, and Muhammad is the messenger of Allah. The

historian, therefore, is demonstrating the existence of Islam in Yemen *before* Muhammad – hardly a deviant view, since Islam is the old religion, the faith of Abraham and all the pre-Muhammadan prophets.*

Al-Hamdani, like Nashwan ibn Sa'id, includes many tales of expeditions made by pre-Islamic kings. One, the unbelievably energetic Malik, reached Soghdia, the lands of the Franks and the Saxons, and the shore of the Atlantic where he set up a statue with

---

* Accounts of bodies found intact recall the recent discovery near San'a of five mummies, wrapped in leather and linen. They are accompanied, like the ones al-Hamdani describes, by wooden plaques. Carbon-14 dating has given their age as around 2,300 years.

the warning, 'He who goes beyond this point will perish.'
Shammar Yuhar'ish, already seen colonizing Tibet, gave his name
to Samarqand which, al-Hamdani claims, comes from the Persian
Shammar kand – Shammar destroyed it.

It is a history made not by the mind but by the heart. But
however wild some of the claims may be, al-Hamdani was insistent
on setting them down, for they attempted to show that the armies
of Yemen had reached as far as those of Islam. Geographically as
well as doctrinally, the sons of Qahtan had got there first.

★

There are, then, two pasts: the past of the archaeologists and epig-
raphers, and the more richly embroidered past of al-Hamdani and
his school. The two versions are not mutually exclusive; each
complements and informs the other. A third past is only beginning
to be charted: that of the mass of curious practices inherited from
pre-Islamic times. Children in San'a, for example, throw their milk
teeth to the sun and call on it to give them the teeth of a gazelle;
farmers in some areas butter the horns of a bull when the sorghum
is sown, to ensure a good crop; Hadrami townsmen go on annual
ibex hunts and present the animal's thigh and forequarters to the
religious authorities – precisely the same cuts that are given to the
priest in South Arabian inscriptions and, hardly by coincidence, in
both the Book of Leviticus and a Carthaginian tariff found in
Marseille.*

And then there is the linguistic past. Arabic, which started as a
dialect of North Arabian and had for some time been the lingua
franca of trade and poetry, seems to have taken over from the old
languages by the end of the third Islamic century. But Yemeni
speech is still haunted by the ghosts of South Arabian. Some words
have undergone strange metamorphoses as they passed through the
twilight areas of meaning between Himyari, Yemeni dialects of
Arabic, and standard Arabic. For example, *wathan* to a Himyari was
'a boundary marker'; today in some dialects it has taken on the extra
meaning of 'an oath'; in the lexicon, it is 'an idol of stone or wood'.

---

* See, on customs involving bulls and ibexes, the articles by Jacques Ryckmans and Walter Dostal in
Arabian and Islamic Studies.

This word association came to mind as I travelled alone late one afternoon across the uplands on the way to Khamir. Here is the territory of the Hashid tribal grouping, who have been powerful for nearly two thousand years. Boundary-stones, oaths, idols, were all around. I remembered the Old Testament curses heaped on those who move their neighbours' landmarks, and the marching lines of little cairns, their shadows lengthening on the bare lime-stone, suddenly took on an aspect that was ancient and not a little sinister. The way into Dictionary Land is often to be found here, where present and past intersect.

★

For some Arabs the past is an ephemeral existence on the fringes of desert or sea; for others it begins with the Pharaohs or the Mediterranean of Phoenician and Classical times. Yemen is different: it is one of those rare places where the past is not another country. I have eavesdropped on tribesmen visiting the National Museum and heard them expressing surprise, not at the strangeness of the things they see, but at their familiarity. Asking the way to al-Qalis, the site of Abrahah's *ecclesia* in San'a, I have been quoted the Qur'anic account of his defeat on the Day of the Elephant as if it had happened yesterday. There is a feeling in Yemen that the past is ever-present.

The most recent past has been eventful: there has been revolution, war, unification and – as I shall relate – a bizarre and doomed attempt to re-erect the old internal border. At the moment, the future is uncertain and there is a sense, more than ever, of people looking back to the distant past with affection, even with nostalgia. It is appropriate. Nostalgia, as far as the Arabs are concerned, was invented by a Yemeni, the poet Imru al-Qays. The settings of his poetry go beyond the land of Yemen, however, for Imru al-Qays was a scion of the noble sept of the Kindah tribe which transferred to Najd, then to the north of the peninsula. It was he who first addressed the remains of a campsite associated with a past love affair.

Stop. Let us weep, remembering where a love once lodged,
Where the sand hills fall between al-Dakhul and Hawmal . . .

The tiniest of traces, the *atlal* – charred sticks, dried goat dung, the minutiae of memory – evoke the deepest passions. 'In the open plain with its wild, parsimonious beauty,' wrote Wilfrid Scawen Blunt in *The Seven Golden Odes of Pagan Arabia*, 'every bush and stone, every beetle and lizard, every rare track of jerboa, gazelle or ostrich on the sand, becomes of value and is remembered, it may be years afterwards, while the stones of the camp-fire stand black and deserted in testimony of the brief season of love.'

Imru al-Qays, born when the great civilizations of ancient South Arabia were in their final decline, is an appropriate figure to end an account of pre-Islamic Yemen. His life was quixotic and marked by the same combination of wanderlust and homesickness shared by so many other Yemenis of his own time and now. His poetry has become – like so much that originates in Yemen – part of the common cultural inheritance of the Arabs. His obsession, almost Proustian, with the *atlal*, resembles the Yemenis' love affair with their past – not so much the concrete past about them, but a past reconstructed from the slenderest historical fact, interpreted not by the mind, but by the heart.

★

We were taking the short cut to Hadramawt across the sands of Ramlat al-Sab'atayn. It was the way the incense had come from Shabwah to Marib, the route followed by the ancestors of Shaykh Zayid and of my Muscat taxi driver. The Safir oil installation to our left was black against a rising sun. A single flame shot silently upwards. The only sound was the hiss of air from the tyres as Abdulkarim, the desert guide, let them down with a twig to grip the sand better. It would be an easy crossing, he said; the sand was still firm from the autumn rain.

We left the tarmac and crossed the first dune. For a while, we saw the traces of passing humans, an oil-can, a mineral-water bottle: twentieth-century *atlal*. The desert, though, had kept its looks, beautiful and frightening. For several hours we went on, at first through a sandscape that looked as if it had been formed by a giant ice-cream scoop. Then, gradually, the dunes began to get lower. In places there was the lightest covering of grass, fading blue-green into the distance.

Lulled by the motion of the car over the gentle sand swell, I began to doze. Images of Iram of the Columns, the city of Ad destroyed by divine wrath, flickered, then burst when I opened my eyes. Iram, they said, was somewhere here, in the middle of nowhere, half way between San'a and Hadramawt.

Suddenly, in front of us, there was a group of buildings.

I sat up and rubbed my eyes. The buildings were still there. Abdulkarim broke a long silence: 'That's the old border post.'

He stopped the car and we got out.

The Iram of the Qur'an had been wiped off the face of the earth. The Iram of legend was a mirage, a reaction to the *horror vacui* of the sands and of history. These buildings were the *iram* of the dictionary: a marker set up in the desert. As a memorial to imperialism, they are fittingly ugly. And unlike camp-fire traces and oil-cans, it would take many years for their cement blocks to be buried or worn away.

We stood for a while, where the sand hills fell away into the distance, and looked. We remembered, but did not weep.

3

Down to the Gate of the She-Camel

'Nowhere have I experienced more strenuous travelling than
in the Yemen . . . I had the cartilages removed from both
knees; apparently I had worn them out.'
Wilfred Thesiger, *Desert, Marsh and Mountain*

IN THE FIRST CENTURY of Islam, a pilgrim named Yazid ibn Shayban was on his way to Mecca when he met an old man on the road. Yazid greeted him and asked him where he was from; the old man replied that he was of the people of al-Mahrah, in the east of Yemen. After exchanging the usual courtesies, Yazid was about to continue on his way when the old man said, 'Wait! Upon my life, if you are of Arab stock then I shall know *you*. The Arabs are founded on four corner-stones: Mudar, Rabi'ah, al-Yaman and Quda'ah. Of which are you?' Yazid said he was a descendant of Mudar. 'Now,' the old man went on, 'are you of the Camelry or the Cavalry?' Yazid thought for a while, then realized the old man meant Mudar's two sons, Khandaf and Qays, and answered, 'Of the Camelry.' 'And are you of the She-Hare or the Skull?' That needed more working out . . .

Nine generations on, the old man's freakishly developed memory showed no sign of flagging. 'Now, this Shayban married three wives: Mihdad the daugher of Humran ibn Bishr ibn Amr ibn Murthad, who bore him Yazid; Akrashah the daughter of

Hajib ibn Zurarah ibn Adas, who bore him al-Ma'mur; and Amrah the daugher of Bishr ibn Amr ibn Adas, who bore him al-Maq'ad. Of which are you?' 'Of Mihdad,' Yazid replied, by now utterly astonished by the performance. 'Do you see', said the old man, 'that I know you?'

The story, appropriately, is quoted at the end of Qadi Muhammad al-Hajari's *Compendium of the Lands and Tribes of Yemen*. The Arabs in general are fascinated by pedigree, some families preserving their lineage back to Adam; but nowhere is genealogy as visible – on the ground – as it is in Yemen. The traditional view is that, starting from the ancient civilizations around the desert fringe, the ancestors spread outwards towards the coasts, giving their names to mountains, valleys and settlements on the way. 'Their inward thought is', as the Psalmist said, 'that their houses shall continue for ever, and their dwelling places to all generations; they call their lands after their own names.'

The problem is that the geo-genealogists who charted the diaspora were over-keen. One example of their inventiveness is the attribution of the site of the Ethiopians' church in San'a – the *ecclesia*/al-Qalis – to an ancestor called 'al-Qalis'. Often, too, they found themselves in a chicken-and-egg quandary – did the tribe give its name to the place, or vice versa? – and usually came out on the side of a personal eponym. There is some evidence in the pre-Islamic inscriptions to suggest that the medieval texts often did have a point, and that a particular clan was in fact associated with a place that took on its name. But when al-Hamdani and his school tried to apply the idea across the board – and then work out the blood-relationships between the names – they had to exercise their considerable imaginations.

I would spend hours at a time lost in the map, following in my mind ancestral routes from the desert to the sea, bloodlines radiating from an ancient heartland. Naturally, it was the *wadis* that formed the main lines of communication, leading up from the desert into the mountains and, from the other side of the watershed, down to the coast.

Most of these valleys were well-worn tracks, cropping up frequently in the texts. But there was one on which the historians and the geographers had almost nothing to say, other than to give the supposed lineage of the ancestor who settled it: Surdud ibn Ma'di Karib ibn Sharahbil ibn Yankif ibn another eight generations ibn Himyar ibn Saba. Wadi Surdud falls to the coast in a virtually straight line from a point a little over twenty-five miles north-west of San'a, and should have been a major line of communication. The main road from the capital to the coast, however, plunges down 3,000 feet then climbs again to its original altitude, covering double the vertical distance of Surdud and snaking across the Haraz Mountains in a series of magnificent but terrifying switchbacks. To find out why Wadi Surdud had been ignored would mean walking it, to the point where it joins the motor road at Khamis Bani Sa'd. Debbie, an intrepid yet sensible walking companion, had fallen in with the plan on the grounds that Surdud is a valley, water runs downhill, and we should not have to do any climbing. In theory.

We left San'a at about nine o'clock in the morning, an early start by Ramadan standards. Our list of equipment was short: walking sticks, a torch, candles, 'Cock Brand' mosquito coils, penknives (mine is a Japanese Swiss army model incorporating a full-sized fork and dessert spoon, which once belonged to the chauffeur of the pre-Revolution ruler Imam Ahmad). Also boiled sweets, cheese spread triangles, two small tins of tuna – all these to be considered as treats – and a staple of festival cakes, made for the end of the great fast.*

We found a shared taxi to the town of Shibam surprisingly quickly and, with the temporal displacement that goes with Ramadan, seemed to get there before we left. Shibam market is full of sensible goods – pots, tobacco boxes, pinstriped jackets without arms, spirtles and so on. We made our way to the military bread ovens to stock up on *kidam*, bread rolls of amazing longevity; they were an Ottoman import, marching-fodder for Anatolian conscripts.

Again with uncanny speed, we found a truck to take us the short distance to al-Ahjir, the head of Wadi Surdud. As she climb-

---

* A sixteenth-century Yemeni traveller considered twenty items indispensable for any journey. His packing list went: kohl applicator, kohl pot, scissors, tooth-cleaning stick, mirror, comb, inkstand, writing-case, penknife, pen-box, staff, overcoat, tweezers, Qur'an, prayer-mat, ablution vessel, belt, victuals, scroll of paper, sewing kit.

ed in, Debbie revealed no more than three gold-embroidered inches of her long Pakistani drawers to the other passengers, all old tribesmen. Their fasting ennui melted away.

'Where are you going?' they asked.

'Tihamah.'

'*Tihamah?* You're going the wrong way. You must go back to San'a and get a taxi.'

'But we want to walk.'

'You'll get lost,' they said.

'How can we get lost?' asked Debbie. 'We'll just follow Surdud.'

The tribesmen looked at each other. 'There's no way down Surdud.'

We began to feel uneasy. These were sons of the land, their ancestors had lived here for generations: how could centuries, millennia of Yemenis be wrong? But they were also mountain men to whom the *wadis* were little known, sources of occasional income from share croppers, to be passed through as quickly as possible.

'You see', I ventured, 'we've heard so much about the attractions of Surdud, we want to see it for ourselves.'

This worked. Even if foreigners do irrational things like sightseeing, and going on foot when comfortable cars are available that all but the poorest can afford, this had struck a chord; the tribesmen were not insensitive to the beauty of their surroundings. They had realized that we were not mistaken, just soft in the head.

Except for one. The truck bounced across a deep rut and he gripped my knee, partly to steady himself, partly for emphasis. 'Have you heard about the *tahish?*'

The word rang a bell.

'The *tahish* – the monster,' he explained.

'What sort of a monster?' Debbie asked brightly.

'It's the size of a cow but it's got a head like a hyena's, with a wide jaw, like this . . .' He opened his mouth and moved his head from side to side like a periscope. Everyone laughed.

I remembered the word. The Ministry of Culture had put on a play called *The Tahish* a couple of years before. Curious, I had done some research, but found only a reference to a *tahishah* in Hadramawt: the gloss on the word was strange and unilluminating – 'a bird unknown to you'. At any rate, the monster

in the play never even appeared on stage, which must have been a relief for the props people. It just roared in the wings and turned out to be nothing more than a figment of mass hysteria, an allegory of the fear inspired in pre-Revolution Yemenis by the tyrannical Imam Ahmad. The *tahish* was a bogeyman, a myth, a Yemeni yeti.

Suddenly the man's head stopped swivelling and his eyes fixed on me. 'Last year the *tahish* ate a man in Surdud. All but his flip-flops.'

Yemen has its share of disturbing creatures. First, there are snakes. Some are benign, like the snake that guarded the Palace of Ghumdan in pre-Islamic San'a. Guardian serpents are still to be found carved, coiled, on the walls of houses – coiled to spring, like the flying snakes that Greek geographers mentioned as watching over Yemen's incense groves. The tails of certain snakes, used as kohl applicators, are said to prevent eye disease. As for the malevolent ones, they are dealt with by the *hannash*, the professional snake-gatherer. One *hannash* I met in the mountains west of the capital was claimed to be able to attract dozens of snakes from a single house by reciting Qur'anic verses; they would slither into a sack and writhe harmlessly. Not knowing any *hannashes* in San'a, the only time I found a snake in my house I decapitated it with a coffee-roasting spoon.*

Then there are scorpions. Very occasionally they are found in bunches of *qat*. Once, a baby one walked out of my bundle and across my lap, and disappeared among the leavings in the middle of the room. I have never seen *qat*-chewers move faster. Another creature that sometimes pops up in *qat* is the *fukhakh*, the hisser – the Yemeni name for the chameleon. Its blood taken externally is a cure for baldness, but its breath makes your teeth fall out. The gecko too is often killed, as it eats the remains of food from round your mouth as you sleep, pisses and gives you spots. Despite this I have been attached to several that have grown up in my house as they are clever flycatchers and converse, like the Hottentots, in clicks. There are few bigger beasts, although hyenas are common and leopards are spotted occasionally. The thirteenth-century traveller Ibn al-Mujawir also noted were-lions in the mountains west of Hajjah. They now appear to be extinct. All the same, who could tell what might be waiting in the unvisited gorges of Surdud?

We said goodbye to the tribesmen where the road entered al-Ahjir. I got my boot caught in the truck's tailgate; Debbie

---

* A Tradition of the Prophet says that snakes found in houses embody spirits, some benign, others malevolent: you should give them fair warning by reciting the call to prayer, and only if they take no notice should they be killed.

descended, again with remarkable decorum. The truck lurched away and we were left looking over the valley. Al-Ahjir is a huge bowl. There is something un-Yemeni in the shape, as though, in contrast to the jagged and geologically young mountains, this is the product of lengthy attrition, like a glacial corrie. Behind us rose the ramparts on which the fortress-town of Kawkaban sits, up in the gods of this huge natural theatre. In front, at the far side of al-Ahjir, was a gap – the lip of the bowl – and although it was too far away to see, we knew that beyond it the land dropped away, down, down to the Red Sea. It is easy to forget how high you are, living up here on top of the mountains and surrounded by more mountains; but the thought of that uninterrupted 8,000-foot descent charged the spot with massive potential energy. I had a momentary vision of tilting the bowl we were standing in and seeing Yemen pour away. (In fact, landslides have occurred here. Eight hundred years ago an entire village slid a mile down al-Ahjir and engulfed the hamlet below. The people of the second village complained to a judge and were awarded the topsoil which had arrived so precipitately on their doorsteps. The people of the first village were permitted to recover their houses.)

The track was good, and we almost skipped down it. All around us was the evidence of long and careful cultivation. 'Al-Ahjir' derives from the old South Arabian *hajar*, a town, and the name is shared with many other anciently inhabited areas. The valley is watered by permanent streams which once powered mills. Grain is still produced, mainly sorghum and a little barley, as well as apricots, peaches, almonds and *qat*.

The motor track soon doubled back to climb around the inside of al-Ahjir, serving a string of villages. We branched off it and climbed down into the empty flood course, turning to look up towards Kawkaban for the last time. We were leaving the familiar and trusting ourselves to gravity, as free as the water which when it rained would tumble over these rocks. Surrounded by Cock Brand coils, we would sleep wherever we were when the sun went down.

A few goats foraged, untended. One was standing on its hind legs in the middle of a thorn bush like the biblical ram caught in the thicket, reaching up to nibble at a leaf; another had scaled a tree and was munching its way, oblivious of the drop, along a slender branch. We neared the lip of al-Ahjir in silence, saving our breath for exclamations of wonder at the great panorama which would open up before us.

It didn't. Through the gap, all that could be seen was a narrow and gloomy canyon.

'I wonder if we've come the right way,' Debbie said. She reached into the pocket of my rucksack for the map and we followed the broken line of the track, down from the spot where we had left the truck, past the villages of al-Zuhar and Silyah, into the watercourse. Here the contours began to look like lines of panic in a Munch lithograph. There were no tracks or settlements; not even, for most of the *wadi*'s length, any of those tiny black squares which show habitations. Mentally I shrunk myself to scale – about the size of a mushroom spore – and dragged myself across the knotty 6-mile squares. We had come the right way. This was Wadi Surdud.

The canyon soon opened up, but in one dimension only – downwards. At the same time the cliffs above us edged closer together, threatening. Boulders underfoot grew larger, and the only sound was of our boots scraping to get a grip on their smooth surface. The cliffs shut out the sky and finally closed on us like a sphincter. We had to double up and edge through a tunnel where the sides of the *wadi* had collapsed, all but blocking it.

Then the gorge opened up a little and we sat down to rest. Debbie pointed to a tree on a boulder, gripping the rock with roots like a spider crab's legs: it could have had nothing to live on but air and dew, and it was flourishing. But the light, the little of it that penetrated, was fading with tropical swiftness. High above us, the cliffs were rapidly caramelizing.

'Don't you think we'd better find somewhere to sleep while we can still see?' Debbie said.

I remembered the *tahish*. This was definitely *tahish* country. 'Yes. But not here.'

We had maybe ten minutes of light. Soon the gorge opened up a little more and the sides were no longer perpendicular. We were standing on a small beach of white sand in the lee of an enormous flat-topped boulder.

'This is the spot,' said Debbie. She began to unload her rucksack on the sand.

I was horrified. 'Hey, are you crazy? This place is going to be slithering with snakes!' In the half light, every twig was taking on terrifying reptilian capabilities. 'Let's go up on to that boulder.'

'You can if you want. I'm staying here,' she said, unfolding her aluminium foil groundsheet. 'I'm not sleeping on a rock when there's all this nice sand around.'

'Well, I'm the one who's got to take your body back to your grieving parents.'

'Well, if you're that worried . . . But tomorrow, *I* choose.'

The top of the boulder was flat: it was not horizontal. We chased the tuna tin, then the candles, as they rolled away. The candles wouldn't stay lit anyway, so we ate our *kidam* and tuna in the dark. After supper I stood on the edge of the boulder, gripping it with my bare toes, and peed; there was a long gap before I heard it hit the sand. I swayed. There was nothing else to do, so we lit some mosquito coils, using the Imam's chauffeur's penknife and the empty tuna tin as supports, and lay down. Debbie crackled on her groundsheet.

It was too early for sleep so we played Botticelli.

'Are you', I asked, ages later, 'a Danish astronomer with a nasal prosthesis?' Debbie had failed on Bartók, but she had got Bacon, Byron and Blondie.

'No, I'm not . . . B . . . B . . .' She yawned.

'Want a clue? It was a *golden* nasal prosthesis.'

A minute later I heard her regular breathing and looked at my watch. Asleep at half past seven. I gazed up at the stars. Framed by the valley sides, their brightness seemed intensified, artificial, like a planetarium. I counted half a dozen shooting stars, and remembered from my research on the valley that in the year 1385 a stone two cubits long had fallen here from the sky. The sliding village, the falling stone – otherwise, the historians were silent on Surdud. I fell asleep wondering what the odds were against being hit by a meteorite.

It was not yet dawn when I woke up, but we needed to get an early start so I made breakfast, opening the *kidam* bag and feeling for a couple of cheese triangles. I glanced at my watch. It was eleven p.m.

Looking over to where Debbie was, I realized with a surge of panic that she was *not there*. The *tahish* hadn't left so much as a corner of her groundsheet. Or perhaps she had moved down on to her beach, where I would find her in the throes of death, writhing with asps. I dislodged the tuna tin, and the noise was answered by a moan and a rustle from below.

'Debbie! What are you doing down there?'

'Down where?'

I felt around for the torch. It too had gone. Then I realized what had happened. Because of the angle, we had slid down the smooth rock. Debbie, on her shiny foil, had gone further. At this rate she would have been over the edge before the sun was up. We found a part of the rock that was not so steeply inclined, but neither of us got any more sleep that night.

That was how it seemed. But what I was jolted out of was sleep, or something like it. The sky had turned violet and the stars were fading; there were twitters from all around, first isolated then joining together. Then I heard what must have woken me – a harsh, high-pitched scream echoing from the cliffs above, then another, then frenzied chattering. Debbie was awake too and we looked at each other, then up at where the sound was coming from. There was a clatter of tumbling scree, more jabbering, a glimpse of something half man, half dog.

'Baboons,' Debbie whispered. The sounds continued, but although we carried on scanning the high places we saw nothing. After a while all was quiet.

The distance from densely cultivated al-Ahjir was short, but we had passed into a secret and unfrequented place. Elsewhere baboons are often captured and killed, but this was their territory and we were interlopers. The sun was coming up, the birds had taken over with a seamless counterpoint of warbling, but we felt we were still being watched from the cliffs by *Papio hamadryas arabicus*.

I remembered the baboon I had met in a San'a street. It was blocking the way, teeth bared. I picked up a stone. So did the baboon. We stood glaring at each other until a group of men came calling, 'Sa'id! Sa'id!', and it scampered off down a side alley. Pet baboons are always called Sa'id, which means 'happy'. They are usually catatonically depressed or in a snarling rage.

We had breakfast and left the rock, light-headed after so little sleep. I needed a caffeine jolt but had to make do with a few gulps of water: there was no indication of when, or if, we would find any, so we had to ration ourselves. Almost on cue and totally unexpected came the sound, mechanical and rhythmic, of a water pump. But as we went on it resolved itself into something different. The sides of the gorge were narrowing again and amplifying the noise like the horn of an old gramophone – not a pump, but water itself, trickling and gurgling. Rounding a corner we saw a stream, only a small one from a side *wadi* but suddenly growing – from where? – as it met the main watercourse. It could only have come from underground. We washed the sleep from our eyes and filled empty bottles, scattering tiny fish.

The stream stayed with us along the gorge and we had to walk through it. It was a delicious feeling, the cold water swilling around the inside of your boots, until you stepped in a deeper part and they filled up with abrasive grit. For the next couple of hours there was relief, then grit, then a stop to undo laces and empty it out, then relief and the cycle starting again. By mid-morning we had two types of stops – boot-stops and bag-stops. Most of the bag-stops were mine, as my sixty-year-old rucksack had no shoulder padding. Every long walk I do I resolve to get another, but have never found a replacement for its bleached and mildew-spotted canvas among the garish hi-tech creations in the shops.

Then, as suddenly as it had appeared, the stream vanished.

'So,' said Debbie, 'that was Surdud.'

We had been looking forward to not carrying heavy water bottles. Now we would have to limit ourselves to sips and lug the stuff to Khamis Bani Sa'd. The sun was getting higher and we sweated down the canyon. During a boot-stop we examined the map and realized we had lost 3,000 feet in height since leaving the truck the day before, which explained the heat: in linear terms there were still three-quarters of the way to go.

Rounding another sharp twist in the gorge, we were heading into the sun and didn't see the woman until we were within speaking distance. She was coming towards us, picking her way nimbly through the stones.

'*Al-salam alaykum!*' said Debbie, cheerfully.

The woman, old and unveiled, appraised us with pursed lips. Her face was blotched with areas of lost pigmentation.* She didn't answer.

I was worried. If you meet an old woman in a lonely place and she does not respond to your greeting, she may be a witch. I wondered whether to exclaim, 'I take refuge with God from witches!' It would cover all eventualities: if she *were* a witch she would presumably disappear in a puff of smoke; if not, she would get the point that it is rude not to respond to greetings.

'*Wa alaykum al-salam,*' the woman said, just in time. 'Where are you from?'

'Britain.'

'And where do you think you're going?' she asked, with sudden and unaccountable anger. We pointed down-*wadi*. '*Ha!* So you're going to spend the festival in Britain!' She folded her arms and looked at us as if we were crazy. 'Well, you'd better hurry up or you won't get there.'

'Actually . . . we're going to Tihamah.'

'That's what I mean. You'd better hurry. The festival's today. Or is it tomorrow. Do *you* know?'

'Well, in San'a they said it's probably tomorrow.'

'*Ha!* You *don't* know!' She shook her head in pity. 'Well I don't know either. Hmm . . . you're going to spend the festival in your wife's village . . . what's it called? *Britain?*'

There was clearly no point in explaining.

'So what's the matter with you, boy? Why don't you ride?'

I shrugged feebly, gestured to the boulders, the towering cliffs, the burning sun.

The woman turned full on me. 'Shame on you,' she shouted, 'starving your wife like this!' She strode off, round the bend.

Debbie and I were left looking at each other, wondering where *she* was going. A full minute later, Debbie asked, 'What did she say you were doing to me?'

'She said I was starving you. *Tija'ja'*. Well, that's the dialect

---

* Ibn al-Mujawir ascribes the condition, known as 'white leprosy', to a number of possible causes: the bite of a yellow fly; an excess of milk and fish in the diet leading to the predominance of moist humours; or infection with the saliva of geckoes.

meaning. In Classical Arabic I think it means "to make a camel kneel so you can cut its throat".'

The gorge kept expanding and contracting like a gut in spasm. At times, there were glimpses far up into the ranges of al-Haymah on the left and al-Tawilah on the right, shoulders and crests looming above like the silhouettes of prehistoric beasts. The sky was clear, except for a few shreds of cloud which had snagged on the higher peaks; the sun glinted off the windows of houses perched on what looked like the least accessible ridges. I wondered, as I always did in the High Yemen, how men could be deluded into thinking themselves eagles.

Suddenly it would all be cut off, this other, higher world. The *wadi* sides would close together, shutting out the sun and confining us in secrecy. Translucent ferns, aliens from temperate places, clung where water dripped down the cliff walls, often where moisture showed itself as little more than a stain. And that was the strange thing. All around was the evidence of erosion, cliffs undercut, niches hollowed out of the rock by eddies, some with a whitish mineral deposit where water had lain and evaporated slowly – like the empty fonts and stoops of a redundant church. Gloom and damp and silence all added to the ecclesiastical atmosphere. It was gothic; not the rational gothic of medieval times, nor the stick-on gothick of Strawberry Hill, but the vegetable gothic of Gaudí, growing, slowly, by subtraction. But when? Here erosion was not a gradual process; these rocks had been subjected to sudden and gigantic forces of water and gravity, the same gravity which was taking us, increasingly painfully, down Surdud.

There was a third type of stop, the map-stop. We knew where we were going but not how far we'd gone; time had little bearing on distance. Triangulating by the sun, the direction of contours, and by elimination, we could at least find where we weren't. Where we were was more conjectural. There were a few scattered habitations marked, not more than half a mile away; but by totting up the contours we realized that the half-mile was both horizontal and vertical, and that the houses were the ones we had seen catching the sun.

It was during a map-stop that we heard an enormous bang. It echoed for perhaps seven seconds, a diapason reverberation on the scale of Notre Dame. And, strangely, there was something in the sound that took me back in time a long way.

Shortly after, a man appeared round a twist in the gorge. He greeted us and came to squat down nearby, his deeply cracked bare feet gripping the rock. His face was that of an old man but no grey showed in the hair escaping from his headcloth. I looked at his gun and wondered how his slight frame coped with the recoil, then remembered that in the school corps we had probably been no more than fifteen when we shot the same .303s. 'Can I have a look?'

He handed me the rifle. Its butt, smooth and patinated, bore a stamp.

'Do you know how old this is?' I asked.

'Old.' He looked at me. 'As old as you.'

I shook my head. 'It's as old as my father.' I pointed to the stamp, a crowned GR and 1916. 'Seventy-six years. This is the mark of our Queen's grandfather, George ibn Edward.'

'George Bush?'

'No, much older. But they're still the best guns – much better than the *ali*.'

The man nodded. The *ali* is the AK47, the standard weapon of contemporary Yemen, but guns like these, simple as they are, are admired in the same way as old daggers.

'I just missed a *wabr*. They move like demons,' he said.

'Why did you want to kill it?'

'For the festival.'

'So a *wabr* is lawful meat?'

'Yes. The meat's good, but you must shoot it in the head. If you get it anywhere else it pisses inside itself and you can't eat it.'

Debbie asked what a *wabr* was. I explained that it was a rock hyrax, a rodent-like creature which is apparently a biological relative of the rhinoceros and the elephant. I had never heard of hyraxes being eaten but knew that their dung is sometimes mixed with warm water and used by rheumatism sufferers as a poultice. They are timid animals, but if cornered are said to fly at their attacker's genitalia.

I handed back the gun. Alongside the AK47, American automatics are to be seen, and the occasional aristocratic hunting rifle. Even in urban San'a many households have something in case of emergency, perhaps an old tommy-gun gathering dust in a store-room; a story goes that many weapons were impounded there in the Seventies during a lunar eclipse, when the San'anis took to the streets to shoot at where the moon should have been. I wondered how this venerable weapon had got here – by way of Lawrence and the Arab Revolt, via the Somme or Vimy Ridge, or as part of a consignment bought cheap by a dodgy Aden trader. The man shouldered the rifle. He said he had to be going to see about preparations for the festival and took his leave, off to hunt the hyrax.

We pressed on for a while, then, more as an excuse to stop than from any desire to eat, sat down to have lunch under an acacia. The *kidam* were running low so, reluctantly, we went on to the festival cakes. They were dissolving into a mass of crumbs, and ants had got into the bag. We picked out some of the more intact fragments and dusted them off. They had a cloying texture, like plaster of Paris. Pudding was a boiled sweet. I read a couple of chapters of a biography of Vita Sackville-West I had brought and lay back.

Debbie was keen to be off. I envied her less aesthetically pleasing but ergonomically advanced rucksack, and grumbled like a camel being loaded as the hard canvas bit into my shoulders. I tried using spare socks as padding but they shed themselves after a few hundred yards. A nail was coming up through the heel of my right boot. Walking in this dry and stony place was ceasing to be a pleasure, and I looked at the patches of shade, longing to give in and curl up again with Vita; there was something of her in Debbie, I thought, striding out like Diana the Huntress. She disappeared round a corner. Then I heard her calling, too far off to know whether it was in distress or excitement. Rucksack bumping, limping to avoid the nail, I stumbled off at a trot and caught up. Debbie was splashing about in a stream. The water had reappeared.

Not long after, we saw signs of cultivation, the first since al-Ahjir. A few tiny fields had been terraced into the side of the *wadi*, way up out of reach of flash floods; they were long abandoned and, like deserted lazy-beds in the Scottish Highlands haunted by memories of the Clearances, there was an air of sadness about them. Soon after this came the first inhabited spot. It would never have appeared as such to the aerial photographers who made our map – the house, more of a byre, was the concave underside of a cottage-sized boulder, smoke-blackened and, even from the far side of the stream, smelling richly of cattle. A woman and a small child stood watching us. The woman replied to Debbie's greeting but waved us away as there was no man around.

We walked on, invigorated by the presence of running water, the late afternoon drop in temperature and the thought that we had passed back into the world of people, leaving behind the beautiful but disturbingly empty upper reaches of Surdud. The way had been tiring but not what you would call difficult. From now on it would be plain sailing. In regularly spaced villages curious but kindly people would invite us to decent meals.

'*Whayyy!*' The voice came from above us, on the left. '*Whaaah!* Where are you going?' A man skipped down the mountainside towards us. He had the same small frame as the hyrax hunter, and carried an axe with a tiny head and a long rough haft.

'Down the *wadi*,' we said.

'You can't. Come and stay with us, then you can go on through al-Haymah to the motor road.'

'Is that your place back there, with the cattle?' I asked.

'Yes, but we don't live there. Our house is up above.'

'How far?'

'Two hours. Three for you,' he added, glancing at our sticks. 'We'll be there not long after sunset.'

'That's very kind of you, but we ought to press on. You see, we're walking to Tihamah.'

The man smiled. 'You can't.'

On walks I was always meeting people whose parents' generation had thought nothing of going on a three-day march to buy a pound of sugar but who, within a few years of the first car coming, had been softened into total reliance on mechanical transport. Pansies. Namby-pambies. Thesiger was right: the motor car had spelt the death of Arab virility. 'But', I said petulantly, 'we've walked all the way from the head of al-Ahjir.'

He raised his eyebrows, impressed. 'I said you can't go on. Listen.' He cupped his ear downstream. Water tinkled pleasantly; a breeze had begun to blow up from Tihamah, ruffling its surface. But there was something else. A deeper, bass note, growing louder as the breeze gathered strength.

'You see?' said the man. 'The waterfall. Come and stay with us, then go through al-Haymah to the motor road.'

Debbie and I held a quick conference. We were speaking in English but the man, his head cocked to one side, nodded in agreement whenever I caught his eye. We had come so far. There was no way we would give up Surdud. It was just the usual assumption he was making that, being outsiders, we were puny.

'Is there *no* way past it?' I asked.

'No. There's no way past it. There's a way down it, but not for you. Come and stay with us.'

'You're very kind, but we'd like to try.'

We must be devil-driven. 'Well . . . I've done it myself. You . . . you do this . . .' he straightened himself up with his arms flat by his sides, 'then you slide, all in one go. At the bottom the water's up to here', he put his hand to his chin, 'when it's low.'

'Is it low now?' asked Debbie.

'Perhaps. But come and stay with us.'

'May God reward your generosity,' I said, 'but we'll try. We're strong – good climbers and swimmers,' I added, without much conviction.

'Then God be with you,' he said, shaking his head. He left us and made for the byre.

Five minutes later we came to a pool at the head of the waterfall. By now, the noise was a roar, though we still couldn't see its source. We ditched our rucksacks and waded in: the water was chilly and came up to our waists. It was still, but with the ominous calm of potential energy. Reaching the far side, I stood astride the lip of the cascade. Only the last few inches of the water's surface seemed to move, then slide over the edge like an endless skein of gunmetal silk before plunging some twenty feet down a chute.

Debbie joined me. 'That looks fun! Who's first?' She wasn't being ironical.

I looked down into the seething cauldron below. It led to a series of smaller cascades. 'Look, we don't even know what's under the surface. There could be rocks – I mean, you could twist an ankle, knock yourself out and drown. And how are we going to get the bags down?'

'So what do you suggest?'

I scanned the far side of the gorge. 'We could lever ourselves down that crack and . . .'

'What crack?'

I pointed to a fingertip-wide fault in the smooth rock. Debbie said nothing for a long time.

For half an hour we weighed pros and cons. Debbie was afraid of the climb; I was afraid of the water. The light went and we decided to sleep on it.

We waded back through the pool, picked up our bags and found a beach of clean white sand. I didn't argue, and was glad to lie down on the yielding surface after the last tortured night on the rock. We finished the *kidam*, treating ourselves to some cheese triangles, and before the end of the first round of Botticelli Debbie was asleep. I had discovered how to make a sort of sleeping bag by tying the ends of my sheet into bunches, and lay, hands crossed on chest, like a shrouded effigy on a medieval tomb, waiting for the slither of reptilian flesh. I slept well.

Another visit to the waterfall in the morning revealed the folly of attempting to go either round it or down it. So we went over the mountain instead.

Scrambling up rock that crumbled like festival cakes, clutching at roots, sending avalanches of scree over cliffs, we passed one point of no return after another. Eventually we found a goat-track that led down, and knew the danger was over. But the goat-track became a hyrax-track, then ended at the brink of a sheer sixty-foot gully. We climbed all the way back, then up a horribly steep slope to the next shoulder of mountain, only it wasn't a shoulder but a shoulderblade followed by a chasm. By now we were almost weeping with frustration. There was to be no more up, we decided, and followed the shoulderblade downwards. It bristled with desert roses and prickly tree euphorbias, and the rock was fissured and rotten like the vertebrae of a decaying carcass. We arrived at the bottom speechless, sweating, hands ripped, and realized the awful truth: six hours after we had started, we were back at the pool.

But something was different. There was no roar, or rather it was much fainter and came from our left.

'We've done it!' shouted Debbie, pointing to the waterfall five hundred yards upstream. It looked insignificant, a milky smear against the rock.

We tore off our sweat-sodden clothes, hung them in a tree, and lay in the cool water. Massaged by bubbles and fine gravel, the sense of disembodiment was bliss, the knowledge certain that this never was, and never would be, a route down from the highlands. We had solved a very minor historical enigma.

I read Vita while Debbie embroidered. The panel she was working on was a private, unconventional map, each triangle or zigzag representing a halt in a *wadi* or on a mountain, or a wait to fix a puncture. I suspected that, Penelope-like, she unpicked it at night, so slowly did it grow. By the time we set off, the afternoon was already dying, the sun raking across the water into our eyes. Looking back, the mountains immediately behind were high-lighted while their upper ranges were blue and unfocused, like the vanishing point of a Claude Lorrain landscape where centaurs live.

We came to a village. It wasn't on the map. The houses were of two storeys, one room below for the animals, one above for people. They looked like the garden houses you sometimes find in the walled demesne of a manor house, except that they were painted with blue, yellow and red diamonds like a harlequin suit. A dog barked, a donkey brayed, sorghum rustled. A woman's face popped out of the sorghum stalks, wished us a happy festival and scolded me for maltreating my wife. I gave her a Stan Laurel look of benign idiocy and left her clicking her tongue. 'Be careful of the *sayl!*' she shouted after us.

The *sayl*, the flash flood. I looked over my shoulder. Surdud smiled in the warm colours of late afternoon, but the blue distance had lost its innocence. Clouds were massing, stacked over the mountains from which we had come. The shallow brook we were walking through, only a few yards wide, was the outlet for a catch-ment area of thousands of square miles: it didn't take much arith-metic to work out the result of even a moderate shower in the highlands. I remembered going up Wadi Sara', which joins Surdud at Khamis Bani Sa'd, sitting on a load of firewood in the back of a truck, chewing *qat* and watching the cloud swirling round the peaks ahead. Suddenly the truck shot up the *wadi* bank with a scream of transmission – luckily I had my foot hooked under the

load ropes – and, with a roar, a chest-high wall of water the colour of oxtail soup boiled past us, inches below the rear wheels. That was a *sayl*, a little one.

Debbie walked nonchalantly on in the middle of the stream. I kept to the edge. The occasional houses we passed – still not on the map – were built high above the watercourse, which at one point narrowed into a throat. Overhangs and undercuttings became sinister in the fading light. There was no longer any doubt about the forces that had sculpted them. Like the Ancient Mariner I dared not look behind.

Just when it was getting too dark to see, the valley opened up again and we camped on a raised bank. It had been sliced away like a cake, but we reckoned we were far enough from danger. I lay on my back, worried less by snakes than by the serpent tongues of lightning licking the high peaks. There was no thunder; there were no stars.

Next day the sky over the mountains was still gravid and threatening. We walked for half an hour before realizing that we were following a motor track: it was so faint, a graffito almost washed away, that it only occasionally showed as a ridge of pebbles separating two barely indented lines. It crossed and recrossed the stream, losing itself in beds of sage which gave off a peppery tang like tomcat's piss. Stands of tall reeds and the odd *talh* tree, a kind of acacia, hid little fields, binding the precious soil together. Behind these were bare mountains, now lower and less jagged. From time to time a drab hamerkop flapped past with a whooping cry, or a huge electric-blue dragonfly hovered out of the way. Tall Goliath herons, each with its territory of double-bank fishing rights, stood trying to mesmerize the water. They were as still as garden statues and hardly bothered to lope into the air as we approached.

Visually it was Arcadia, but the pain of rucksack straps and blisters nagged like toothache. I knew how the ancient tyrants must feel, punished in a nether-world of tantalizing beauty by endlessly repetitive trials. I examined my feet: they were pallid, repulsive, like those troglodyte salamanders that live in permanent darkness. The heat was increasing. When we weren't walking through water we were crunching across a fine layer of silt at the stream's edge where it had cracked and curled up into huge cornflakes. More hamlets appeared, shimmering clusters of five or six houses on rocky spurs above us, each a little more prosperous as we got closer to Khamis Bani Sa'd, but the motor track was still as faint, a sporadic line on the palimpsest of the *wadi* bed. Dogs lay in pools of mud, and when one of them charged at our legs in a frenzy of barks I turned and chucked a stone, ripping the shoulder strap of my rucksack. The dog slouched off, grinning.

We stopped for lunch under a *talh* tree. Weaver-bird nests dangled from its branches like hairy fruit. I pictured rock hyraxes flying at them, teeth bared, in training for the day when they were cornered. We forced down the remaining fragments of festival cake. Food was beginning to occupy every corner of our thoughts. We knew that with each step we were nearer the port of al-Hudaydah and baked fish, blackened on the outside, succulently flaky on the inside, eaten with tomato, chilli and goat cheese relish; nearer to *fattah* of fresh bread soaked in ghee and dark, pungent acacia honey; nearer to mutton, tender as butter, baked slowly with mountain herbs in a clay oven, all washed down by icy Canada Dry Cola; and nearer to *shami*, the doyen of *qat*, raced down from the peaks of al-Mahabishah with the dew still on its asparagus-thick stalks, *shami*, fuel of dreams . . .

Somebody was calling us. We waved and passed on but he caught up with us in seconds. 'Shame on you for not stopping! Come and have lunch with us.'

Good manners require a refusal. We made the feeblest possible excuses and followed him up a rough track into one of the perched villages. It smelt of smoke and goats. In his one-roomed house, with his wife, parents and young son, we had our first decent meal for four days: spongy *luhuh* bread, like a big flattened crumpet, dipped into milk and chillis; broth with fenugreek; and boiled goat meat.

Until the Gulf crisis, Rashad had worked at a laundry in Riyadh. He hadn't seen his family for three years, which was typical of many rural Yemeni men who worked overseas. Surprisingly, he expressed little rancour over being thrown out – with nearly a million of his countrymen – by the Saudis, and hoped to go back. Just when was in the hand of God.

They wanted us to stay the night, but we brushed aside warnings that the *sayl* would carry us away. Rashad thought we might make it to Khamis that day if we hurried, but it was another four hours' hard walk. There was no chance of meeting traffic on the track: a vehicle might pass by once or twice a year. A greater contrast with Riyadh and its eight-lane highways could not be imagined, but Rashad had taken it all in his stride, as he had the appearance of these two shabby foreigners.

Again, the afternoon cloud was stacking over the mountains behind us, and people we passed shouted, 'The *sayl!* Be careful!' Debbie said that death by drowning held no fears for her now she had a good meal inside her, and something of her blasé attitude began to rub off: from keeping to the stream's edges, ready for the life-or-death rush up the bank, I started to follow her course down the middle of the *sayl* bed. It rained, great gouts the temperature of blood, but we weren't bothered: the danger was rain in the mountains.

It was now five o'clock and from what Rashad had told us of *sayl* timing we knew the threat was past. More worrying was the thought that we had at least another couple of hours before Khamis and would be walking in the dark: even after a real lunch, we were determined to get a ride from there that night, down to al-Hudaydah and its baked fish.

Rounding a bend we saw something totally unexpected: a man fishing with a rod and line. When we got closer, we saw that the hook was baited with maize.* He confirmed Rashad's estimate of the time it would take to reach Khamis.

'I don't suppose you've ever seen foreigners up this way,' said Debbie.

The man thought. 'Foreigners? Loads of them. Someone from San'a came here, oh, it must have been five years ago.'

The light went. Debbie plunged on, I lagged behind, stubbing my toes on rocks and cursing the nail in my boot. Debbie, who like Wilfred Thesiger had spent her early years in the British Embassy in imperial Addis Ababa, seemed to have inexhaustible reserves of stamina, while I wallowed in increasingly frantic self-pity. A dog howled, making me jump, and I remembered a story told by a San'ani friend. A man walking along just such a *wadi* at just such a moonless hour had stepped on something, a formless, squashy something. Suddenly all the dogs started baying. The

---

* Habshush mentions that fish called *awshaj*, a type of barbel, were caught in Surdud and elsewhere by poisoning with *dafar* seeds and sold to the Jews. Mountain tribesmen long considered fish to be an inedible kind of worm.

man went on. Soon afterwards he developed a tumour in his leg: what he had stepped on was a *jinni*. I borrowed Debbie's torch, which she disdained to use, and followed its pathetic stain of light.

Then I saw familiar shapes looming ahead. 'We're nearly there!' I shouted. 'See those mountains? They're opposite Khamis, where Surdud joins Wadi Sara'. I remember them well.'

Squinting into the gloom, I soon realized I hadn't remembered them at all — mountains all look much the same at night with no moon and no stars. I saw more familiar shapes but kept my mouth shut. Khamis Bani Sa'd might as well not exist: I would wake up in San'a, the baboon-haunted nave of Surdud forgotten as I was jolted out of this nightmare by the *petit mal* you experience as a false footstep in the first moments of sleep.

But we arrived. The sound of dogs and the smell of human habitation told us it was Khamis. We floundered through the confluence of Surdud and Sara' for another twenty minutes, stepping on squashy things, setting off choruses of barking: the *jinn* could go to damnation.

At last we climbed the steep track that led up to the tarmac of the al-Hudaydah road. There, bathed in neon, was a shop, its doors open and beckoning, a fridge humming next to stacked crates of Canada Dry. 'Debbie!' I croaked, 'Let's celebrate.' I stumbled over to the shop.

As I reached for the bottle opener a truck appeared, heading for al-Hudaydah. Debbie flagged it down and called to me. 'Come on! We might be here all night.'

I handed back the unopened bottle, the condensation deliciously cool in my palm, picked up my rucksack and staggered to the truck. I hauled my wrecked body over the tailgate. Debbie followed, decorously, and only a little more stiffly than at Shibam. There were half a dozen other passengers in the truck. Mechanically, we answered their questions – where we were from, where we were going, where we had come from.

'Shibam. On foot.'

There was a pause. '*Why?*'

'We, er, wanted to save money,' I said. And we had – a little over a pound. Our questioners fell silent. The wind rushed past, undoing my headscarf.

Peering ahead over the cab roof, I could just see the nick, like a gunsight, in the ridge of rock through which the road passes into the coastal plain of Tihamah. The nick is called Bab al-Naqah, the Gate of the She-Camel, after an unmistakable humped rock by the road. I've tried many times but I've never made out the She-Camel. Perhaps it is lack of imagination. Or perhaps too much imagination, which turns these igneous outcrops, these last ripped

margins of the High Yemen, into a bestiary of stone guardians: herds of camels both dromedary and Bactrian, marine iguanas, spiny anteaters, mastodons, stegasauri, centaurs, griffins, manticores, chimeras, *tahishes*. Even Britain's first woman prime minister is there, in profile.

★

After Bab al-Naqah the land is flat. In the dark, we couldn't see Tihamah; but we could smell it. Warmth and humidity released distant and near-subliminal odours of smoke, dung, roadside dead dog, jasmine. And somewhere, even here, was the smell of the sea.

Across this vapour-filled plain came the outsiders – merchants and adventurers, diplomats and soldiers, Ayyubids, Mamluks and Ottomans. It is the proper way to enter Yemen. Today, most people land at San'a Airport and see the place inside out. But not all outsiders came this way. One, al-Hadi, the first Imam, came out of the north. In Sa'dah he founded a line of scholar–warriors who ruled, until only a generation ago, for more than a thousand years.

4

Gorgeous and Disorderly

'There is not a people on earth whose power once waxed
great, but misfortune swept them away in its flood . . .'
                                        Wahb ibn Munabbih (d. AD 732)

HIGH NOON at Sa'dah *qat* market. I was on my way in when a
man grabbed me by the arm and gestured to a line of cob-
blers, their corkscrew curls bouncing as they hammered. 'These',
he said, 'are Jews.' There was a pride in his voice. It was like the
people of an English village pointing out a pond containing the last
examples of a rare species of newt – no one would have thought
twice about them had they not been in danger of extinction. The
danger is real: the Jews of Yemen used to number perhaps 75,000,
scattered across the country. After five decades of emigration, there
are now a few thousand at most, living in communities around
Sa'dah and Raydah. The last resident Jew of San'a died in 1992. An
eccentric, he spent his final years in a packing case.

    In the thick of the *qat* market, I squatted to inspect a pile of
green bundles. A Jew, indistinguishable from the other *suq*-goers
except for his sidelocks, came and squatted next to me. In no time
at all the three People of the Book – Muslim, Christian and Jew –
were going hammer and tongs at their ancient rivalry: trying to get
the best price.

    Wandering around with my *qat* under my arm, I realized that
Sa'dah is a true architect's city. The noble, tapering forms of the
buildings recall Lutyens's Whitehall Cenotaph but are dictated by

materials, not aesthetics. Houses are constructed rather like coil pots, but on a huge scale: a complete course is slapped down and left to dry before the next one, slightly thinner in section, is added. Each course is a seamless band of mud, and the technique gives a sinuous, plastic quality to the buildings. Small towers with loop-holes and projections have the appearance of faces – Easter Island faces. Sa'dah buildings are inhabited sculpture, mud at its most glorious.

Near Sa'dah's Bab al-Yaman – as in San'a, al-Yaman here means 'the south' – I was taken aback by a strange sight: the Great Mosque, a sober, blank-faced building, has erupted on its southern side into a rash of domed tomb chambers, some sprouting trefoil parapets, some ribbed like lemon-squeezers or jelly-moulds. Among all the tapering cuboids these tombs are an alien arrival – appropriately so, as they include the resting place of an incomer whose successors, although they were to dominate much of Yemen for over a millennium, were always set apart.

Yahya ibn al-Husayn was a descendant of the Prophet through his daughter Fatimah, who married the Prophet's cousin Ali ibn Abi Talib; he was therefore not of Qahtan but of Adnan, tradition-ally the founder of the Northern Arab line. Born and raised in al-Madinah, he was summoned, in AD 897, to arbitrate in a tribal dispute which had been raging around Sa'dah for three hundred years. Thus the two markedly different elements, tribes and imam, embarked on a contrapuntal relationship based on mutual need. Yahya adopted the title 'al-Hadi ila al-Haqq', the One Who Leads to Truth, and struck coins bearing the Qur'anic verse: 'Truth has come and falsehood has vanished, verily falsehood is a vanishing thing!' The first Zaydi Imam of Yemen left no doubt that he ruled by divine right.

Al-Hadi was in his late thirties when he arrived in Sa'dah: he was to die only thirteen years later. Often strapped for cash, his rule was limited to the northern city, with San'a under his control for short periods; but he attracted an immensely loyal following. Biographers tell of his great physical strength – of how, for example, he could stand his ground hanging on to the tail of a camel while its front end galloped over the horizon, and of how he could rub the inscription off a coin with his fingers: he impaled enemies on his lance 'as one spits locusts on a twig'. He was endowed too with healing powers, and the seals from his letters were said to have cured dumbness, quinsies and chronic diarrhoea. Al-Hadi, it is said, also fought with Dhu al-Fiqar, the sword of his ancestor Ali ibn Abi Talib,* and like Ali he was both a warrior and a scholar, the ideal for holders of the imamate.

The Zaydi sect, which al-Hadi led, was named after Zayd ibn Ali ibn al-Husayn ibn Ali ibn Abi Talib, who was killed in Iraq in AD 740.† Like other Shi'ah groups it has its origins in the rise of opposition to the caliphate in the eighth century AD. The Zaydis first achieved political power in AD 864 in Tabaristan on the southern shore of the Caspian Sea, and although Zaydism originally dictated that there should be only one imam, a special dispensation was made because of the great distance between there and Yemen. In theory the imam could be chosen from any of the *sayyids* – descendants of the Prophet – providing he possessed various qualities including justness, soundness in mind and limb, and courage. The imamate was not hereditary; neither was it elective – a prospective imam had to proclaim himself in a process known as *da'wah*, then be confirmed by the other *sayyids*. That Imam Yahya and Imam Ahmad both appointed crown princes was to be a bone of contention among their peers and a major factor in the final collapse of the imamate.

★

The old Sa'dah of the Zaydi imams is now, like most Yemeni towns, ringed by a belt of sprawling development. At first sight, the place seems to consist entirely of mechanics, oil changers and *bansharis* (puncture repairers). All the paraphernalia of transport make it look like one huge truck-stop.

The history of Arabia is one of perpetual motion, and the

---

* The sword, of ancient Yemeni manufacture, was found embedded in a column in Sa'dah by a later imam of the fourteenth century AD. It passed into the hands of the Rasulid sultan al-Ashraf, who had its authenticity confirmed when, after having sex, he found himself unable to lift it from its hook until he had bathed. One Dhu al-Fiqar is now displayed in Istanbul, although there are other claimants.

† Zayd's naked body was exposed on a rubbish dump for five years. Tradition says that his paunch drooped, miraculously, to conceal his pudenda.

settled Yemenis have from time to time been caught up in this as much as have the desert nomads. In pre-Islamic emigrations and Islamic conquests, and as migrant workers, Yemenis have always been on the move. Compare Arabia as a whole with medieval Europe: while the Arabs were covering phenomenal distances, the West, from the end of the Roman Empire until the end of the fifteenth century, tended to stay at home.

Thus, roads have a significance for the Arabs verging on the sacrosanct, and in Arabia one of the most important rights is the right of passage. The Islamic era begins with a journey – that of the Prophet Muhammad from Mecca to al-Madinah; pilgrimage is one of the Pillars of Islam; *sabil Allah*, the Road of God, is short-hand for all the exertions expected of a good Muslim. The English antonym to journeying, 'home', encrusted as it is with semantic barnacles, is not that far from the Arab's *a'ilah*, his dependants – an inviolable repository of honour; except that the Arab's home is movable.

All the more extraordinary, then, that despite all the comings and goings we still find Yemenis where they were centuries – often millennia – ago. The tribes al-Hadi mediated between, for example, still live in the same places eleven hundred years on. Few Englishmen can prove continuous occupation of one spot since Saxon times.

At a place where the puncture repairers are most densely concentrated, a turning marked by an oildrum leads north, following the old pilgrimage route towards the Hijaz and the birthplace of al-Hadi. We will follow instead the highway heading south down the backbone of the mountains. It is Yemen's spinal cord, and wherever the head has been sited, this road has ultimately controlled communications with the body of the country.

The journey begins with the emergence of the imamate in Sa'dah and ends with its eclipse in Ta'izz. As a ruling institution, its power was intermittent and often localized. It was under almost constant pressure from shorter-lived dynasties and foreign powers. But this pressure produced some outstanding leaders, like Abdullah ibn Hamzah, who fought the Kurdish Ayyubids, and al-Qasim, who defeated the Ottoman muskets with stones and founded a dynasty which reunited Yemen. Then, during the eighteenth and nineteenth centuries, the imamate fell into decline. Visiting in 1763, Niebuhr described the pomp of Imam al-Mahdi Abbas as 'gorgeous and disorderly'. The later al-Mansur Ali, famed for his profligate palace building, would regularly consume an aphrodisiac, Habshush informs us, prepared from the engorged pizzles of thoroughbred donkeys. The potion made him 'stronger than a Nile crocodile'.* A string of imams were born of slave-girls, and eventually the system crumbled into anarchy: one imam held the office on four separate occasions, each time under a different title; the imamate was sold for a night for 500 *riyals*; *sayyids* in San'a were dragged off the street and elevated temporarily to the imamate in order to legitimize Friday prayers. Playfair,

---

* The British Indian naval officer Cruttenden, who visited al-Mansur in 1836, describes the Imam's stately procession to the Great Mosque, mounted on a magnificent white charger, his hand resting on the shoulder of 'a confidential eunuch'. The Imam, however, lived a private life marked by 'gross sensuality', and within a month had been dethroned, insulted and immured in a dungeon.

writing in 1859, said, 'At the present day, Yemen can hardly be said to have any government at all.' Finally came the brilliant but flawed Hamid al-Din family: Imams Yahya and Ahmad, last of the scholar-warriors. Accompanied by the ancient trappings of power – the great tasselled parasol, and the executioner's sword named Purity – they ruled Yemen by divine right until, Canute-like, they were overwhelmed by the flood-tide of the twentieth century.

★

South of Sa'dah you pass through a region of vineyards. Crumbling watchtowers peep over mud walls. Pre-Islamic poets mentioned the growing of grapes in this region, and an ancient quiet hangs over the place, as though it were Naboth's vineyard before the days of Ahab.* But the signs of man soon disappear and the landscape turns to one of windy upland, blasted trees and sudden mountains like Jabal Maghluq, a tortured unclimbable mass, split down the middle like a cracked molar.

About sixty miles south of Sa'dah you reach Harf Sufyan, the market place and metropolis of the Bakil tribe of Sufyan. It is a temporary-looking town where a passing tumbleweed would not be out of place. A turning leads north-east to the Barat massif, home of Sufyan's cousins Dhu Ghaylan whose two branches Dhu Muhammad and Dhu Husayn are a paradigm for the gordian complexities of tribal relations: their subsections form the longest entry in al-Maqhafi's *Gazetteer of the Land and Tribes of Yemen*. Perhaps because they were often used by the imams as troubleshooters in Lower Yemen, Dhu Muhammad and Dhu Husayn became bywords for backwardness. The historian al-Wasi'i, writing in the 1920s, accuses them of being 'up to their necks in ignorance, heartlessness, violence and dissoluteness', and goes on to say that they tried to eat soap and thought that sugar-loaves – the conical, paper-wrapped kind you can still find in the San'a *suq* – were artillery shells. Another writer says that they

---

* The Sabaean word for a vineyard is *wyn*. Its similarity to the supposedly Indo-European root (*oinos*, *vinum*, wine, and so on) is striking, and makes one wonder where viticulture was first practised.

threw away rice thinking it was dead maggots and, never having seen mirrors, shot at their own reflections.*

Whatever their former lack of gentility, the people of Barat live in extraordinary houses. The building technique is similar to that used in Sa'dah, but here huge buttresses are added either side of the door, and the whole edifice striped in bands of ochre, orange and cream. The effect looks edible, like a rich confection of caramel and fudge. One unusual advantage of building in mud was revealed by a story told me in Barat. During fighting between Dhu Muhammad and Dhu Husayn, an aged artillery piece was brought into action. The storyteller and some friends were quietly chewing *qat* when they heard an explosion and saw a shell pass, like a country-house ghost, in one wall and out of the other, just above head height. It was, he said, not a unique experience.

After Harf Sufyan, the road rises on to a higher, even barer plateau. This ends at the town of Huth and the turn-off to the most famous of the northern centres of scholarship, the airy fortress town of Shaharah, a place that could stand as a symbol for the traditional Zaydi mix of the learned and the warlike.

On my first visit to Shaharah I left San'a at lunchtime and was in Huth in little over two hours. There were another forty miles to al-Madan, a major-looking place just north-west of Shaharah which, according to the picnic table sign on the map, was a market. The first third of the distance was on a 'Road, Loose Surface', better than a 'Motorable Track' and far superior to an 'Other Track'. The remainder was a 'Road, Metalled' which continued to the coast. It would take little over an hour, and I could spend the night in al-Madan and get up early for a bracing six-mile walk to Shaharah.

I got out at a filling station and looked for the road. There was nothing but a narrow dusty lane, and I cursed the taxi driver for setting me down at the wrong place. All the same, I checked with the man in the filling station. Yes, it was the Shaharah road. It took about three hours to get to the foot of the mountain.

---

* The soap story is also told, by Fynes Moryson (*An Itinerary Containing His Ten Yeeres Travell . . .*, London, 1617), of the Irish: 'when they found Sope and Starch, carried for the use of our Laundresses, they thinking them to be some dainty meates, did eat them greedily'.

'*Three hours?* But it says there's an asphalt road . . .'

The man shook his head. I felt cheated. A journey without maps was fair enough, but not one with a totally misleading map. And it had been prepared by the British Ordnance Survey, in tasteful colours. 'Users noting corrections or additions' were asked to send them, pencilled in, to Surbiton: the map would be replaced. When? In ten years' time, after millions more of taxpayers' money had been lavished on charlatans who could conjure sixty-mile roads out of nothing? My feelings mellowed slightly when I noticed, in very small print, 'Road Under Construction'; but, eighteen years after the phantom red line was printed, it still does not exist in reality.

Much of the journey to the market village beneath Jabal Shaharah was made in the dark, and I spent the night on a metal workbench in a welding shop. Next morning, with bruised hip bones, I hitched a ride up the mountain in the back of a truck. The road climbed ever more steeply and, for the last section, turned into a series of large steps. It was here that supporters of Imam al-Mahdi Husayn saw him floating down the steps – after his death in battle in AD 1013 – along with Jesus.

Shaharah air is rarefied and brittle, stinging the nostrils after the muggy lowlands. The place is a retreat for study, a bleached ivory tower with a hint of refined asceticism. Shaharah developed its own tradition of *belles lettres* and became a pillar – literally, if on a giant scale – of the faith. It is also an eyrie, a lookout from which no movement of armies below would go unnoticed.

Although Shaharah seems impregnable, it fell to the Turks in 1587 but was retaken by Imam al-Qasim, who used it as his headquarters and died there in 1620. After that it was never captured, and even the Egyptians in the 1960s could only bomb it from the air. Its greatest moment of glory came in 1905, when a large Ottoman force was beaten off in hand-to-hand fighting at the gates.

Now, although the mountains round Shaharah are a prosperous *qat*-growing area, the town itself is a bit forlorn. For better or worse, its future may depend on tourism. In 1982 this was just beginning, and a grand house had been turned into a simple but impressive *funduq*. I called in to leave my bag and ask about lunch, and the woman in charge told me to go and pick up a chicken. Ten minutes later I returned with a scraggy and comatose bird, handed it over and set off for a walk.

The walk took me, inevitably, to The Bridge.

Shaharah is, like Jabal Maghluq, a split mountain, and The Bridge that joins its two halves has to be capitalized because it is one of *the* images of Yemen. Neither does it disappoint, a honey-coloured arc soaring over a dizzy chasm of dark rock, built around a hundred years ago. Beneath it are the stumps of an earlier structure.

I was back at the *funduq* at 2 p.m., after shooting at rocks with some undress policemen and visiting the prison, where I drank tea out of a rusty bean tin with the leg-ironed inmates. A German couple had arrived, fashionably weathered by a life of smart travel destinations. Their safari clothes were hi-tech, the sort which would pack away into a Coke can. (My own wardrobe comprised a shirt inherited from someone shot dead in Northern Ireland, a pair of Hong Kong cotton trousers nearly gone at the right buttock, and boots reinforced with bits of tyre.)

After a strained international greeting, a sort of Red Indian 'How!', the Germans went back to their digestif *qishr*. They looked happily well-fed, and I was looking forward to my own lunch. A girl brought it in. Something was missing – the chicken. I asked where it was and she summoned her mother. 'Where's the chicken?' I repeated, glancing at the Germans.

The woman looked me straight in the eye and said, 'The cat ate it.' It was an act of God and I could hardly ask for my money back, but as I dug into cold rice and vegetables I heard a sound from the Germans. I thought it was a purr, but it was the auto rewind of a camera.

Tourism in Shaharah is now big business. The local tribesmen have a monopoly on trucking foreigners up the mountain and – quite rightly – do well from it. As always there is a flip side: women drawing water from the cistern are too picturesque for words, and many tourists have shown surprisingly scant sensitivity as to where they point their cameras. It is even rumoured that a former French ambassador brought a magnum of champagne to drink on The Bridge, under cover of darkness. One only hopes, given the roughness of the road, that he chose a *marque* that travelled well.

★

It was in Shaharah that I saw my first *bara'*. It was at the time of one of the Islamic festivals, and there was a tense excitement in the air. A man was heating a large copper drum over a fire. When it was tuned he began beating it, a single insistent beat. Men and boys, bright in their festival clothes, appeared and formed a circle. It had soon reached forty or fifty strong. Another rhythm came in, higher pitched, syncopated, and as sharp as pistol shots, and the circle began to revolve. Every so often, it twisted, reversed and dipped. *Jambiyah* blades flashed in unison. Then the circle became still and a pair of older men entered the space in the middle. They began advancing towards each other, then retreating, describing more complex circles around the pivotal point. The rhythm speeded up; someone began to shoot off-beat tattoos on an assault rifle. Despite all the weaponry and the warlike sounds, there was a delicacy in the movement. It was awesome to watch, but enchanting.

I have purposely not called it a dance. Dancing, for the tribesmen, is frivolity, and has its own time and place. Ethnologists have called the *bara'* an expression of tribal solidarity. Certainly, each tribe has its own steps; and with the display of weapons and connotations of honour, it may resemble the medieval tournaments of Europe. But whatever it is, it is not dancing.

In the days before I came to realize this, I dropped a brick at a wedding *qat* chew in a remote mountain region. One of the chewers was an unusually traditional *sayyid*, and when I asked him why he hadn't yet joined in the dancing, the gathering fell suddenly, horribly silent. Then someone whispered, '*Sayyids* don't dance . . .' Seeing my consternation, the *sayyid* chuckled and said, 'We don't dance; but we can do the *bara'*!' He gave a signal to the drummers, got up, and did a solo turn in the middle of the room.

The tribes around Shaharah are members of the Bakil confederation. Bakil and Hashid, the other main northern grouping, are traditionally traced back to eponymous ancestors. The two are brothers, great-great-grandsons of Hamdan; Hamdan is an eighth-generation descendant of Kahlan, son of Saba and brother of Himyar. Between them, the names Hashid, Bakil and Hamdan have dominated northern Yemen since well before Islam. But from the earliest inscriptions onwards, there is often confusion over whether a tribe, a person or a place is being referred to. There are also instances, up to recent times, where a whole clan, because of a disagreement with its 'lineage' group, has left Hashid for Bakil or vice versa. In fact, a look at the dictionary shows that the two names are connected to verbal roots meaning to ally or mix. Genealogy, then, has probably as much to do with place and politics as time and descent, and membership of the tribe often means not so much kinship as citizenship.

Al-Hamdani said of the Qahtani family tree that 'its roots are deep, and therefore its branches are lofty'. He might have added that the branches would be impenetrably entangled were it not for the grafting and layering of the genealogists. It is precisely because the tribal family tree represents something more complicated than bloodlines that it has lasted so long. At the time when the Hutu-Tutsi problems were brewing in Rwanda, Abdullah ibn Husayn al-Ahmar, Paramount Shaykh of Hashid, said to me, 'Tell them we are not like the tribes of Africa!' If they had been, the Yemenis would probably have wiped themselves out centuries ago.

The *qabili* – the tribesman – is an ambivalent figure, particularly for the town dweller who regards him as both noble and savage: savage in that *qabili* equals yokel, hick, hayseed (and irretrievably so – a proverb says that 'the *qub*', the tribesman's indigo headcloth, will always leave its mark on a man's forehead, even if gentility shines out of his arse'); noble in that a townsman of tribal origin – and most of them are – will declare with pride, 'We, our family, are *qabilis*.'* Pride stems from honour, honour that is almost as tangible as a suit of clothes and which, like clothing, protects and decorates. Honour can be brought into the most everyday transactions. If you give a taxi driver a hundred-*riyal* note for a short ride, by saying 'Give me *qabyalah*' – what a tribesman would give – you are honour-bound to accept whatever he hands back, he not to

---

* The contradictory nature of mountain tribesmen was noted by the journalist Walter Harris, who visited Yemen in 1892. 'The Yemenis', he wrote, 'are the aristocracy of Islam. Wild in appearance, their manners are perfect.' The manners remained perfect even when Harris did his party trick – administering electric shocks with a small generator he carried in his baggage.

overcharge you. *Qabyalah* is, perhaps, a species of gentlemanliness, a first cousin of fair play.

Stories abound of the heroism and incredible magnanimity of tribesmen. Here is one from the history of al-Wasi'i: 'A man who had killed another fled and took refuge, unwittingly, in the dead man's house. Hot on his heels came a group including the victim's brother. The victim's father, who was shaykh and judge of the place, learnt that it was his son who had been killed. However, he kept the killer under his protection and calmed his fears. Then the brother demanded that his father try the killer, who still did not know that his victim was none other than his protector's son. In the presence of the two parties [that is, the killer and the victim's brother] the shaykh ordered blood-money to be paid. The killer then asked for permission to go to his own people to collect the money, after which he would return and pay it to the brother. At this the shaykh said, "I have judged that you should pay blood-money as justice demands, but since your victim was my son I absolve you from payment. This is because you took refuge in my house and in order that you may benefit fully from my protection and feel no fear. So, go to your people in peace. In God is my recompense for all I have lost." The killer immediately burst into tears and wept so greatly that he almost fainted, but the shaykh calmed him and said, "No blame attaches to you, my son. Go on your way with a clear conscience." And the killer answered him saying, "I weep because I do not know how one such as you can be allowed to die." '*

Since the 1962 Revolution, everyone has become, symbolically, a tribesman – *sayyids*, butchers and other non-tribal groups included – by adopting the *asib*, the tribesman's upright dagger. Liberty, equality, fraternity: it could be a tribal warcry. In southern Yemen, where the Party outlawed tribal names, tribalism is now undergoing a renaissance.

Some urban intellectuals and technocrats view tribalism as a dangerous and potentially anarchic force. Many San'anis remember the sack of their city by the tribes in 1948, and the old tribal

---

* Tribal generosity sometimes became a fetish. Doreen Ingrams says that travellers who did not stop to accept hospitality from the Buqri family in Hadramawt would be shot at.

slogans, one of which went: 'We are thieves, we are highwaymen, we wear our skirts above our knees!'*

Distinctions between city and tribes are blurring. But the *bara'* has yet to be demoted to folkloric display. For the moment, the drums will beat on, the blades will flash, the circle will wheel and dip. And the brows of intellectuals and technocrats will remain furrowed as they try to work out just how it seems to adapt itself to the rhythm of the times.

★

Khamir, a town eighteen miles south of the Shaharah turn-off, is in the Hashid heartland. It has a prosperous yet dour look to it: you are out of the region of mud and into one of stone. Nothing softens the uncompromising angles; buildings are devoid of the spun-sugar fripperies of San'a plasterwork. The town looks less like a community than a convocation of pele towers. But soon after Khamir you come to the pass of Ghulat Ajib, and here, behind an abandoned petrol tanker, there is a sudden change. The ground drops to a vast and fertile plain, Qa' al-Bawn, a great carpet of little dun and green compartments unrolling to the horizon and strewn with villages and farmsteads. At the first town of the plain, Raydah, I once picked up a taxi to San'a. It was early afternoon, chewing time, and the passengers were in voluble mood. The man next to me was from the Sharaf al-Din family, descendants of a sixteenth-century imam who had settled in the fortress town of Kawkaban. We soon got on to the favourite subject of *qat*-chewers: *qat*.

'Our ancestor, Imam Yahya Sharaf al-Din, tried to ban this,' he said, handing me a branch. 'But the religious scholars and doctors in Mecca wouldn't support him. They said *qat* wasn't a drug. Now, the Saudis say it is a drug, but only because they know we'd sell it to them and get rich.'

I suggested that his ancestor must have made himself highly unpopular.

---

* Another version runs, 'We are thieves, we are highwaymen, our knees are nailed!' Having nailed knees has something of the English expression 'putting hairs on your chest' – or even 'lead in your pencil'.

'Ah, except for the *qat* business, he was a great man. He defeated his rivals the Tahirid sultans. His son captured two thousand of their followers, cut off every second man's head, and had the others carry them back to San'a. Dreadful times . . . a thousand heads . . . A great family.'

The act was a hard one to follow. The Sharaf al-Din family, exhausted by their subsequent fight against the Ottoman invaders, retired from politics to their fastness of Kawkaban where, for the past four and a half centuries, they have been writing poetry and running genteelly to seed.

We passed through the town of Amran and on to the last of the al-Bawn plain, where a cement factory puffs away like a beached tramp steamer. As the road rose, the man from Bayt Sharaf al-Din looked across to the west, to the distant and misty escarpment where his family held sway. Kawkaban, the Starry One, named because of the lavish use of plaster and white stone in its buildings, runs along the cliff edge like a row of gleaming incisors. Crows and kites scud past its windows, spying out carrion a thousand feet below in Shibam.

The taxi passed through a landscape of extinct volcanic cones before beginning the descent to the San'a plain. One of the curious features of this road down the mountain spine is that, even though it seems to drop in a series of huge steps as you journey southwards, the total altitude lost is negligible. The effect is like one of those *trompe-l'oeil* drawings where the eye climbs a staircase and, without appearing to descend, ends at the point where it started.

For some time the road had been skirting the territory of Arhab, a Bakil tribe. Arhab was the goal of probably the most eccentric traveller the Muslim world has ever seen. The Reverend Joseph Wolff, an Anglican clergyman born a Jew, had convinced himself that Arhab were none other than the Rechabites, a group of nomadic teetotal Hebrews.* In 1836 he arrived in San'a, having distributed along the way Arabic copies of the New Testament, *Pilgrim's Progress* and *Robinson Crusoe*, and intending to bring Arhab into the Church of England. His reception was cool, but he avoided any serious incident. Wolff was less lucky when (following a spell as a curate in Massachusetts) he arrived in Bokhara eight years later claiming to be the Grand Dervish of the United Kingdom, Europe and America. This time he was on the trail of Stoddart and Conolly, two British officers who had been imprisoned by the Amir Nasrullah Khan. In Bokhara he discovered that his compatriots had been beheaded, and escaped the same fate only because the Amir found his appearance uproariously funny (the clergyman was travelling in full academic regalia). After these adventures, Wolff retired to his Somerset vicarage and never left England again.

Some decades later Habshush saw, in the house of a Jew of Najran, a copy of the New Testament which seems to have been

---

* This curious people also features in the work of another Anglicized Jew, Disraeli's 1847 novel *Tancred, or The New Crusade*.

one of Wolff's. Its owner, not surprisingly, kept it well hidden, which makes one wonder whether in some byre or woodshed around San'a there may still exist a wormy Bunyan or Defoe. The latter was an ironic choice for a Christian missionary, as it was probably inspired by a twelfth-century Andalusian's account of how a foundling child on a desert island grew from *enfant sauvage*, via Plato and Aristotle, not to Christianity but to Islam.

To the west, we passed the turn-offs to Tuzan and Madam, where rich volcanic soil nourishes grapes and *qat* of rare quality, before reaching the eastern end of Wadi Dahr.

Wadi Dahr is one of the world's surprises. I first saw it at 9.47 a.m. on a Thursday late in 1982. We slewed off the road by a petrol station and laboured up a slope of disintegrating red rock. The bonnet of the car flapped open and shut, as if gulping for air. I had no idea where we were heading. Then my host hit the brakes and we slid to a stop in a cloud of red dust. The dust, settling, revealed a view: picture several square miles of intensive cultivation, shockingly green, transposed to a setting of tawny rock, then dropped far below the surface of the earth.

Over a thousand years ago, a visitor looked down on Wadi Dahr and exclaimed, 'I have travelled the length of Egypt, Iraq and Syria, but never have I seen the like of this.' Earlier this century, the sons of Imam Yahya had a small cave here fitted with glazed doors so they could chew *qat* surveying the scene. Today, people do the same, but in parked cars on the cliff edge. Yemenis are connoisseurs of landscape and colour (a San'ani friend once dismissed the Royal County of Berkshire – 'There's too much green'); here, the distance to the valley floor enables the eye to take in everything at once, as in a diorama. The prospect is neither of this world nor the next, but of another Eden.

Down in the valley, we were magicked into a secret world. Labyrinthine paths twisted between walled vineyards, *qat* plantations and orchards of pomegranate, peach and apricot glimpsed through gates made of twigs. Some of the entrances were so small that I expected to see a bottle of pills labelled, like Alice's, 'Eat Me'. Parts of this enormous *hortus conclusus* remain invisible behind high walls and handleless doors, like that in Holman Hunt's *Light of the World*.

In this weird sunken landscape, it came as no surprise to catch a complete palace in the act of vertical take-off. Dar al-Hajar, the Palace of the Rock, stands on top of a huge pillar of stone that has popped up out of the valley floor like a jack-in-the-box. The building itself is not a folly but a standard, if rather grand, San'ani mansion constructed in the 1920s by Imam Yahya, the abode of a comfort-loving stylite. The folly is all nature's for putting the rock pillar there in the first place.

Strange happenings might be expected in such a place as Wadi Dahr, and one in particular is still remembered by its older inhabitants. About fifty years ago, a man bought a house near the little *suq* to the west of Dar al-Hajar. He moved in but found the place haunted by a poltergeist which would bang about the house and upset the pots. Having tried all the usual means, the man appealed to his neighbour Imam Yahya, who wrote to the spirit commanding it to be gone. Even this attempt failed. In desperation, the man proposed to the poltergeist that he would no longer try to exorcize it provided they could live together in peace. The cohabitation was successful, and for some years the spirit would run errands, finding lost possessions and going to market. In recent years it has been less active. A neighbour commented that 'Even the *jinn* grow old.'

The Yemeni poltergeist, *idar al-dar*, appears in one account as 'a beast of Yemen which copulates with humans. Its semen consists of maggots.'* An old house I once lived in was inhabited by an *idar*, but it did nothing more disturbing than smoking a water pipe outside my bedroom door every night, at around one in the morning. Others are known to take snuff.

★

On the morning of 17 February 1948 the unsuccessful exorcist, the hammer of the Turks, al-Imam al-Mutawakkil ala Allah Yahya ibn al-Mansur bi Allah Muhammad Hamid al-Din of the al-Qasimi dynasty, descendant of the Prophet, Commander of the Faithful, ruler of the Mutawakkilite Kingdom of Yemen and one

---

* The great ninth-century polymath al-Jahiz's *Book of Animals*. Al-Jahiz, 'Popeyes' (his real name was Abu Uthman Amr ibn Bahr al-Basri), was reputedly killed by his own library when the piles of books he worked among collapsed on top of him.

of the most remarkable monarchs of the century, set out to inspect a new well at a farm of his south of San'a.

The Imam was travelling in a single car, accompanied by a small grandson, his Prime Minister Qadi Abdullah ibn Husayn al-Amri, and two soldiers. As was his custom, he left the main body of his escort at Bab al-Yaman, to save money on transportation. While the vehicle was passing along a narrow point in the road at Sawad Hizyaz it came under a barrage of fire that killed all its occupants. Yahya's body was found to have fifty bullets in it. He was in his eightieth year. He had never seen the sea.

According to one account, the first shot was fired by one Muhammad Qa'id al-Husayni, a shaykh of Bani Hushaysh. It was he who checked the Imam's body and found the old man still alive. 'You've got as many lives as a cat!' he said, and finished Yahya off with a bullet in the heart.

The ambush was led by Ali Nasir al-Qarda'i, a shaykh of the Murad tribe and a remarkable character in his own right. A poet and warrior, he had fallen out with the Imam twenty years before and had been imprisoned in San'a, but was able to escape by having a pistol and *jambiyah* smuggled into his cell in a tin of ghee. Later, Yahya pardoned him and sent him to occupy Shabwah, claimed by the colonial government in Aden. The British responded by dispatching a force under the Master of Belhaven, and after a short battle between the two scions of fighting stock, al-Qarda'i was ejected. Under the gentlemanly terms of surrender, the shaykh was allowed to take his rifle on to the aircraft which would take him home to Bayhan; but he realized that the plane was in fact heading for Aden and, in what may have been one of the first aerial hijacks in history, he forced the pilot to take him to his intended destination. On landing, al-Qarda'i bought a sheep and gave the aircrew lunch. He interpreted the incident, naturally enough, as a plot devised by the Imam and the British to get rid of him, and said,

> The trick was hatched by San'a and London,
> Plotting together, *sayyid* and Christian!

Belhaven's version claims that 'the RAF very handsomely flew him back to Beihan [*sic*] to save him the long desert march'.

Whether the regicide was the result of a personal grudge or, as al-Qarda'i's supporters claim, stemmed from a genuine desire for political change, will always be open to question. Al-Qarda'i's original reluctance to kill Yahya was assuaged by a *fatwa* issued by opposition *sayyids* permitting the assassination; it was a strange alliance, between a fastidious and urbane religious élite and a tribal leader who decorated his rifle butt with ibex beards and who, in his youth, had lost an eye and most of his nose in a fight with a leopard.

Yahya Hamid al-Din was born in 1869 and spent his early years, like any young *sayyid*, in the pursuit of knowledge – Qur'anic exegesis, jurisprudence, grammar, and so on. His father was proclaimed Imam in 1889 and went into opposition against Ottoman rule; he and Yahya, his only son, were to spend the next fifteen years moving from one northern fortress to another, whipping up funds to buy tribal support and fighting a guerrilla war against the forces of occupation. Following his father's death in 1904, Yahya was accepted as Imam. Thus began the imamate's strange Indian summer.

Yahya spread the word that he was here to replace with the *shari'ah* the corrupt and worldly rule of the Ottomans. Relying on a combination of charisma and cash, he had the capital surrounded in less than a year. The 1905 siege of San'a was just one in a series of trials undergone by the city's long-suffering inhabitants, but it was the worst. People were reduced to grinding straw for bread and to eating cats, dogs and rats. A horse was sold as meat for four hundred silver dollars. There were, it is said, cases of cannibalism. By the time the siege was raised by Turkish reinforcements from the coast, around half the population had died of hunger.

Yahya retreated to Shaharah, but his campaign continued. A succession of governors were sent to Yemen by the Sublime Porte, but the Turks realized they were losing ground and came to a power-sharing agreement with the Imam. After the First World War, they left for good.

The three decades of Imam Yahya's reign were stable, but to the point of stagnation. Yahya was no delegator, and the bulk of the administration rested in his hands. On one level, security was better than ever before. Muhammad Hasan, an Iraqi military adviser who lived in San'a during the 1930s, claimed that only one policeman was needed to keep the entire city in order. Offenders in country regions were brought to book by having military units billeted on their villages: the soldiers had to be provided with everything, including *qat* and tobacco, until the criminal was handed over. Muhammad Hasan also approved of the hostage system. Yahya kept some four hundred young male relatives of tribal leaders in San'a, which 'brought benefits no constitutional laws can match'. The Iraqi, however, deplored conditions for women ('outwardly beautiful, they yet have no *psychological* beauty'), which resembled those in his own country fifty years before. As the twentieth century progressed Yemen – in the eyes of foreigners, and particularly other Arabs – went backwards in time until, towards the end of the imamate, it seemed to them to be firmly stuck in the Middle Ages.

Few outsiders were as complimentary as Muhammad Hasan. A Syrian agricultural adviser, Ahmad Wasfi Zakariyya, claimed for example that the Imam kept boy hostages fettered in 'schools of evil and wretchedness' (a later visitor, Lady Luce, described the hostage system as 'a sort of compulsory Eton'). But it was the sense of claustrophobia that weighed heaviest. The British entomologist Scott complained constantly of the lack of freedom to travel. Ahmad Wasfi put it more dramatically: 'He who enters Yemen is lost, and he who leaves it is reborn.'

In external relations Yahya, despite his maxim that he would 'rather see his people eat straw than have a single foreigner in his land', was not an all-out isolationist. His reconquest of the coastal plain of Tihamah from the Idrisi *sharifs* in 1925 was due in part to arms and technicians sent by the Italians, and during both his reign and that of his son Ahmad there was a small but persistent Italian presence. The British tried to counter it in 1940: their secret weapon was Freya Stark, sent to show Pathé newsreels to the ladies of the royal court. To the blandishments of oil companies, however, Yahya remained immune. When an American company offered $2 million for exploration rights, he retorted – with visionary cynicism, some would say – 'And how much will it cost to get you out?'

Politically, the outside world was tapping insistently on the

Imam's front door; economically, Yemen was far from self-sufficient, and through the tradesmen's entrance at Aden came a constant stream of goods — essentials like paraffin, and luxuries like Ovaltine, for which the Mutawakkilite princesses had a particular penchant.

A few carefully selected Yemenis were sent abroad — those who could pose no possible threat to the monarchy. They included al-Sallal, the future first President of the Republic, and Hasan al-Amri, who was to defend San'a against the Royalists in the Seventy-day Siege of 1967–8.

At home, by whittling away at the tribes' independence, Yahya did not endear himself to those who, after all, had brought him to power. He also incurred the anger of the *sayyid* class by forcing them to recognize Ahmad as heir to the imamate. In circumventing the process of *da'wah* he was treating the institution like a hereditary monarchy. The two systems could not co-exist.

For many, however, life went on as it had for the previous thousand years. Among the loyal supporters of the status quo was the historian Abdulwasi' al-Wasi'i, author of *The Relief from Care and Tribulation in the Events and History of Yemen*, written in 1928 and one of the last great annalistic accounts of the imamate. In this, unruly tribes are put down by righteous and valiant princes, who bear the honorific 'Sword of Islam', and the humdrum life of good and bad harvests is punctuated by marvels: demonic sheep, giant hailstones, a false prophet, and a clairvoyant madman who reveals a treasure. Al-Wasi'i warns — ahead of his time — of the dangers of cigarette smoking, which 'causes a worm to grow in the brain'.

A slightly later contemporary, Isma'il al-Washali, also wrote an annalistic history. Again, local events are carefully recorded. There is, for example, the story of the cat in Milhan which was struck by a bolt of lightning while sitting on a drum and sealed unharmed under the drumskin. But in al-Washali's history, the outside world is beginning to impinge. The author lived in Tihamah, where he had witnessed the coming and going of Turks, Idrisis, Italians and British. There is much fascinating detail on an eventful period in Tihami history but perhaps even more interesting is his reporting of happenings further away, and particularly of new inventions.

Some he was able to see for himself, like the telegraph, which on one occasion 'brought word of the destruction, by a comet, of two cities of India whose people are infidels. They are cities of Amrika in the Land of the Franks.' The wireless telegraph arrived soon after: al-Washali suggests that it works by means of mirrors. Later, in 1917, the first telephones and moving pictures appeared in Yemen. Other inventions are reported second-hand, like the 'land steamer' on the Hejaz Railway, the 'steamer which flies in the air' built by the Germans, and the aeroplane – two were brought down during fighting between the Ottomans and the British near Aden, 'perhaps with a magnet'. In the very last entry before his death in 1937, al-Washali records the arrival of foreigners – probably Scott and his party – who had come to collect insects and other vermin. To the end, the Franks remained inexplicable.

Unlike most other twentieth-century Arab leaders whose image proliferates as their power grows more absolute, Imam Yahya maintained a total ban on representations of himself. Apart from the Islamic strictures on portraiture, it had been rumoured during his fighting days that he would only die if he were drawn or photographed. Another Syrian visitor in the 1920s, to whom the Imam had said, 'You may photograph anyone and anything you like – except me,' described him thus: 'His countenance is grave yet bright, his frame evenly proportioned, and his face tawny and round with a few smallpox scars. He has a high forehead, large cranium and small mouth. His eyes are dark and glint magnetically. His nose is short and broad, and his beard black. He has small hands and feet.' According to those who knew him, the sketches of Yahya which a number of visitors drew from memory bear little resemblance to him.

Yahya has been condemned for many faults, chiefly his isolationism, but also his miserliness (after his death the rebels discovered a cache of tens of millions of gold sovereigns and hundreds of millions of Maria Theresa dollars). But unlike Imam Ahmad, he is rarely charged with tyranny, although his functionaries were often overbearing and corrupt. And none would deny his credentials as a traditional Zaydi scholar. He published occasionally in the international Islamic press, and it was even suggested by the Lebanese Islamic reformer Muhammad Rashid Rida that Yahya assume the caliphate, in abeyance since the fall of the Ottomans. Despite an early Islamic prophecy that San'a would get a turn as the seat of the caliphate, he refused.

In his personal life Yahya was an ascetic. His only indulgence was *qat*, and even this he gave up on his physician's orders. Perhaps his greatest failing was that he expected others to emulate him. He banned music and imprisoned one of his sons for riding a 'fiery bicycle'. The national anthem, chanted by massed troops after the end of Friday prayers, went:

> O you who disobey our master and transgress his orders,
> There is a day you will surely see,
> A day when the heads of children will go grey
> And birds stop dead in the sky!

Scott summed the Imam up: 'If anyone on earth can say, "I am the State," it is the Imam of Yemen.'

During Yahya's reign, the trumpets were blown every night at three o'clock Yemeni time – three hours after sunset. This was the signal for everyone to go home and turn in. The whole nation was, symbolically, tucked up in bed by the High Victorian paterfamilias whose love for his people, his children, ultimately stifled them.

The coup of 1948 was intended to set up a constitutional imamate, with Abdullah al-Wazir holding the title. It had the support of many prominent members of the *qadi* class, learned families of Qahtani tribal origin who resented the patronizing attitude of the *sayyids*. For some, the descendants of al-Hadi were still incomers a thousand years on.

The idea had been to kill Ahmad, at the time Governor of Ta'izz, and his father simultaneously; but the revolutionaries lacked all but the most basic means of communication and had to depend on bicycles to carry messages. Worse, news of the coup – including a complete list of the intended revolutionary government – had been leaked to the foreign press a full month earlier. Also, the manner in which the old imam was disposed of shocked many of his subjects. The princes in San'a mustered enough support to win back Qasr al-Silah, the fort that dominates the city, while Ahmad rushed up from Ta'izz. One account claims that he had dogs slaughtered before the tribal leaders, in a grotesque and shaming parody of the *aqirah* ceremony in which sheep or bullocks are slaughtered as a plea for aid. In the event, the tribes streamed into San'a to carry out Ahmad's revenge.

The Sack of San'a lasted for seven days, and according to the historian al-Shamahi was carried out by 250,000 tribesmen. They vandalized and plundered, taking anything movable − including doors and windows: some of the plunderers were themselves plundered by latecomers. Ahmad had shown the strength of his hand but carried righteous vengeance beyond the limit. It is understandable that he never lived in the capital again, and no wonder that the San'anis backed the Republic from the start.

Less than a month after his proclamation as Imam, al-Wazir and the other ringleaders were executed. It took ten blows of a blunt sword to sever al-Husayni's head. Al-Qarda'i, who had held out on Jabal Nuqum for twenty days, slipped away but was caught and killed. For two months his head, which even in life Belhaven had compared to that of a month-old corpse, stared down with its one eye from Bab al-Yaman. The warrior-poet's very last verse, uttered with the curious snuffling sound that came less from his mouth than from the gaping hole above it, had been:

> To Yahya ibn Muhammad I say:
> We shall meet once more − on Judgement Day . . .

★

South of the spot where Yahya was assassinated, the road passes through a fertile valley whose pumpkin fields are interspersed with shallow terraces of barley, before dropping down in another huge step. From the top of the step, the Yislah Pass, the view on to the plain of Qa' Jahran is immense. Red-winged grackle wheel and whistle overhead; from below comes the distant chug of irrigation pumps. Although the plain lies indisputably beneath you, it is actually higher than San'a. It took the introduction of altimeters this century to reveal the fact, so complete is the illusion of continuous descent.

Down on Qa' Jahran the road, for once, is straight. Here, huge dust devils wobble and pirouette over a land that 5,000 years ago was marsh and lake. People say that the sky in these parts is cracked, and the wind pours in through the holes. Dhamar, the largest settlement of the plain, is a prosperous town. Seen from the road it is the usual hotch-potch of eateries, stores and filling stations – 'a confused or despersed city', as the Englishman Benjamin Green saw it in the early seventeenth century; but its origins are ancient and, unusually, there is a visible link with the city's presumed eponymous founder. Pre-Islamic inscriptions built into the Great Mosque there mention Tha'ran ibn Dhamar Ali, the Himyari ruler whose bronze statue, together with that of his father, dominates the entrance hall of the National Museum in San'a. (The statues are the joint work of two sculptors, one with a Greek name and the other Yemeni; they depict their subjects as typical Hellenistic athletes – foreskins and all.)

The men of Dhamar are the canniest in Yemen and, proverbially, a Dhamari is worth two San'anis. There is a story behind the saying: some years ago two San'anis and a Dhamari were travelling together. In those days, cotton sleeping bags were used to keep out the cold and the fleas. During an overnight stop the San'anis decided to play a trick on their companion and, as he slept, they burned holes in his bag with coals from the water-pipe. The Dhamari did not appear to stir but realized what was going on, and when the San'anis were asleep he slipped out of bed and cut off their donkey's lips with his *jambiyah*. Next morning, the San'anis roused the Dhamari, shouting, 'Look! Look! The stars have fallen and burned holes in your sleeping bag!' 'I know,' he replied sleepily. Then he pointed to their donkey: 'Even the donkey's still laughing about it.'

Typically, the account of the thirteenth-century traveller Ibn al-Mujawir centres on girls, whose suitability for marriage can be judged by observing how hard they bargain in the *suq*. The medieval Syrian geographer Yaqut also writes on the women of the region. Of two villages south of Dhamar he says, 'Nowhere in Yemen are the women lovelier. Adultery is widespread and people come from afar in search of wantonness.'

Another story, if true, would give some substance to Yaqut's comments. Ludovico di Varthema, a Bolognese gentleman traveller, was captured in Aden in the early sixteenth century. The Portuguese had been trying to seize the city, so the Tahirid governor's suspicions were justifiable. Varthema was taken to the Tahirid capital Rada', south-east of Dhamar, and incarcerated. In no time at all one of the Sultan's wives became inflamed with passion for the fair-skinned prisoner (luckily, her husband was away at the time). She would come and contemplate him, Varthema says, 'as tho' I had been a nymph'. Later, she took to feeding him eggs, hens, pigeons, pepper, cinnamon, cloves and nutmegs. In order to extricate himself, the Italian decided to feign insanity. This he did by attempting to convert 'a great fatt sheepe' to Islam; but the plan backfired when some of his captors began to suspect him of being a holy man. The case was resolved, however, when he urinated over some religious scholars sent to assess him – 'whereby', Varthema says, 'they agreed that I was no Sainct, but a mad man.' Eventually, he persuaded the Sultana to let him go to Aden to visit a genuine holy man for a cure, and from there he escaped. Not long ago, I bumped into Varthema in the British Museum. He was in the Print Room and still travelling, a gnome-like figure with staff, scrip and hairy knees, striding out lustily along the bottom margin of Holbein the Younger's world map.

For two and a half centuries following Varthema's journey, Western visits to the Yemeni interior were sporadic. The first organized European expedition since the Roman Aelius Gallus's abortive military adventure took place in 1763 and was funded by the King of Denmark. This time the aim was scientific, and the group included the celebrated Swedish botanist Peter Forskaal, a student of Linnaeus. But the expedition fell victim to Tihami malaria, and when its members arrived in Yarim, the next large town on the road south from Dhamar, Forskaal was already exhausted by fever. He died shortly after.

Seven years after it started out, the expedition returned to Denmark. Of the five members who had left Copenhagen, only the Frieslander Carsten Niebuhr survived. The combined knowledge he brought back was of inestimable value, and the book of the expedition became a best-seller. It included the first significant contribution to European cartography of Yemen since Ptolemy. The title of Niebuhr's map is inscribed on a parchment scroll which, appropriately, unrolls to reveal a branch of the choicest *qat*, *Catha edulis Forsk*. The botanist would have approved.

The Sumarah Pass south of Yarim, which Forskaal ascended tied to the back of a donkey, is the highest point of the road from Sa'dah to Ta'izz and the divide between Upper and Lower Yemen, Zaydi and Shafi'i. Western writers have dwelt too much on supposed implications of the division. The two schools of Islamic thought have never been seriously at odds, doctrinally or otherwise. What does happen south of Sumarah is that rainfall increases: the people here, al-Hamdani said, 'live up against the udders of the sky'. More rain means more crops, which make the area irresistible to tax-gatherers. While further north the medieval and later states usually left the tribes to their own devices, here in Lower Yemen an overtly tribal system has long been buried under layers of centralized bureaucracy.

Together with port dues from Aden, the lush farmland south of Sumarah provided the cash for that most magnificent of Yemeni dynasties, the Rasulids. Between the thirteenth and fifteenth centuries they ruled Lower Yemen and made Ta'izz a wealthy and cosmopolitan capital, cultivating literary figures and scholars of religion. One of these, however, proved something of an embarrassment to them. To visit him, we must temporarily bypass Ta'izz, along a road that continues southward through a fertile *wadi* before arriving at the foot of Jabal Habashi. Here is the town of Yafrus, the centre of devotion to the Sufi *wali* and poet Ahmad ibn Alwan. He was born glowing: later, his sanctity was confirmed when a green bird landed on him. The Rasulids tolerated him as a sort of *memento mori* − perhaps surprisingly, as some of his poetry is forthright in its condemnation of them. For example, he warns the reigning sultan,

> Shame on you for building lofty palaces,
> When your subjects live in dungheaps!

Ibn Alwan died in 1267 but his popular following survives; the mosque at Yafrus is always full of lunatics taken there in the hope that the *wali*'s influence will bring about a cure. On the *ziyarah* or annual visitation to Ibn Alwan's tomb, Benjamin Green says, 'The goast of the said saint is said to walke, and telleth them of many strange things, which they houlde and doe beleeve infallible, and with these and the like abominable falshoods is theire develish sect maintained.'

The place has an undeniably strange atmosphere which proved all too much for Imam Ahmad. As Governor of Ta'izz in 1939 he was less tolerant than his Rasulid predecessors, and had the *wali's* tomb chamber demolished.* It has been rebuilt, and the mosque itself remains intact, a pair of bosomy domes rising above a host of lesser ones against a backdrop of green mountain.

Some visitors were overwhelmed by the fecundity of Lower Yemen. One of these was Ibn al-Mujawir, who passed through in the time of Ibn Alwan. On a certain pass in the region, he says, are two rocks in the shape of vaginas, which are said to menstruate. 'I did indeed see something like blood on them, but was unable to confirm whether it was blood or not.' One of his scientific friends suggested that the liquid might be *mumiya*, mummy, since 'the origin of human mummy is a substance which condenses in rock and flows from it. Some people say that the rocks give off a bad odour, but I smelt it and found it otherwise . . .'

South of Yafrus the vegetation becomes even lusher. The asphalt finally gives out at al-Turbah, some 340 miles south of Sa'dah. Since Ta'izz, the road has dipped beneath the 5,000-foot contour, but here the altitude rises again, the highlands' last fling before they drop into the empty southern coastal plain.

★

Ibn Alwan's reprimand to the Rasulid sultans was ignored, and not long after his death Sultan al-Mu'ayyad built a showpiece palace, al-Ma'qili, just east of Ta'izz. The palace was decorated with gold and marble; pleasure gardens were laid out, with cisterns and fountains that rivalled the *jeux d'eau* of the Alhambra, its contemporary at the other end of the Muslim world. Now, only some bits of a cistern are left.

The Rasulids were true renaissance princes, active in many

---

* Mainstream Zaydi opposition to Sufism has always been implacable. One imam cured a lunatic maidservant by having her fed bread baked on a fire fuelled by *Al-Fusus*, a famous tract by the Andalusian Sufi Ibn Arabi. A similar prescription also cured an eighteen-month bout of diarrhoea.

branches of the sciences. A set of chronological tables produced for al-Mu'ayyad are the most detailed for any location in the medieval Islamic world. Another ruler, al-Ashraf, personally constructed an astrolabe, now in the New York Metropolitan Museum of Art, and made the earliest known reference in an Arab text to a magnetic compass. Others wrote scholarly treatises on agriculture. At a time when a large part of the Islamic world was still in ruins from the Mongol attacks, Ta'izz was the repository for much that had been lost elsewhere.

The Rasulid city, with its extraordinary buildings, must have looked strange to visitors from further north. For the Rasulids, spiritual and temporal beauty were closely linked and their mosque-schools, like the Ashrafiyyah with its twin minarets, were enclosed by covered terraces from which their glittering capital could be surveyed. The city itself turned its face not to Yemen's mountain interior, but to Aden and beyond the sea. Together with new ideas in science and architecture, lavish gifts were exchanged between the Rasulid court and the rulers of Egypt, the Levant, Persia and India. A glass vase enamelled with the Rasulid blazon, a five-petalled rosette, has been found in China, and was perhaps part of the gift sent by Sultan al-Muzaffar to the Chinese Emperor to persuade him to allow the circumcision of Muslims. The gifts that flowed into Yemen included menageries of animals – leopards, elephants and 'grammatically-speaking female parrots'.

The Zaydi Imam al-Mutahhar's epitaph on al-Muzaffar, who by the time of his death in 1295 had not only brought Hadramawt under his control but had also composed several scholarly works (including one on the magical properties of gemstones), may serve for the Rasulid dynasty as a whole: 'The one whose pens broke our lances is dead.'

In this century, Imam Ahmad was less kind to the memory of that brilliant dynasty, and used the palace-builder al-Mu'ayyad's tomb as a petrol store.

Ahmad, in general, followed his father's policy of isolation. (He did commission a US corporation to conduct a geological survey of the country; after the 1962 Revolution, the resulting map was found hidden inside a wireless set.) Nothing, however, could stop the flow of money into Ta'izz via Aden. During his thirty-odd years there as Governor and then Imam, the city grew enormously. Yet there could be no greater contrast to the Rasulid palace of al-Ma'qili than Ahmad's Ta'izz residence next to the Turkish barracks. The building is now a museum, entered through a cramped courtyard and a series of guardchambers. Visitors have commented on the palace's tatty air, and on its contents which, for the writer Eric Hansen, 'brought back memories of my middle-class American childhood in the 1950s'. Given the benefit of time, the objects could become *objets*, but at the moment the senseless duplication of possessions, with whole rooms given over to scent bottles or fountain pens, is reminiscent of the boudoir of Miss Havisham or Imelda Marcos.*

Ahmad's last residence is in its way as alien as the first Imam's resting-place in Sa'dah; but while the palace suggests that he was an introverted hoarder, Ahmad was also a lover of the dramatic and extrovert gesture. In front of the building there is now a busy traffic intersection, but in 1955 it was a place of execution.

Ahmad, who for some time had seemed to be living the life of an invalid recluse, had been besieged in his palace by army units led by al-Thalaya, an officer unhappy with the Imam's authoritarian rule. Ahmad was persuaded to sign abdication papers which gave the throne to his brother Abdullah. In fact, he was playing for time. When the Imam was certain of support from irregulars and local shaykhs he burst out of house arrest, sword in hand, and by force of character alone made his former guards join the attack on the rebels. He also sent a warning in verse to Abdullah, saying that the rebellion had lit a fire which, 'If right-minded men do not put it out, will be fuelled by corpses and heads.' True to his word, Imam Ahmad had Abdullah and another brother, Abbas, decapitated in Hajjah. Of the other ringleaders, thirteen were executed here in Ta'izz. When it came to the turn of Qadi Abdulrahman al-Iryani, he bowed his head. The executioner raised his sword, smeared with the blood of those he had already dispatched. Suddenly the Imam called 'Stop!' Shortly afterwards, al-Iryani was released. He went on to become second President of the Yemen Arab Republic in 1967.

---

* A hoarding instinct seems to have run in the family. Robert Finlay, Assistant Surgeon to the British Mokha Residency, who treated the ruling Imam in 1823, wrote in his diary: 'The rooms His Highness occupied during his sickness were so full of horse trappings, jimburs [*jambiyahs*], swords, matchlocks, pistols, organs, common empty bottles, bales of piece goods, broad cloths. English silks, etc. etc. that there was scarcely room left for him to move. On his pillow were fixed 6 gold and silver watches, all going.'

A photograph of Ahmad (unlike his father, he did not object to being portrayed) shows him watching the executions, surrounded by family and courtiers. The Imam sits in the middle, his great bulk clothed in white, his face framed by a dense beard (dyed black – it was said to have gone grey prematurely during a fight with a *jinni* who was guarding a treasure), a white turban on his shaved head.* The eyes, the famous exophthalmic stare said by his detractors to have been deliberately induced by sleeping with a rope tied round his neck, study the scene with shrewd yet bemused appreciation. We cannot see it, but clearly the sword is poised to fall. The other onlookers display neck-craning concentration, knuckle-biting suspense, and in one case laid-back boredom. One of the little princes in the foreground ignores the spectacle completely and is playing with something in his lap.

There was something superhuman about Ahmad. A visitor in the 1920s said, 'When I placed my hand in his, it was like touching an electric current.' During his campaigns against the Tihami tribe of al-Zaraniq he claimed to be bullet-proof; and like the Prophet Solomon and the first Zaydi Imam, he was said to have the *jinn* under his control. Ahmad cultivated such rumours, and others which claimed that – again like Solomon – he could also control wild animals. Often he could be glimpsed in a high window of the palace, stroking a tiger. The tiger is still there, a cuddly toy sitting on top of a wardrobe.

Throughout the 1950s opposition to the Imam grew. Pamphlets denouncing the imamate flew from the presses, the airwaves buzzed shrilly with attacks on Ahmad from Nasser's Cairo. The Imam could not beat them, so he joined them. In 1958 the Mutawakkilite Kingdom became part of the United Arab Republic, now renamed the United Arab States; its official capital was al-Hudaydah. Egypt and Syria had found themselves the strangest bedfellow but Nasser, who had spent so long calling for Arab unity, could hardly refuse. Ahmad had dealt a masterstroke.

During the 1950s Imam Ahmad developed a passion for Heinz

---

* Until recently Ahmad's personal barber was still at work in Ta'izz. I have been shaved by him, and admit that as the blade passed over my throat, I felt a frisson at the thought of where the hand holding it had been.

Russian Salad. At some time in the same decade, he became dependent on morphine following the administration of the drug during an operation, and in 1959 he left for Italy to be cured of the addiction, taking with him a retinue of 140 staff. The visit was a success; the only hitch occurred when the Imam's guards rushed on to the street brandishing their *jambiyahs* – some *paparazzi* had swarmed up trees in an attempt to snap the royal harem.

On his return via Egypt his famous meeting with Nasser took place. The Imam refused to rise from his bed to greet the President, an omission which strained their relations to breaking point. Yemen's membership of the UAS was withdrawn in 1961, when Ahmad publicly belaboured Nasser in verse for his unIslamic socialist policies.

Back home, dissent continued to simmer. While Ahmad was away the Hashid paramount shaykh, Husayn al-Ahmar, considered staging a coup and setting up the malleable Crown Prince al-Badr as Imam in place of his father. Ahmad was furious, and in his speech on landing at al-Hudaydah he displayed his talent as a showman to the full. In verse, he threatened his opponents with 'blows so hot that fire will turn to ice'; he vowed, in prose, to lop off heads and 'smash stuck-up, corrupt noses with a pickaxe'; and – the final flourish – he brandished a sword: 'My blade burns with thirst for the blood of the necks of those who desire to snatch rule from its rightful owner! If there be any here whose veins throb with such satanic insinuations, let them come forward. Here is the horse, here is the battleground, and if anyone calls me a liar then let him be put to the test!' Had the circumstances of his birth been different, the Imam might have had a glittering career as a Hollywood villain.

Two years after the speech, also in al-Hudaydah, Ahmad's challenge was taken up when three army officers emptied their revolvers into him at point-blank range. Having turned his body over to check he was dead, the assassins fled. In fact, the Imam had survived the attack. His opponents began to wonder whether his claim to be in league with the supernatural was not entirely baseless.

Imam Ahmad died in Ta'izz, of natural causes, on 19 September 1962. In the words of one revolutionary, which recall that other far-reaching event in Yemen's history, a dam had collapsed.

Ahmad's son al-Badr was proclaimed Imam. A week later, the tanks moved in on the new monarch's ironically named residence, Dar al-Bashayir, the Palace of Good Tidings. Al-Badr escaped down the long-drop of a lavatory and fled San'a as Abdullah al-Sallal, a trusted officer of Imam Ahmad, took over with the blessing of Cairo. At long last, some pointed out, power was once more in the hands of Qahtan's descendants.

Al-Badr and the Royalists, for their part, found an eager backer in the Saudis and this, together with Nasser's support for the fledgeling Republic, sparked off what became a proxy ideological war. By the end of 1964 around 60,000 Egyptian troops were in Yemen. Their use of napalm foreshadowed events in Vietnam; the Saudis, true to the memory of Imam Sharaf al-Din and to their own pre-modern image, offered a bounty for severed Egyptian heads.

The Royalist cause attracted several foreign soldiers of fortune and at least one eccentric. Bruce Condé, an American, had originally become attached to the royal court in the late 1950s because he shared with Prince al-Badr 'a consuming interest in postage stamps'. Through Condé, the Mutawakkilite exchequer profited from foreign sales of Yemeni stamps. The American fell from favour but was back during the war, this time – according to Thesiger, who travelled with him and thought him 'a strange character' – as Major-General Prince Bourbon Condé, Postmaster-General in the Royalist Government.

Of the mercenaries, the most notable was Colonel David Smiley, an ex-SAS man who had fought the Jabal Akhdar rebels in Oman. His exertions there were followed by a spell as Scottish contributor to *The Good Food Guide*, before taking command of the fifty or so British, French and Belgian soldiers in the Imam's forces. Among Smiley's responsibilities was keeping the mercenaries supplied with parachute drops of beer, scotch and brandy from a depot in Saudi Arabia. He took up the command on condition that he be allowed to return to the UK for his children's school holidays; it was to come to an end in the summer of 1966, when he was appointed a Gentleman-at-Arms to Her Majesty the Queen.

Cairo soon realized just how crippling was the cost of maintaining a huge military presence in Yemen, and with the 1967 war with Israel the Egyptians needed every soldier possible at home. Al-Sallal, too much a creation of Nasser, was ousted in a bloodless coup – 'bloodless,' said *The Independent*'s obituary, 'because no one lifted a finger to defend him' – and replaced by the more tradition- ally minded Qadi Abdulrahman al-Iryani, who had escaped the executioner's sword. The Saudis, terrified of the Left, breathed a sigh of relief and gradually withdrew their support for the Royalists. The Revolution had resulted not in the destruction of the old socio-political edifice, but in a reshuffling of its constituent blocks. It resembled, perhaps, the French Revolution more than the Russian. But, like everything else in Yemen, it was not quite like anything else on earth.

The tribes have proved the most durable element in the struc- ture. They had always had a love-hate relationship with the Zaydi imams, sometimes falling dramatically foul of their nominal ruler. In 1727, for instance, the imam of the day killed the paramount shaykh of Hashid with his own hands, impaled his head on a lance and galloped off towards San'a shouting at the tribesmen pursuing him, 'Your idol, Hashid and Bakil!' The tempestuous affair came to an end in 1960, when Imam Ahmad had Shaykh Husayn al-Ahmar and his son Hamid executed. Poor Hamid, not yet thirty, had spent his life since the age of eight as a hostage attached to the court.

Hamid's brother Abdullah is the present paramount shaykh. A 'progressive' after the Revolution, Shaykh Abdullah is now leader of the Islah Party, which represents a conservative – though not traditional Yemeni – strain of religious thinking. He is the most powerful tribal leader in the country, with tens of thousands of armed men at his disposal. He is also Speaker of a democratically elected parliament. This seeming paradox may titillate Western commentators and Arab intellectuals, who view the tribes as an inherently anarchic force. The contrast, as so often in Yemen, is imagined.

In his role as Shaykh of Shaykhs, he must 'gather the word' of his people. As Speaker, he gathers the word of Parliament. In tribal terms he is, by virtue of his position, *hijrah* – set aside and unassail- able. In Parliament, he puts aside party allegiances and is, in a sense, made *hijrah* by the Speaker's chair.

Urbane, charming, but still a tribesman in his speech, Shaykh Abdullah's very appearance is a compromise: he wears the long coat of the religious scholar, but the ordinary headscarf and upright dagger of the tribesman. One wall in his San'a house is a pictorial history of Yemen over the last forty years, beginning with photographs of his father and reaching the present via shots of himself in Revolutionary government posts. Next door, however, he has built a new house, its entrance front surmounted by the upright *jambiyah*, the blazon of *qabili*-dom. Inside, another wall tells a different story: it is carved with his tribal genealogy back, almost, to the year dot, with names he has given his bandolier-hung sons, like Qahtan and Hamdan. The ancestors are being resurrected, the lineage made permanent in stone.

★

Al-Sallal, rehabilitated from exile, was brought out every year to reminisce on the anniversary of the 26 September Revolution until his death in 1994. In the *suq* you can still buy tin tea-trays commemorating his first official meeting with Nasser. The Egyptian, with his boyish smile, looks like a used car salesman; al-Sallal appears surprised, as if he hadn't expected to be the chosen one who was to end a thousand-year dynasty. As the market for commemoratives goes, the trays must rank as something of a flop.

Until his death in August 1996, the last Imam of Yemen resided in the English Home Counties, in the bosky purlieus of Bromley. His father, however, was not allowed to rest in peace. It is said that after Imam Ahmad's death some tribesmen tried to break into his tomb. Their intention was not to desecrate it, but to check that those eyes of his were shut, once and for all.

5

Emerald, Amber, Carnelian

'Of this will they assure you, those who know:
Ours is the Green Land – look to the hills!
For the Watchful One blesses them with rain
In times when all His creatures thirst.'
                    Dhu al-Kala' al-Himyari (d. AD 1014)

AL-SUKHNAH means 'Hot', and the place was living up to its
name. A drop of sweat fell from the tip of my nose into my tea
with an audible plop. I was too drowsy to mop my face. The
torpor was due not so much to the febrile Tihamah night as to the
Egyptian soap opera on the TV across the yard. The plot: poor
boy, factory worker, falls in love with boss's daughter . . . The rest
was predictable. Even the calf tethered next to my string bed
seemed to be following it. That highly coloured world of gilt
what-nots and candy limousines, the 1,001 cliffhangers (camera
zooms to startled face) – it's all been done before, long ago, by the
suq storytellers. But it did seem strange in this dun place where the
mountains meet the plain.

Al-Sukhnah, though, is no ordinary Tihamah town. The name
comes not from the climate but from the hot springs which bubble
up at the base of the mountains, and the town dates back only to
the days of Imam Ahmad. In his declining years, Ahmad spent an
increasing amount of time here, stewing his corpulent frame in
water heated by underground fire. Al-Sukhnah was also the setting
for his one and only press conference. The journalist David

Holden was engrossed by the Imam: 'His face worked uncontrollably with every utterance, his hands tugged at his black-dyed beard, and his eyes . . . rolled like white marbles only tenuously anchored to his sallow flesh.' Again, it was the eyes.

Early that evening I had found the bath in a clump of shabby, block-like buildings. There were three pools of varying temperature, from very hot upwards: the first was just bearable; the second I dipped a toe into; the third was hot enough to boil a lobster. The bath-keeper told me that the temperature varies from season to season. At the moment it was 'quite cool'.

The waters of al-Sukhnah are said to be good for rheumatism and skin diseases. I had come out of curiosity, and to loosen my limbs for an unrest cure in the mountains of Raymah.

★

Anyone who had not been there before would need some persuading that Jabal Raymah existed at all. But it was there, invisible behind the post-prandial Tihamah haze. Al-Mansuriyyah market, the departure point for the mountain, was settling down for the afternoon, and potential Raymah passengers were drifting away alarmingly. The Landcruiser taxi would leave only if it was full; earlier, the *suq* seemed to be packed with Raymis on their way home, but they couldn't provide a stable quorum and the taxi-driver had spent the last three hours appearing and disappearing with shrieks of differential and clouds of dust, like a *jinni* in a huff, trying to round them up.

I was the eye of the storm, the queue of one at the taxi stop. Raymis would come and use me as a timetable, getting the latest travel information then dashing off to make some last-minute purchase. All the last minutes mounted up. I should have been recording the manners and customs of Tihamah market-goers, but all I remember is an old man on the pillion of a motor cycle, brandishing a pair of crutches to clear a passage through the crowd. Several people were felled, as if by the scythes on Boudicca's chariot wheels.

A man was shaking me by the shoulder. I must have dozed off. 'Come on! You're holding everybody up.' He dragged me away by the hand. Waiting for the taxi in an orderly English way I had forgotten that the world, and not least al-Mansuriyyah, was in a state of perpetual flux. To paraphrase the pre-Socratics, you could not stand in the same queue twice.

The man was soon ahead of me. I had the longer legs but while I shuffled, he skipped, the result of a lifetime of mountain paths. Even dressed in a suit and tie, his gait would still have given him away as a mountain man.

The taxi was packed. I followed my acquaintance to a place on the roofrack, but one of the fifteen or so passengers inside was ejected and I was pulled in instead. A woman in the back admonished me when I protested. 'Shame on you, Professor. Old people like us deserve to travel in comfort.' She was old enough to be my grandmother.

We were off. The driver selected a cassette and turned the stereo on full. A rhythmic slapping and a noise like a vastly amplified comb and paper, just recognizable as a *mizmar*, a double reedpipe, came from the single working loudspeaker. We passed the turning to al-Sukhnah, then entered a landscape of carefully pollarded trees and bullrush millet, invaded in places by patches of rock and euphorbia. Ahead, Raymah hovered, a spectral mountain. It rises to over 7,000 feet and is the bulkiest of all the ranges that overlook Tihamah, the 'Climax Mountains' on Ptolemy's map,* but in the afternoon vapours it is on top of you before you have a complete idea of its size. The road became increasingly steep, rounding the bases of huge honeycombed stacks.

After the village of Suq al-Ribat, where we bought *qat*, the road climbed ever more steeply. On either side, near-vertical slopes were covered with a dense layer of creeper-hung trees, a rare survival of the aboriginal forest which once cloaked the entire range. Rising out of these was the lighter green of inhabited places, pyramidal peaks and dizzyingly steep flanks of mountain. The landscape, seen through a moving frame of windscreen, looked as fanciful as a Chinese watercolour.

Raymah, like much of Yemen, is an upside-down place. In other mountainous countries, people tend to live in the valleys;

---

* The old Arabic name for Raymah was Jublan, from a certain Jublan ibn Sahl of the line of Himyar. His brother Wusab gave his name to the next range south.

here in Yemen they seem to choose the most inaccessible ridges and summits for their dwellings, places only fit for eagles. Why? Is it for defence, or because of the climate? Or for the view? Or is it just contrariness of nature that makes them build on seemingly impossible peaks, where calling on the neighbours means a trek of hours along goat paths, and *qat* sessions are arranged by walkie-talkie?

The defensive argument is strong. Power-hungry outsiders have always lusted after Yemen's strategic location, for whoever controls its western seaboard controls the entrance to the Red Sea. Time and again, invaders have occupied the coast, where it is easy to land large forces, but have left their backs open to attack by the mountain people. Even the Ottomans, with their advanced weaponry, only effectively held the cities and were for ever busy resisting assaults led from mountain strongholds like Shaharah. They were given little freedom of movement by a tough landscape and a tough people. A sixteenth-century Turkish commander summed up his problems when he said, 'Never have we seen our army founder as it did in Yemen – every force we sent dissolved like salt.' Three hundred years later, another Turkish general commented on the mountain tribesmen of al-Haymah that he could take the whole of Europe with a force of a thousand such fighters. Things hardly changed when the Egyptians brought air-power into the anti-Royalist conflict of the 1960s: mobility in the air means nothing if ground forces cannot follow it up.

Retreating to the mountains in time of war is, then, understandable; but to live there permanently, expending so much effort against gravity – why? Perhaps a walk along Raymah would answer the question.

A *mizmar* tape is hypnotic by the third hearing, and the *qat* was beginning to take effect when the top came into view. For the last section of the road the driver even used four-wheel drive – to avoid doing so seems to be a point of honour among Yemeni drivers. About three hours after leaving al-Mansuriyyah, we arrived in al-Jabi, the metropolis of Raymah, entering it from beneath the walls of its fort. From here, if you are up early enough, you can see across Tihamah to the sea and, some say, to Africa.

I finished my chew at the *lukanda*, a corrugated iron flop-house, watching American all-star wrestling on Saudi TV. The picture was soon blotted out by snow on the airwaves, and I went for a stroll in the keen evening air. Stopping for cigarettes, I was impressed by the range of goods in the shop. Mini stereo speakers sat next to air rifles, depilatory cream jostled against tins of lychees.

The shopkeeper was an ex-resident of Jeddah who had left Saudi Arabia before the Gulf crisis in 1990. The Saudis kicked out his less fortunate compatriots, like our host in Wadi Surdud, who were still there when Kuwait was invaded. Up until then they had enjoyed a special status which allowed them to work without finding a Saudi 'guarantor'. By their reaction to Yemen's stance on the Kuwait crisis – that all possible efforts should be made to find an Arab solution before calling in non-Arab forces – the Saudis had deprived themselves of a huge part of their service sector and had reduced hundreds of thousands of their Arab brothers and sisters to penury. Many of them reached Yemen with only the possessions they could carry, leaving behind their sole source of livelihood. By early 1991 perhaps a quarter of the cars on Yemen's roads belonged to these refugees in their own land, and reception camps were crowded and insanitary. The economic backlash has been severe, with huge losses in hard currency income and in aid from the Gulf States and elsewhere, and a massive fall in the value of the *riyal*. Other poorer Arab states – those which supported the US-led force – were silently paid off by having their debts rescinded. Yemen, however, remains a little-publicized victim of the Gulf crisis, a martyr to conscience in a world of *realpolitik*.

Back at the *lukanda* most of the other guests were asleep under the neon striplights, cocooned in tartan blankets like Henry Moore's sleepers in the Underground. I climbed up a ladder to a broad shelf at the back of the room and fell asleep thinking of the walk that lay ahead.

★

Nothing in the world, I thought as I started out along the track, sets you up for a walk as well as a plate of steaming fried liver at six in the morning at 7,000 feet. To the left, a small plateau ended in a row of houses and then nothing; to the right there *was* just nothing, or rather a huge vertical drop ending in a sea of vapour rising from Tihamah. A couple of crowded trucks passed, heading towards al-Jabi.

Shortly after, the motor track began a huge arc round the outer flank of the mountain and I struck off on a well-trodden footpath to cut off the corner. For a while the going was easy; then the path crossed a rock face and became little more than a crack with a long plunge to the left. I picked my way gingerly, sending little avalanches over the edge. A group of young children squeezed past me and skipped along on their way to school in the town, oblivious of the drop.

As the path levelled out I saw that a change had taken place. Away from the seaward-facing slopes the terraces had a different look – they were either bare or, where there were crops, growth was stunted. The contrast was stark, the result of a sudden climatic variation: a detailed weather map of the western mountains would be made up of a patchwork of micro-climates, each dependent on the exact topographical aspect of its location. Raymah weather is certainly strange: I have seen snow in the month of June.

In one of the bare fields an old man was taking a rest from ploughing while his donkey munched alfalfa. The bundle of fodder stood out against the khaki earth like an exclamation mark. The man beckoned me over and poured some *qishr*, husk coffee, into a tin can; the bite of ginger was instantly refreshing. I asked him, as one does, about the rain.

'In Kusmah,' he said, 'they've had some good downpours, but here . . . well, it has spat a few times this year. We have to get our water from the spring down there,' he pointed to a patch of green, probably a thousand feet below, 'and that's almost dry. We had some water engineers here, but if there's no rain in the first place there's nothing for them to engineer.'

It was hard to know what to say. It would have been cold comfort to point out that this was merely another in a series of droughts which, punctuating Yemeni history, have killed thousands. At least, with all the imported wheat around, people would not die as they did just the other side of the Red Sea. 'Can't you drill a well?'

The man laughed. 'The shaykh was trying to collect money, but how can we come up with . . . oh, a million or more? We were thinking of getting the boy from Ta'izz – do you know the one? He can see water through rock. "Drill here," he says. "There's grey rock, then black rock, then water at 400 feet." And he's always right, praise God. But you still have to get the machine in and drill.' He crumbled a lump of earth in his fingers. The wind blew it away before it hit the ground.

'May God bless you with rain,' I said, getting up to leave.

'Amen,' he replied.

I waved to him before I rounded the mountain. As he raised his arm, the sun caught the brilliant white of his *zannah*, and I thought of the enormous effort that had been expended in washing it.

Back on the motor track, each step raised a puff of dust as fine as talcum powder. Rocks underfoot were polished smooth by spinning tyres. I stopped in the meagre shade of an overhang, where drill holes showed that the cliff had been dynamited away. My throat was dry and I wondered where I could get water. Then, around a corner, I saw a car parked on the shoulder of the mountain and quickened my pace.

The car was a Layla Alawi, the latest model of Landcruiser which the Yemenis named after a curvaceous Egyptian actress (she was furious). It would have a cooling compartment between the front seats, packed with drinks. A man stood next to it, looking at the view.

I greeted him and was granted a lacklustre reply from the back of his head. He turned in a studied way and, for a moment, I was taken aback by his appearance. Over an immaculate *zannah* with buttoned Mao collar he was – even in the heat of the sun – wearing a black sheepskin-lined greatcoat, not the usual countryman's baggy version but cut with a swagger. It was the sort of coat a White Russian prince would wear. In his belt, behind a vastly expensive *jambiyah*, was a chrome-plated Smith and Wesson with ivory grips. A perfectly trimmed moustache swooped down to sharp points on either side of his chin. He looked like Lee Van Cleef after a successful night at the poker table.

'Er . . . Have you got any water?'

The man paused to think. 'No.'

'Is there anywhere I can get some?'

He was looking at my ancient, fly- and mildew-spotted rucksack. 'No.'

For a time I surveyed the view. I had never met anything like such a stony response in Yemen. Well, I would engage him in conversation. 'Not much rain, is there.'

He clicked a Yes.

Silence.

'Are you from al-Jabi?'

He clicked a No.

'Kusmah?'

A shake of the head.

'So . . . where are you from?'

'Bani Abu al-Dayf,' he said, with a pained sigh.

An unusual name. Rendered literally, The Sons of the Father of the Guest. I couldn't resist. 'Ah, you must have been called that because of your hospitality to passing strangers.'

He burst out laughing. The pose was gone. 'I'm sorry,' he said, 'but I really haven't got any water.'

We said goodbye. Someone I met on the road later knew the man with the Layla Alawi and said that he'd made a killing in Riyadh, running a juice bar.

It was lunchtime. The two or three villages I passed showed no signs of activity. They sat on outcrops, ringed by dense barriers of prickly pears. These, although they are found all over the country, are not native to Yemen, as their Arabic name – 'Turkish figs' – suggests. (In Greece they are called 'Frankish figs' and the scientific name, *Opuntia ficus-indica*, proposes yet another origin; in fact, they came from the Americas.) But they are welcome invaders, for their fruit is wonderfully refreshing.

I turned on to another footpath. By now the humidity boiling off Tihamah had risen enough to cut out the harshest rays of the sun. Another vista opened, and another micro-climatic region. This time it was moist, and there were even some mushrooms. It was tempting to lie down, surrounded by rising cloud and the scent of thyme; but Kusmah, the day's destination, was still a long way off.

Back on the path, a boy overtook me. I caught up with him and kept pace for a while. Then, suddenly, he stopped and gazed intently to his right. I couldn't see what was holding his attention until he picked up a stone and flung it. Something tumbled over the little terrace wall. A long, thin tail twitched. A chameleon. It tried to get up but he threw another rock which caught it in the middle and it lay still, its visible eye revolving feebly. I like to think that it may have changed colour, gone through its palette in a chromatic swan-song, but we pushed on. I soon realized I could not keep up with the boy, who was about ten, and told him to go ahead. Later, I met him coming back from the market below Kusmah. It was still half an hour away but he had been there, done some shopping, and was on his way home. I began to feel that the old woman in the taxi to al-Jabi might have had a point.

In the market I was collared by a voluble and slightly crazy old man who gave me a run-down on the US election campaign. He lost me when he got on to the relative importance of the various primaries. The sun was going down, the mist was coming up, and

I abandoned him in Iowa. My knees were crying out for the horizontal, but I set out for the final pull up to Kusmah. At first I tried to keep up with the last in a string of donkeys carrying sacks up from the market. As it climbed, it farted rhythmically inches from my nose and it was a double relief to get to a level stretch of path.*

Kusmah is built on a ridge at the south-western end of the

---

* The pro-Ottoman historian al-Nahrawali recorded that on one occasion Yemeni forces retreated after their commander's donkey farted – they took it as an omen of disaster. The Raymis – judging by the flatulence of their donkeys – must have a lot of bad luck.

Raymah massif. From below it has an imposing presence; when you get there it is a pretty ordinary large village, with one irregularly cobbled street lined with shops, all selling the same things. Gaps between the buildings open on to distant views over the Kusmah midden and the prickly pears that thrive on it. I made for the single eating house and ordered a plate of beans as the sunset prayer was called. With a cough, a generator cranked into action and the striplights flickered on. The clink of tea glasses, the hiss of the paraffin stove, the thud of the generator — all were sounds of arrival in a mountain town. The breath of donkeys hung in the air outside.

There were two people in Kusmah I was keen not to bump into. The first was the self-styled *umdah*, or mayor. On an earlier visit I had spent a couple of hours in his house at the top end of the ridge, and the entire time had been taken up with his prostate trouble. I was willing to forgo a further session on the mayor's leaky plumbing. As I sipped my tea, the other major annoyance of Kusmah stalked past in his striped pyjamas, stately in a pained sort of way. I quickly stared into my beans. After my previous escape from the *umdah* I was passing the school when this man, graduate of a university in the Nile Delta and Kusmah's principal pedagogue, had shot — if that's the right word for a fat, middle-aged Egyptian — out of his religious instruction class and dragged me in. I was a choice and appropriate piece of what the theorists of teaching call *realia*, educational *objets trouvés*.

Fifty pairs of eyes were on me.

'What is your name, sir?' the Egyptian asked in English.

'Tim.'

'No! "*My name is Tim.*"'

'Oh, yes. Sorry. *My name is Tim.*'

'And where are you from, Professor Tim?' He rolled his r's like a big car purring.

The interrogation continued in English. The children, of course, understood nothing. Nor were they supposed to: they were a primary class, and English instruction is only given in middle and secondary schools. After establishing my basic credentials of nationality, marital status, religion and so on, he changed into Arabic.

'Come here, Ali.'

A small boy in the front row jumped up. Teacher's pet, I thought. The Egyptian put one arm round each of us – with some difficulty because of the vast difference in height – and stood beaming. The room was in suspense.

'Now. How many eyes has Professor Tim got?' he asked the class.

'Two!' they shouted.

'And how many eyes has Professor Ali got?'

'Two!'

'How many ears has Professor Tim got?'

'*Two!*'

'And Professor Ali?'

'*TWO!*'

'How many . . . noses has Professor Tim got?'

'One!' There were a few 'twos' from the back of the class.

The questioning went on until we had covered all mentionable parts of the body. Our respective religions were then re-established. 'So, although Professor Tim is a Christian and Professor Ali is a Muslim, God has created them the same in all respects.'

'But he's taller!'

'Silence! This', said the Egyptian, finally releasing us, 'is proof of the oneness of His creation.'

A bell rang and the pupils charged out. I admired the teacher's exposition of so elemental a truth, and told him so. 'Naturally', he said, 'we must use such methods here. The people are so very . . . *simple.*'

I said that, to me, the pupils seemed very bright, that school education to them was something new and that, moreover, it was appreciated far more than in the West. And in Egypt, I nearly added. I could have done – he wasn't listening anyway. But then I didn't pay attention to his tirade against life in Kusmah compared with the pleasures of Tantah. For an Arab returning to the cradle of his race – and getting paid vast sums of money relative to his potential earnings at home – it all seemed ungrateful.

Well-meaning people in Yemeni villages have often billeted me on a teacher with whom, they suppose, I will have much in common. With Egyptians the reverse is true. It is different, though, when the teacher is Sudanese. Although their spindly Nilotic forms, Giacometti men clad in robes of purest white, are more suited to the wide savannah than to the mountains, all the Sudanese I have met seem to have an affinity for Yemen and its people. And when they get together the Sudanese party, unlike the lugubrious Egyptians and their homesickness encounter groups.

I looked up from my beans, paid and left. Outside, I glimpsed the teacher's broad back nearing the end of the street, the turning-point of his solitary *paseo*, and for a moment I felt sorry for him. But I went quickly to the *funduq*, found a room to myself and, undisturbed except for a tiny girl who appeared cat-like round the door and asked me if I was an Egyptian, read for a while then fell asleep.

Kusmah is on the watershed, and another climatic border. From here to al-Hadiyah, my final destination, was a hard day's walk. There was no motor track, but there was at least the prospect of well-made footpaths.

The path zigzagged down the flank of the mountain. It was heavily scented and slippery with dew. I passed a party of women on their way to collect fodder for their cattle: many of the mountain women keep at least one cow, which gives them a degree of economic independence. The money they make will usually be turned into gold, and these women were well off – their heavy chokers and large pendants, swinging against flared dresses of Japanese synthetic brocade, caught the sun as it rose over the mountain tops. People looked prosperous, and it was good to see houses being built in every village.

The track crossed a dry stream bed then turned to follow the side of a mountain mass set at right angles to that of Kusmah. Villages clung to the steep slope all the way along it and from now on the path was beautifully built, of large stone blocks fitted together in a careful jigsaw pattern. Fresh donkey dung everywhere showed that this was a principal highway.

The path wound for much of the way between high stone walls enclosing terraces. They were overhung with coffee trees and ferns, and gave the place a churchyard feel. Now and again, water channels opened up on the left to give views of the great sugarloaf of Jabal Zalamlam. Then the path dropped down into a deep valley scattered with houses, their window ledges glowing with the autumnal colours of drying coffee berries.

Coffee has a special place in the Yemeni's heart. As a modern symbol for Arabia Felix, the coffee tree appears on stamps and bank notes. The anti-*qat* lobby makes the largely unjustifiable charge that coffee trees have been rooted up to be replaced by the more valuable crop, but optimum growing requirements for the two trees are different. Certainly, though, the heyday of coffee production is over. As early as 1738 an English traveller in Egypt noted that Yemeni coffee was being adulterated with cheaper beans from the West and East Indies. The Yemenis themselves have always sold the beans, *bunn*, and drunk *qishr*, made from the husk.*

If coffee used to be the prime export crop, the staple for home consumption has always been grain, as traditional dishes show. There are scores of bread varieties, and these are used in dips, like *saltah*, or to soak up broth, milk or ghee. Porridge- or *polenta*-like dishes such as *asid* or *harish* are common. Within a limited but delicious range, the Yemenis are connoisseurs of food, suffering the furnace heat of a crowded eating house that makes the best *saltah*, or queuing – sometimes for hours – for special *sabaya* bread during Ramadan. Before *qat* caught on (probably in the fourteenth or fifteenth century) food seems to have been the national obsession. Ibn al-Mujawir says: 'Their talk is of nothing but food. One will say to another, "What did you have for breakfast?" and he replies, "Millet bread with two kinds of milk," or, "Layered bread and oil." Another asks, "What did you eat for supper?" and his friend replies, "A round of wheat bread and four *fils*-worth of sweets – altogether it came to six *fils!*" Or you will hear someone say, "I've eaten enough today to last me three days! Bread and milk and sugar candy – I gorged myself until I was bursting . . ."'

Sorghum is the most widely grown cereal, and has been since

---

* Pedro Páez, one of two Jesuits captured off the south coast towards the end of the sixteenth century, records that in Hadramawt they were given 'Cahua, made from the rind of the fruit Bun, in place of wine'. The Arabic *qahwah* – by coincidence originally a word for wine – went through various English spellings including 'coho', 'cohoo' and 'coughe', before ending up as 'coffee'.

ancient times: the names of the different varieties derive from those of the old South Arabian seasons. Life itself turns on the harvest, *surab* (another pre-Arabic term), as the bachelor's prayer shows: 'Be patient, O my prick, until the harvest, or I'll chop you off!' To pay the bride-price would be impossible without the money generated by a good crop.

Another legacy of the so-called Age of Ignorance before Islam is the widespread use of star lore, by which farmers overcome the problem of the lunar Islamic months being out of step with the farming calendar. The rising of certain stars divides the seasons, and in some places ancient rock gnomons are used to calculate sowing times. Another rich source of farming lore is the collection of verses of Ali ibn Zayid. Star lore in particular has been formalized, often versified in mnemonic form to give information like when to cut wood so it won't get wormy, and when the fleas will start jumping – as if one needed to know.

The minutiae of astral calendars fascinated the inquiring minds of the Rasulid rulers. They were both patrons of science and scientists themselves, and married local star lore with the latest international developments in astronomy. Their heritage is very much alive, and a number of astral calendars are in print today. In terms of varieties grown, Rasulid rule also marked the golden age of Yemeni agriculture, and the sultans imported fruit trees, herbs and flowers from as far away as Sind. A contemporary list of products includes exotica like cannabis and asparagus. Their passion for all things agricultural took off at Sabt al-Subut, a date festival centred on Zabid which reached Bavarian *Bierfest* proportions. People came from all over the country to drink wine made from dates and wheat flour, and to be entertained *al fresco* beneath the palms by three hundred camel litters full of dancing girls. The bash lasted for weeks and ended with the revellers going to the sea on bejewelled camels for a mixed bathing session. As a result there were, Ibn al-Mujawir says, 'many divorces and many marriages'.

Coffee, a more sober crop, is associated with the Sufi mystic al-Shadhili, founder of the modern town of al-Makha. He is reputed to have introduced it from Ethiopia in the early fifteenth century and made use of its stimulant properties to spend more time in prayer and contemplation. In Yemen it has never attracted the faintly racy image that went with the London coffee-house or the *espresso* bars of the 1950s, although elsewhere in Arabia some of the more extreme members of the puritanical Wahhabi sect have disapproved of its aroma of unorthodoxy.

★

Some women called me over from the yard of their house in the valley bottom. There were no men about and, although they were far from nubile, I sat at a demure distance on a wall. One of the women went inside the house while the other went on feeding a cow.

'Come on, my dear, eat,' she said, coaxing a bundle of dry sorghum stalks wrapped in greenery into the cow's mouth.

'Can't she see it's a trick,' I asked, 'I mean wrapping up the sorghum like that?'

'Oh, she knows. But if you don't do it she'll eat nothing at all. It's a game.' The woman held an unwrapped stalk out to the cow. It shook its head like a truculent child.

The other woman appeared with a tin bowl full of *qishr*. All around, on large metal trays, coffee beans lay in the sun. I remembered *The Dispute between Coffee and Qat*, a literary contest composed in the middle of the last century in which each tree vies with the other in praising itself and belittling its opponent. The coffee tree says: 'When my berries appear, their green is like ring-stones of emerald or turquoise. Their colour as they ripen is the yellow of golden amber necklaces. And when they are fully ripe they are as red as rare carnelian, or ruby or coral.' The nearest jar of Nescafé was far away.*

I said goodbye and set off on the track, which zigzagged up one of those stegasaurus backs like the one we had crossed in Surdud. I was still panting when I got to the yard-wide ridge. I hung my jacket on a prickly pear and sat down. Two men appeared from the direction of a solitary tower further down the ridge. They were dressed in spotless white *zannahs*, lounge-suit jackets and highly polished loafers. Not a bead of sweat showed on their faces. They

---

* The eighteenth-century French visitor de la Roque said, wistfully, of *qishr*, '*La couleur de cette est semblable à la meilleure bière d'Angleterre.*'

greeted me without stopping, leaving behind them a strong scent of rosewater. The scent was still there when I looked up to the left ten minutes later. The men were far above, white flecks moving against the dark green of the mountain.

In an hour or so (a great deal of effort is compressed into those five monosyllables) I reached a village, unimaginatively – if appropriately – named al-Jabal, the Mountain. I propped myself up against a shop doorway and gulped down a can of ginger beer. Flavoured with chemicals resulting from decades of research, packed in al-Hudaydah under franchise from a German firm in a can made from the product of a Latin American bauxite mine, furnished with a ring-pull which was the chance brainchild of a millionaire inventor, and brought here by truck, then donkey, for my delectation, it wasn't nearly as refreshing as the *qishr*. The ground was strewn with empty cans, each saying in Arabic and English 'Keep your country tidy', and I wondered for a moment whether to put mine in my rucksack until I found a litter bin; but the nearest one was several days away, so I placed it at one end of the counter. The shopkeeper picked it up and threw it on the ground.

From al-Jabal to al-Hadiyah is downhill. At first the path was covered with rubbish, but soon there was just the odd sweet wrapper or juice carton as a reminder of the world of creation and corruption. The afternoon cloud rose, swirling past at speed, forced upwards by the cooling of Tihamah and channelled between the sides of the gorge. Everything but the rock wall either side of the path was cut off and I walked in silence. It was like swimming. Only once was the silence broken, by girls' voices singing a snatch of antiphony as they gathered fodder high above on the cliffs. The last note of each phrase was held, then let out with a strange downward *portamento*, like an expiring squeezebox.

About half an hour out of al-Jabal, a strange thing happened. For perhaps a minute the cloud parted, revealing two conical peaks directly in front and, below, a field of cropped turf, like a green on a golf course and perfectly circular. Then another column of cloud rose and shut out the vision. The precise geometry of the field's shape and its vivid colour, and the way in which it had been revealed so unexpectedly and then veiled over, made it a mysterious sight. It had seemed to hover. It was the sort of place where you might bump into al-Khadir, the Green Man.*

I half thought I had imagined the field and that the path would continue prosaically downwards, but I soon reached it. Once on it the perspective was different and its shape not apparent, a *trompe-l'oeil* but seen too close to work. A few cattle lay round the margin of the field. They took no notice as I stood watching them and seemed anchored to the ground, oblivious of the intruder in their tiny, circular paradise.

After the field, the mist gradually disappeared and the other-worldliness was gone. Once more the path was beautifully maintained – it had to be, for it passed through an unbroken string of hamlets and carried a constant traffic of heavily laden donkeys. The boys who drove them had their *zannahs* hitched up and tucked behind their daggers. I stumbled down; so did the donkeys – but at twice the speed; the boys danced on stork-thin legs. Even the ones coming up danced.

I stopped to rest, and to look at the vista of receding mountain flanks sprinkled with little houses. Somewhere on this very path, Baurenfeind, the artist of the Niebuhr expedition, had stopped more than two centuries before to sketch the original drawings for the plate, 'Prospect among the Coffee Mountains'. It was the expedition's first experience of highland Yemen, and they were captivated by the scenery, the people and the flora. The coffee trees, Niebuhr wrote, were in blossom and 'exhaled an exquisitely agreeable perfume'. It was a landscape in which, despite its natural ruggedness, the hand of Man could be seen everywhere.

Niebuhr's original *Beschreibung von Arabien* was at first ignored; but the French and then the English translations were hugely popular when they came out some years later. They had touched the spirit of the new age – the age of burgeoning Romanticism and the Picturesque. Up to then, the reading public had been

---

* Al-Khadir is a fearfully complex figure, variously considered a prophet (Elijah?), a saint or an angel. Some authorities have him as the brother of Qahtan. An eighth-century writer said that al-Khadir, whose name is really an epithet, was told during a visit to the Fountain of Life: 'Where thy feet touch the earth, it will become green.' He is still alive and well, and people occasionally bump into him in Yemen's western mountains.

given an Orient almost entirely of the imagination, colourful but savage. Now Europe began to look at the East through new eyes: Southey wrote of a garden 'whose delightful air/ Was mild and fragrant as the evening wind/ Passing in summer o'er the coffee-groves/ Of Yemen'; George Moore, in *Lalla Rookh*, of 'the fresh nymphs bounding o'er Yemen's mounts'. They had read their Niebuhr. Baurenfeind's plates, too, contributed to the new way in which people looked at mountains. Hitherto, mountains had been forbidding places, ignored or feared. Baurenfeind recorded a different image, of mountains dotted with folly-like dwellings, sculpted into terraces and covered with crops – in a word, humanized.

The light was beginning to go and the mountains were turning to amber, then carnelian. The humidity was increasing. The path levelled out and entered a *wadi*, snaking along the side of the valley through banana terraces which resembled a Rousseau jungle. I was half expecting to glimpse the shade of Baurenfeind sketching from a terrace wall, and when an old woman called out to me from above the path, I jumped. She laughed, and offered me some mouth-snuff. I was tempted but, not being used to it, didn't want to find myself retching for the sake of a quick nicotine fix.

After the airy peaks of Raymah, al-Hadiyah smelt fetid and unhealthy, although in Niebuhr's day it had been something of a hill-station for the European coffee merchants, a retreat from the even clammier heat of Bayt al-Faqih down on the plain. (The latter was sometimes rendered in English as 'Beetle-fuckee' – probably a reflection of the merchants' feelings towards it rather than simple bad spelling.) I arrived in al-Hadiyah just after dark, knees jellified by the relentless descent from al-Jabal. I had arranged to stay in the English midwife's house; she had left the key with her neighbours as she was away – something of a relief, since it would save a lot of tongue-wagging.

The electricity went off early, interrupting me as I flicked through *Diarrhoea Dialogue*, the only reading material I could find in the house apart from *Where There Is No Doctor* – a book no hypochondriac should ever open, for its refuses to mince the strong meat of medical problems from leprosy to yaws. I made up a bed on the roof. A frog croaked softly from a pot of geraniums;

elsewhere, geckoes clicked; and the night was alive with other, unidentifiable, susurrations.

Not long after dawn the flies woke me. No trucks would leave for Bayt al-Faqih until later, so I walked to al-Hadiyah's main attraction, the waterfall. This plunges over a cliff in a single dizzy drop, then cascades in a series of deep pools. The path to it wriggled through rocky undergrowth and was home to dozens of glossy black millipedes; some were nearly a foot long and looked like pieces of self-propelled hosepipe.

When I reached the waterfall I found it empty. Little more than a dribble of moisture stained the rock. Only when it rained on the high places would the waterfall come to life, a roaring column of white against the dark cliff.

I sat there watching the dragonflies and thought of my absent hostess, delivering babies up in the mountains where the waterfall had its source. Horizontally she was no distance away; vertically, she was in a different world where climate, crops, dress, buildings, even speech, were different from those of al-Hadiyah. Any study, agricultural, ethnographic or dialectological, of Yemen's mountains would have to use a three-dimensional projection to map these variations. But in spite of the contrasts encountered over the vertical, the mountain people are bound together by a tenuous lifeline of water.

Rain for the Arabs is *barakah*, a blessing; and it is particularly so for Yemen where the great majority of cultivable land is rain-fed. In poetry, rain is a metaphor for human as well as divine generosity; historically, water is the reward of just government, and drought the punishment for profligacy. The beneficent rule of Imam al-Mutawakkil Isma'il in the mid-seventeenth century caused an increase in the water table, and even British policy in Hadramawt was said to have resulted in heavy rains there in 1937 (followed, it should be noted, by seven years of drought and famine); in contrast, Imam al-Mansur Ali – he of the donkey-pizzle aphrodisiac – made the wells run dry.

Barakah is for God to grant or withhold, but intercession can pay off. When there is no rain, the entire male population climbs to the high places and starts a litany – 'Give us rain, O God. Have mercy on us, O God. Have mercy on the dumb beasts, thirsty for water, hungry for fodder.' A sacrifice is made and left to the birds of the air.* And if the rain comes, they do everything possible to hold it back. This is the function of the terraces which are so much a feature of the Yemeni landscape.

Yemen's terraces, its hanging gardens, contouring voluptuously round the flanks of mountains or perched, sometimes dinner-table sized, in what are often no more than vertical fissures, are not just a way of making a level surface. More important, they act like a cross between the pores of a giant sponge and the locks of a canal. The rain is trapped by them and contained in subdivisions separated by little bunds, before being released to the next level down in a slow and measured cascade. In slowing the downward flow of rainwater, too, terracing enables more of the *wadi* land to be cultivated. A torrential downpour, unchecked, runs away to waste and takes with it the *wadi's* precious topsoil. The mountain men, as masters of the whole system, tend also to own the valleys and farm them out to sharecroppers. It is a system that calls for continual maintenance. The collapse of one terrace will affect the flow of water, and this in turn will lead to the destruction of terraces further down. Terraces must be kept planted so that the roots of plants consolidate the soil. The delicate balance can also be upset by the building of a surfaced road, which will speed up the flow of water and force streams into new channels.

People have to live at the top. If they didn't, the upper reaches of the *wadis* would also be uninhabitable, and cultivable land restricted to a few central plateaux, the hot and malarial coastal regions, and great inland *wadis* like Hadramawt and al-Jawf. The mountains would in time be stripped bare from top to bottom. Since the protective covering of forests was felled, the history of mountain Yemen has been that of a war waged against loss of land. The weather is, at the same time, the mountain farmer's reason for being and his antagonist.

And what an antagonist! Millions of tons of water, sizzled out of the Red Sea, fried off Tihamah, bounced up the wall of the escarpment and colliding with the cold highland air, pour down

---

* A story in al-Hajari's *Compendium* tells of some cattle rustlers who sacrificed a stolen bullock as part of the rain-prayer ceremony. Rain fell, but on the territory of the bullock's rightful owners.

on Milhan, Hufash, Bura', Raymah and the Two Wusabs. Evaporation and potential energy; blessing and destruction. This is why the Raymis live like eagles, why Yemen looks like nowhere else on Earth.

Gazing up at the terraces hanging all around above me, this ultimate symbol of the Yemenis' co-existence with their land, I began to understand why al-Hamdani and the other geo-genealogists had turned mountains into ancestors. Lineage seems to have been relatively unimportant in pre-Islamic Yemen. It was the North Arabians, the rootless nomads, who developed the science of genealogy to give themselves a sense of continuity. At the same time, they looked down on settled farmers as peasants, with all the scorn that the word implies. As Islam spread over the Near East, the desert Arabs came across huge populations of settled serfs, in Egypt and the Fertile Crescent, working land which was not theirs.

Yemen was different. Here, the old civilizations had been based on agriculture. When these broke up, settlers moved further and further into the mountains, cutting down ancient forests and terracing the slopes. They were owner-occupiers, yeomen not serfs; and they still are – Yemen has remarkably few big landowners. Ali ibn Zayid, the Yemeni Hesiod, summed up their feelings: 'The tribesman's glory is the soil of his home.' Pride for the Yemenis is in land, not lineage.

To express these feelings and demonstrate the antiquity of the link between land and people – perhaps even to make a political point, that Yemen refused to be marginalized by a super-culture which idealized desert values – al-Hamdani and his school used the super-culture's own idiom: genealogy. By making placenames the names of ancestors, they were literally planting the Qahtani family tree in the soil of Arabia Felix. It was an extraordinary landscape that they depicted, and – like the corner of it shown in Baurenfeind's plate – the most remarkable thing about it was the way in which it had been humanized.

And yet, for the West, the nineteenth century created a different image of Arabia. Explorers like Burton and Palgrave – and, more recently, the neo-Victorian Thesiger – portrayed a landscape of sterile sand where only individual qualities of honour and courage could ensure survival. Desert values were resurrected and romanticized, and they struck a chord with Europeans of a more puritan age. The chord still reverberates; received images have crowded out this other Arabia.

★

I wandered round al-Hadiyah *suq* and sat for a while at the base of a huge tree. Its exposed roots formed a knobbly bench, burnished by generations of backsides. The tree, a *Ficus vasta Forsk.*, was of great age; perhaps Niebuhr, Forskaal and their companions had sat there, too, and botanized. It was lunchtime when I found a truck to Bayt al-Faqih. I sat chewing *qat*, wedged between sacks of coffee on the cab roof. Down in hornbill country we passed a group of women whose faces were stained yellow with turmeric. They wore fake plaits made of hanks of wool, and purple straw hats the size of teacups were perched over their foreheads. I glanced back at them and noticed that Raymah was gone, melted into the mist.

6

Dugong City

'Be'old a cloud upon the beam,
An' 'umped above the sea appears
Old Aden, like a barrick-stove
That no one's lit for years an' years.'
Rudyard Kipling, 'For to Admire'

IN 1992, A SENIOR religious figure in Aden complained in the
press about the city's great number of bars and other dens of
lewdness. A senior Socialist Party official replied in an open letter:
'Since the erudite shaykh, as a son of Aden, must know the location of these establishments, then he should inform the authorities
at once.' Nothing came of the cleric's complaint. But the fact that
it had been made at all was significant. It was perfectly justified
but, somehow, not on – as if a mullah had barged into a reading
from Omar Khayyam shouting, '"A Flask of Wine, a Book of
Verse"? *Infidels!*' Aden was *supposed* to be different. Perhaps its days
as a place where anything went were numbered. I decided to
investigate before it was too late.

A desultory fight was going on in the street outside. I ducked
under the blows, made it into the lobby, and paid. My eyes took a
few seconds to adjust to the gloom. A disco globe winked rheumily
at a circular room with a small stage and dance-floor. Around this,
men in *futahs* sat drinking beer. So far the erudite shaykh would
have heartily disapproved. I'd just found an empty table when a
voice, inches from my ear, made me jump. 'Supper?' it lisped. 'Do

you want supper?' I looked round into a black face. Even in the half-light it was clear it had been subjected to heavy-handed maquillage. I nodded. The waiter – it was, just, male – hovered slightly, pirouetted, then glided into a recess. While I waited, the band came on and started to tune up. Again, the hot breath on my ear: '*Shibz.*' The monosyllable was rich with quivering suggestion; perhaps he was a fan of Zsa Zsa Gabor. With little flourishes, as though his nail varnish wasn't quite dry, he deposited the plate of chips and a bottle of beer, and melted back into the gloom. Surprisingly, the chips were hot and the beer cold.

The band struck up a Lebanese hit of the '70s, a strobe was switched on, and a dancer appeared from another recess. The girl looked half-Vietnamese. She had buck teeth and was wearing an Alcanfoil bikini. Slowly, she cranked herself into action. The performance was not so much a dance as a series of little spasms, like the dying stages of an epileptic fit. I could have made a more erotic job of it. Still, some of the men in *futahs* got up and began thrusting banknotes in the direction of her bra. They tended to miss, and another waiter came to shadow the dancer like a referee at a boxing match, stooping to pick up the fallen notes. Each time he stood up he carefully rearranged the two remaining strands of hair on his scalp. I ordered another beer.

The girl showed her first spark of vitality when the music stopped and she ran off stage. Then the band broke into a sort of Egyptian glam-rock number and, unexpectedly, the floor filled with young men dressed in Paisley pattern shirts and pleated trousers. The number of pleats seemed to reflect their prowess at dancing. One particularly energetic youth – a twenty-pleater – shone out: his pelvis was articulated in extraordinary places, and spurts of sweat shot from his forehead. These were the *mutamayk-alin*, the Michaelesques – the fans of Michael Jackson.

I was enjoying the spectacle when, suddenly, it was blotted out by a mountainous figure which interposed itself between me and the dancers. This time the sex was in no doubt – a pair of stupendous breasts could be seen shuddering beneath her *abayah*, like a couple of hippos trapped in a marquee – and the woman, as far as I could see the only one in the place other than the dancer, was gesturing to me to get up and join her on the floor. I was wondering what would happen if I declined when a scrawny man staggered into her and threw up. The vomit just missed her. She went off, disgusted, to look for another partner, while the scrawny man collapsed into a chair next to me. In the light of the strobe, the process of vomiting had looked comical, like an early animated film. The man groaned and I poured him some water.

Up on stage the lead guitarist did a little virtuoso break and the band went into a Queen song, 'I Want to Break Free', a bit fast but very competent. The Michaelesques went wild. The big woman was down there with them like a whale among her pilot fish. Even the scrawny man dragged himself up to join them.

The song finished, the main lights went on, and in seconds the place was empty. I caught sight of the buck-toothed dancer slipping out in her *abayah*; the scrawny man's vomit lay beside me on the floor, still slightly *mousseux*.

★

St Bartholomew, on his way to India, is said to have stopped off at Aden and exorcized a devil from a well on Sirah Island. The devil had been a nuisance to the Adenis for centuries, belching fire and bad-egg smells at them when they came to draw water. According to Ibn al-Mujawir, the well was dug by the Indian *afrit*, or demon, Hanuman. Also appearing in the traveller's account is the Prophet Solomon, who expelled a ten-headed beast from Aden in what appears to be another version of the St Bartholomew story, with echoes of the *Mahabharata* and the Book of Revelation.

The saint's visit is, of course, a legend; the well-devil can be explained away as a geyser. But Aden has had plenty of other bizarre inhabitants and unexpected visitors: the fifteenth-century Sufi superman al-Aydarus, who saved a sinking ship by going into a trance and flinging his tooth-cleaning stick at the peak of a mountain, which flew off and blocked the hole in the ship's hull; the Ottoman admiral Sulayman the Eunuch, 'more a beast than a man', who invited the ruler of Aden to inspect his flagship and hanged him from the yardarm; Haines, the 'sultanized Englishman', who in 1839 founded Aden's modern trading fortunes and died as a result of a stay in a Bombay debtors' gaol; Air Commodore McClaughry, the 'aerial beduin', relaxing on his veranda with a cigar and an enormous Chinese fan; people like Hugh Scott, on his way to collect 27,000 insect specimens in the High Yemen, who thought Aden was 'an interesting and likeable place'; others like Vita Sackville-West who thought it 'an arid, salty hell' and 'precisely the most repulsive corner of the world'; Rimbaud, who indulged his ennui above a godown in Crater; all the transients who ebb and flow round great ports – merchants from Ptolemaic Egypt, from Cutch, Canton and Coromandel, Abyssinians and Persians, Hindus who burnt their dead and Parsees who left them to the vultures on towers of silence and wore hats like coal-scuttles, traders out of Conrad, adventurers out of Buchan; all the apparatus of trafficking – pilots and port officials, Jewish customs men, Rasulid treasurers counting the moneyboxes bound for Ta'izz, Somali stevedores who wore their hair like the cords of a Russian poodle, smeared with brick-red clay; Yemenis from the mountains going to live in Cardiff, Welsh conscripts from the valleys coming to die from heatstroke; dark-skinned seamen from Dar-es-Salaam, acne-faced ratings from Rostov-on-Don; President Salim Rubay' Ali, found guilty in 1979 of 'loathsome mistakes' and shot; and, strangest of all, those two other visitors from northern lands who came treading on Britannia's sullied train, surrounded by a crowd of commissars, *apparatchiks*, ideologues and ballet instructors – Marx and Lenin. With all these comings and goings, why should Aden not have been host to a demon from Hell and a disciple of Christ?

The setting, for a city so full of ghosts, is appropriate. A British naval officer who passed by in 1830 described it as 'very remarkable, looking like an island, very high and rugged at the Top with small buildings or Turrets on different Peaks'. In contrast to the tamer Red Sea havens, Aden is a port of call for the Flying Dutchman or the Ancient Mariner; if it did not exist, Mary Shelley, or Gustave Doré, would have dreamed it up.

Aden's craggy profile was formed by the volcanic activity suggested by the well-devil story and investigated by a party of medieval notables; they lowered a rope into the Sirah well and, when they drew it up, found that its end was singed. As a result of its topography, Aden is not one city but a series of settlements separated by outriders of the central peak, Jabal Shamsan. It is a hemmed-in place, a nightmare for claustrophobes; the tenth-century traveller al-Muqaddasi thought it no more habitable than a sheep-pen. And there is always a creeping suspicion that the ever-lasting bonfire, the volcano below, has only been damped down, not extinguished: a Tradition of the Prophet states that the appearance of fire in Aden, 'molten, slowly flowing . . . which will devour anything it overtakes', is one of the signs of Doomsday.

On the ground, the geography of Aden is confusing. It would be clearer if we went for a spin out of Khur Maksar aerodrome with the shade of McClaughry and saw the place from the air.

Taking off, we leave the sprawling mass of low buildings and markets at al-Shaykh Uthman and wheel southwards over the orderly but peeling rows of villas beyond the creek, the *khur*. The tall structure at their southern edge is the severely air-conditioned Aden Hotel, not so much a place of habitation as a giant refrigerator. In front of it a causeway begins, following the line of a former aqueduct which supplied most of Aden's sweet water. Grubby flamingoes forage in the shallows and the odd pelican clambers into the air.

Reaching the old Turkish wall, outside which only the well-guarded would venture in early British days, we gain height to cross the escarpment. Here the Aden peninsula begins, a rough oval five miles by three, most of it uninhabitable. Following the shore clockwise we come first to the original town, the volcanic crater which gave the area its name under the British. Here too was the port, now silted up and used only by the smallest craft, which brought the city its early prosperity. Overshadowed by a frowning gorge under the lip of the mountains to the west, a series of curiously shaped cisterns built in pre-Islamic times – the Aden Tanks – can just be seen. Vita Sackville-West thought they looked like the penguin house at London Zoo; they take on a more sinister aspect at twilight, when the call to prayer fades away into a whine of mosquitoes and the sound of air rushing through the clefts of rock above.

Continuing clockwise past Sirah, we cross the narrow peninsula of Ra's Marshaq and then follow an empty coast of cliffs and coves. Some three miles on, a long sandy beach opens up with a headland, the Elephant's Back, at its far end; the hulk rusting in the

shallows was a gunboat, dive-bombed as it lobbed shells over the Elephant during the troubles of 1986. Then there is a string of small sandy bays separated by promontories where, on the verandas of once-grand villas, overworked administrators would relax with a sigh and a sundowner, watching the strange backlit profile of Little Aden to the west as it melted with the afterglow.

Here the wide Back Bay opens out, and we cross the headland the British called Steamer Point and come to al-Tawwahi, which they developed at the expense of the old harbour. The streets are broader and the buildings grander than in Crater. At Prince of Wales (now Tourists') Pier the liners of P&O, Lloyd Triestino and the Hansa Line would discharge their passengers through a little neo-Gothic building – not a suburban church but the Arrival Hall – into a world of postcards, duty-free and the obligatory trip to the Tanks before they went on to Singapore or Southampton. It was these, and other non-human cargoes, that made Aden at its height in the late 1950s the greatest port in the world after New York. Now the harbour is home to a number of long-term invalids, rusting away at their moorings under the gaze of a miniature Big Ben up on the mountainside.

Over another rocky bluff and the headland of Hujuf, and the last component of this scattered city, al-Ma'alla, opens out. We cross a cluster of oil tanks, the magnet that attracted shipping in later years, and follow a long canyon of apartment blocks, Martyr Madram Street.

Swooping low over Workers' Island (formerly – *plus ça change* – Slave Island) we curve round to the west along a low, sandy coast with a few bushes and a clump of early 1960s buildings to the north. This is People's (formerly Federation) City, which the British built as capital of the ill-fated Federation of South Arabia.

A final ascent takes us over Little Aden, which the French tried to buy in 1862. This second peninsula is as craggy as Aden proper. Together they hold the great bay in a crab-claw grip. Beyond Little Aden stretches a hazy and sparsely inhabited coast, all the way to Bab al-Mandab and the Red Sea.

As you scud back over the bay it is all too easy to see through the misty eyes of nostalgia the white prows, the memsahib frocks and hats, the cotton ducks and gleaming mess kits of the British masters of Aden's heyday. The 1960s, after Suez had struck midnight at the imperial ball, lie outside nostalgia's periphery. Aden is a feast of faded magnificence for young fogey travel writers and for the Adenis who, never having had it so good, fled Marxism; as it is for some of those who stayed and, even now, sometimes wipe away a tear at the memory of Empire. They forget the cock-ups that surrounded the British departure, that the coolies finally laid down their cheery grins and took up arms. The changes that took place after 1967, so sudden and extraordinary, have for many engendered selective amnesia over what happened immediately before.

It is time to lay the imperial ghosts. Aden, at Unification in 1990, was proclaimed Yemen's commercial capital. It has the dramatic presence to rival Sydney or Manhattan as one of the world's great maritime destinations. More important, it has the strategic location to equal Singapore or Dubai as a centre of trade. In 1992, it still tottered along a narrow divide between the quaint and the seedy.

★

Aden's topography is the main factor behind its equally bizarre human geography. On the map it is an appendage to Arabia, a geological haemorrhoid, or something alien that has run aground. The Adenis know that they don't fit into the traditional tribal picture of society. They have not grown from the land but have snagged on it, brought on tides sweeping down the Red Sea or across from India.

The racial mix is ancient. Ibn al-Mujawir noted that all sorts of nationalities lived in and around Aden, particularly Ethiopians and Somalis. Most incomers have been transient, ebbing and flowing with the port's fortunes. The greatest influx came in the last century. Lord Hardinge, Governor-General of India in the 1840s, feared that free-port status would make Aden 'the resort of all the loose population of the Red Sea coast'. His worries turned out to be justified: some twenty years later Hunter wrote that 'the morality of the inhabitants of Aden is not of a high order' and singled out the problems caused by divorced women. The Jews of Aden, who had some unusual monopolies including the cleaning of ostrich feathers, came in for his particular disapprobation, being 'not, as a rule, very cleanly in their habits, only washing and changing their clothes once a week'.

Not to be outdone by San'a, Aden claims antediluvian origins – Cain is said to have worshipped fire here, and a tower on Jabal Hadid is billed as the site of Abel's grave. When the Himyaris first came to power in the north they found it difficult to protect caravan routes to such a distant spot and developed Muza in the region of al-Makha; in the first century AD the *Periplus* said that Aden, which it calls 'Eudaimon Arabia', was only a village.

However, by Ptolemy's day Himyar had extended its rule and 'Arabia Emporium', as the geographer calls it, regained its importance. A number of dynasties ruled Aden in the medieval period. Under the Rasulid sultans the trade of Aden greatly increased to compensate Mongol depredations in the Gulf, but its fortunes fell with those of its masters. Their successors, the Tahirids, recognized Aden's great potential and revived the port by introducing preferential duties.

It was during Tahirid times that the great Sufi holy man of Aden, Abu Bakr ibn Abdullah al-Aydarus, lived. His superhuman doings, in addition to the toothstick exploit, included making the sky rain milk during a famine. Today, the saint's annual festival is still by far the largest in Aden. Al-Aydarus, however, did not monopolize the miraculous. His predecessor Shaykh Jawhar had a cat called Sa'adah, Felicity, which would indicate how much lunch to prepare by miaowing the number of guests. One day Felicity was found to have miscounted, until it was realized that she had subtracted two of the guests because they were Christians.

By the end of the fifteenth century, Europeans had discovered the Cape route to India; in no time Aden, the Eye of Yemen, caught the eye of Renaissance Portugal, and it was lust at first sight. The Portuguese traveller Duarte Barbosa wrote that Aden 'has a greater and richer trade than any other port in the world', and his countrymen, whose king had assumed the title 'Lord of the Navigation, Conquest and Commerce of Arabia', tried in 1513 to capture the place from its Tahirid rulers. Where they failed, the Ottomans succeeded twenty-five years later; but the Turks were tied up subduing the mountain Yemenis and allowed Aden to deteriorate, using it as a punishment posting. The first British ships to visit, early in the seventeenth century, found Aden in a state of decay and turned their attention to al-Makha. In the late 1830s there were about ninety stone houses, much dilapidated, in Aden. Most of the population existed, according to an English visitor, in 'low crazy cabins of matting or yellow reeds'.

★

My first sight of Crater brought about a strange temporal displacement, the shock of the not-so-old. Once through a cutting in the volcano's rim, the road descends then flattens out into a scene curiously familiar to Britons of the pre-Habitat age. Passing what claimed, in large letters, to be a Rootes Group car showroom, I entered an eerily realistic mock-up of a 1950s city centre in the English Midlands – one that had been blitzed, then rebuilt by architects who had ration-book budgets and a nodding acquaintance with Bauhaus. In most of Britain, townscapes like these have been razed or post-modernized. Here the style lives on, needing a lick of paint, Coventry in the sun.

Above the road, the theme of provincial England continues in a neo-Gothic church set on a basalt eminence. St Mary the Virgin, built in 1869, together with Christ Church, Steamer Point, took over from the 'divine sheds' which were previously the focus of the settlement's Christian worship. It is now CID headquarters. Instead of pews there are metal desks; above, a grubby asbestos roof is out of kilter with the line of the gables. Further up from the church I came across a broken concrete slab commemorating the Norfolk Regiment. From here on, the rough path is strewn with dog turds bleached by the sun to the colour of Cheshire cheese. An extermination order was issued against the dogs of Aden eight hundred years ago; they managed to kill one, and the rest escaped to the rocky heights where they hid by day, and still do. 'I seek refuge with God from their bite,' Ibn al-Mujawir exclaimed, 'for it is poisonous on account of the little water they drink.'

In the heat of noon, when even the dogs are laid low, Crater simmers. As I looked over the town, it struck me that, improbable through the natural setting of Aden is, it was nothing to this vision of home – but home misplaced in both space and time. The transposition of England to the East was, in the root sense of the word, disorientating.

Down in the middle of Crater, the vision was dispersed. The older houses are a combination of warehouse and dwelling, a couple of storeys boxed in by screened verandas to catch what breeze there is, a vaulted godown below. On the other side of Jabal Shamsan in al-Tawwahi there are similar buildings, but a greater sense of space and elegance. Here lived most of Aden's European community.

The Crescent Hotel* in al-Tawwahi uses veranda screening on a huge scale. At first sight, it promised to retain something of the old maritime grandeur. Built in 1932, its lobby had the feel of an ocean liner, with large expanses of dark wood and simple lines. But in the dining-room the napery was crusty and fly-spotted fans hung motionless. There was a miasma of fried fish, but no food. The bar was grotesque. Nursing-home tapestry sofas and club chairs had collapsed *in situ*, as if someone had forgotten to remove the mortal remains of departed inmates; the carpet was tacky with spilt Sirah beer (God knows where it came from – my bottle, warm and produced after a long search, was 'the last one', and the regulars were drinking Stolichnaya); surreal murals included a lady's leg being swallowed by a giant banana, Carmen Miranda's final exit. The hotel is a period piece as much as Le Baron in Aleppo, which lives off its T.E. Lawrence connection and is at least clean. When I first saw it, the Crescent's grandeur was not faded, but rotten.

Someone had advised me to eat not in the Crescent, or the nearby Rock, a monument to 1950s schmaltz, but in the Chinese restaurant in al-Ma'alla. Here you might have found yourself in the company of a Cuban delegation or a knot of Party stalwarts who would slip into Russian over sweet-and-sour squid and Stolly.

The Ching Sing was at the end of a mile-long gash of almost identical apartment blocks in Novosibirsk-brutalist style.

'I didn't realize the Russians had built so much,' I said to the taxi-driver.

'The Russians? Oh, they didn't build anything. It was the British.'

In 1963 Johnston, the High Commissioner, described the half-finished Martyr Madram Street (quondam Queensway) as 'a sort of triumphal way'.

For me, it recalled more closely the description of Aden by Harold Ingrams, the pioneering British administrator of Hadramawt: 'For soulless, military officialdom did its best to see that nothing picturesque or beautiful was ever allowed to raise its head among the depressing, severely practical, and utterly

---

* The name comes from Prince of Wales Crescent (itself commemorating the 1875 visit of the future Edward VII, who was presented with three ostriches in allusion to his heraldic badge).

uncomfortable barrack-like structures it erected itself.' The sentence is telling. It illustrates the peculiarly British gulf that separated the Arabist from the professional administrator, the open-minded from the philistine, or – in the eyes of some – the dreamer from the pragmatist. Ingrams, who responded joyously to the 'peculiar cachet' of Hadrami architecture, was appalled by Aden, a literally outlandish carbuncle of a place but the reason for his being in that distant flawed Shangri-la of Hadramawt. The tension is one that lasted from the earliest days of the British in Aden until 1967. Inevitably, it was soulless military officialdom that came out on top.

★

'Like a pair of resurrectionists', on a dark night in January 1839, two men prowled around Aden's graveyard. They were looking for a choice and movable specimen of the finely carved marble grave slabs littering the ground. One of them was John Studdy Leigh, 24-year-old supercargo of an English trading vessel that had put in at Aden. Next morning he ascended 'Djebel Shunsum' with some companions: they had a picnic breakfast, raised three cheers and waved the Union Jack. 'We left as usual with escaladers like ourselves a memorial of our visit in a claret bottle, which we had emptied.'

It was still some months before the British flag was to flutter more permanently over Aden, but Leigh, an adventurer with a patriotic bent, embodied the soul of the new age. The Napoleonic Wars had marked a turning-point, and just as the Great War a century later loosened corsets and raised hemlines, so Waterloo condemned the powdered wig to its block. The last of the Hanoverian kings had sired ten bastards, but now the debris of the Regency party was being swept away: on the throne sat Victoria, virgin and immaculate, and Aden was the first imperial acquisition of her era.

British interest in the area was not new. The little island of Mayyun, or Perim, in the Bab al-Mandab Strait had been garrisoned in 1799 to prevent the French from sailing to India; but they were soon forced out of Egypt by the Battle of Alexandria, and the British out of Mayyun by lack of water. What brought them back was the need for a coaling-station for the new steamships on the Suez-Bombay run. The first steam-powered vessel to sail the route was the *Hugh Lindsay* in 1830, and the decade that followed saw a flurry of activity in search of a suitable stop near the mouth of the Red Sea. The Island of Suqutra was tried but abandoned when the troops succumbed to fever. Aden was the obvious choice.

The man chosen to take it over, Captain Stafford Bettesworth Haines, belonged to a recent and more swashbuckling past, the age of Clive and the English nabobs. He was to run Aden for sixteen years by a mixture of chicanery, blandishments, and brute force, which earned him the contempt of Victorian Bombay society who dubbed him the 'sultanized Englishman'. His portrait does indeed give him a foreign and disreputable air, a corsair forced into a stiff collar. Had he ended up further off the beaten track, like Rajah Brooke in Sarawak, he would have escaped the snooty opprobrium of the Establishment, but in Aden he was caught between the East India Company's Secret Committee in London and the Governor of Bombay. The military in particular were wary of the way in which he courted local rulers and encouraged trade. His dreams of Aden's mercantile renaissance resembled those of Raffles in Singapore, but Bombay wanted to straitjacket him within the town's defences. Haines's character was a curious amalgam: Bombay accused him of going 'against the spirit of the age' when in 1851 he hung the corpse of a would-be murderer in chains at the Barrier Gate; later, on trial for peculation, he was to assert that 'goodwill, kindness and respect . . . will do more than even the bayonet can in Arabia'. Ultimately, Haines was – like the city he created – a misfit.

British relations with the tribes were uneasy for the first three decades of their rule in Aden. Their immediate neighbours the Abdali Sultans of Lahj, from whom Haines had taken the port, proved the most fickle; the Fadlis, who controlled the coastal region to the east and whose sultan was described by Playfair as 'a very old man, but . . . bold and reckless, delighting in marauding excursions and hazardous exploits', were the most inimical. The tribes launched a number of unsuccessful attacks on Aden from 1840 onwards, but by the 1860s the British claimed to have broken their spirit.

At first, the people of the hinterland did not know what to make of the alien presence, this cuckoo in the South Arabian nest. So they gave British Aden honorary tribal status, with Haines as eponymous patriarch: the new Adenis became known as Banu Haines.

Haines and his successors realized that Aden, whose only natural resource was salt, had to be supplied from the interior. They began to pay out protection money to the neighbouring rulers, and Bombay came reluctantly to accept that it had spawned a monstrous offspring which grew and grew as the network of treaties and stipends ramified.

Haines's problem was that he was a lax bookkeeper. British policy towards Aden, whether controlled by the East India Company, the India Office or the Colonial Office, was to be steered to the last by the men in Accounts, and when the auditors found a shortfall of £28,000 in the records he was shipped off to Bombay, never to return. He was cleared of embezzlement but held responsible – as a gentleman – for the deficit.

The cuckoo in the nest, meanwhile, kept growing; Haines's successors continued to sign *ad hoc* agreements with more and more distant rulers. It was not until the turn of the century that Ottoman expansion from the north forced the British to consider fixing a limit to their sphere of influence, and it took until 1913 for Whitehall and the Sublime Porte to ratify a border treaty. This delineated a boundary running north-eastward from Bab al-Mandab. The following year, the two powers went to war and the treaty was rendered meaningless. On this slender legal basis was Yemen partitioned.

★

The clash of the two empires in South Arabia* was not so much a sideshow as a freak show which might have been funny had it not been grotesque, ludicrous and – even by First World War standards – incompetent.

British and Ottoman forces arrived at Lahj simultaneously, and

---

* For an account of which I have drawn on the late Dr Robin Bidwell's article in *Arabian Studies*, VI, 1982.

exhausted, on the evening of 4 July 1915. Almost the first casualty was Sultan Sir Ali ibn Ahmad al-Abdali, who was mistaken for a Turk and shot by a sepoy as he rode out to greet the column from Aden. He died shortly after. Following this inauspicious start the British, outnumbered, withdrew, and the Turks marched on to take al-Shaykh Uthman; their raiding parties reached as far as al-Ma'alla – unopposed, since the naval-gazing British had all their big guns pointing out to sea.

The saviour of Aden was Sir George Younghusband, brother of the more famous Younghusband of Tibet. He was called in with the message, 'The Turks are on the golf course' – not a metaphor, as Aden Golf Club's links were on the isthmus south of Khur Maksar. Sir George later provided the epitaph for the Lahj fiasco: 'the army sat down and incidentally began to die of heat . . . Some said advance but most said retire and did so.'

The British under Younghusband quickly retook al-Shaykh Uthman and set about fortifying the isthmus, to the dismay of the Golf Club. For the rest of the war they and the Turks glared at each other across no man's land, like Tweedledum and Tweedledee, and occasionally lobbed shells. Transit passengers in Aden would ride out to the barbed wire, hoping to catch a bombardment. It was altogether a chivalrous affair. The Turkish commander refrained from interfering with Aden's water supply, and on the British side the only unpleasantness was, as usual, financial, with London and India wrangling over who should foot the bill. In the end, they went Dutch.

Of the two imperial dinosaurs one expired gracefully at Versailles; the other began a long Middle Eastern suicide when Balfour opened its veins with his promise of a Jewish homeland in Palestine. Death was slow, its final throes in Aden played out not to the stately measures of Elgar but to the sound of grenades and snipers' bullets.

★

'I am an Imperialist,' Harold Ingrams had said in the 1941 introduction to *Arabia and the Isles*, 'and equally certain that the vast majority of Arabs in the Aden Protectorate are too.' In the 1966 edition Ingrams felt obliged to furnish a ninety-page apologia for the sentence. In the intervening years, everything he and the few men like him had achieved had crumbled to dust.

The treaties which Haines and his successors had signed with minor potentates had left the map of southern Yemen a crazy patchwork of states, most of them miniscule. These were divided into a Western Protectorate, extending inland from the coast 100 miles either side of Aden, and a far bigger Eastern Protectorate, largely made up of Hadramawt and al-Mahrah. During the 1930s, Ingrams had succeeded in bringing peace to the Eastern Protectorate. The Western Protectorate, however, remained unsettled. Following the Ottoman withdrawal, Imam Yahya had loudly asserted the unity of Yemen and had occupied parts of the Western Protectorate; the British had responded by bombing raids on the Imam's domains, and Yahya had accepted the status quo but without dropping his claim to rule all of the Yemen. From the late 1940s, however, the British pursued a forward policy in the Western Protectorate, imposing their 'advice' on its rulers. The new Imam, Ahmad, reacted by encouraging rebellions against the British who, in turn, sent in troops. Ingrams viewed this British interference – which he called 'Englishry' – with dismay.

Worse was to come. Having lost their hold on the Suez Canal at the end of 1956 the British decided, urged on by America and Cold War paranoia, to compensate by enlarging the Aden base. To this end they greased the Protectorate rulers' palms liberally in the hope of gaining their goodwill and assurances over its future. In 1959 they tried to impose order on the free-for-all by setting up the Federation of South Arabia. Eventually, a dozen rulers signed up; those of the larger Eastern Protectorate states refused, partly because they were unwilling to share potential oil wealth with their neighbours. The idea was to create something like the United Arab Emirates-to-be, but while Britain could hand each federation ruler a ministerial portfolio, it could not give them the loyalty of their subjects.

The British had lost Suez, but in trying to cling on to it they had also lost their prestige and – in the eyes of many – their conscience. Cairo Radio was there to tell anyone who did not already know, and at a period when cheap transistors were turning the airwaves into a genuinely mass medium. The Aden government suggested lamely that its good relations with Aden and Protectorate Arabs were 'unimpaired'. In stark contrast is the report of an eye-witness, David Holden, who described news of the British defeat over Suez running through Aden's back streets 'like an orgasm'.

Nasser's finger pointed not only at the British but also at the Indians who had come to dominate commercial and political life in the Colony. New laws introduced in 1955 meant that four members of its Legislative Council were now elected, but the mass of the population – Arabs from the Protectorate and further north – had no vote. 'Never since the heroic days of Greece has the world had such a sweet, just, boyish master,' said the philosopher George Santayana of the British. If Suez proved that Britain had grown into an embittered and tyrannical old man, then electoral policy in Aden was all too close to that of Athens in ancient times, where a semblance of democracy teetered on a mass of unenfranchised non-citizens.

Yet, for two or three years after the start of the Federation, Aden boomed. There was a lot of money about, and the new refinery at Little Aden was in full swing. For the British, or at least the Conservative government, the worm in the apple was Abdullah al-Asnaj. With his podgy and deceptively innocent features he bore a resemblance to Harold Wilson, whose opposition Labour Party courted him. The al-Asnaj-led trades union movement, encouraged by the unlikely trio of Wilson, Nasser and (for very different reasons) Imam Ahmad, was able to cause serious disruption. A lot more was on the way.

*

Life for the British went on, though it seems, with hindsight, to have been tinged with a Buñuelesque surrealism. The Fisheries Department was looking into the possibility of catching sucker fish, which after a ten-day training period could be used to hunt green turtles; the fish only required feeding and exercise, 'like pets', and the turtles could be made into soup and toilet preparations. On the surface of the water the Reverend J. Fisher buzzed about Back Bay distributing spiritual sustenance not, like his Beatrix Potter namesake, on a water-lily leaf, but in his new launch *Speedy II*. His Excellency the Governor, Sir William Luce, spoke of the need for secondary industries in Aden for fear that perhaps the large sums spent there on Her Majesty's Services might one day be reduced. 'No matter how unlikely such things may appear in the near future,' the *Port of Aden Annual* commented, 'wise men should listen to wise guidance.' Not to worry. A 1962 Defence White Paper had pronounced, with the sibylline certainty of the Queen of Hearts, that the base would be maintained for at least ten years. That meant a lot more balls to be bowled down the wicket at Steamer Point (157,000 in 1962), a lot more chukkas to be played at the Khur Maksar polo ground. There seemed to be no croquet enthusiasts; in these last looking-glass days of the Colony the flamingoes grazing on the nearby beach didn't know how lucky they were.

For six months of the year, the 1963 *Welcome to Aden Guide* told newcomers, you could enjoy a climate normally available only to wealthy invalids (even if, as the Federal Army Commander Brigadier Lunt admitted, it was too warm 'to wear a tweed suit with any degree of comfort'). Never mind the other six months and the expense of cook-bearers, the suggestion was that in Aden everyone could be a nabob, or at least a nob.

This was far from the case. As usual in colonial outposts, social stratification was more pronounced than at home. Even the beaches were segregated to prevent officers, other ranks and civilians catching sight of each other's flesh. Social streaming had always been a part of Aden life. In the 1930s, the British were the A Stream, notable Arabs, Parsees and other non-British VIPs the B Stream; the C Stream was the Rest. In the 1950s and 1960s it was no less rigorous. New accommodation for refinery staff in Little Aden was arranged in four grades, from detached through semis and terrace houses down to flats, the latter equipped with yards 'for purdah ladies to take the air'. The roads were named after English counties.

Aden's emblem at this time might well have been the stuffed dugong, or sea cow, displayed to gullible ratings as a mermaid: it was a creature more of sea than land; it was beginning to come apart at the seams; it was monumentally ugly; and it was billed as something it was not. Despite the sun, the sea and the servants,

Aden was a more a mixture of Gibraltar, Crewe and Hell with duty-free facilities.

With the post-Suez influx of servicemen and camp-followers, the old Arabists and other enthusiasts were being squeezed out. For them Aden, the Eye of Yemen, had always been its eyesore, a place to be left as quickly as possible for bracing trips into the Protectorate; now they were seeing the Colony inundated by tens of thousands of outsiders. Khur Maksar became a bungalow jungle, and Arabic 'Adan' was transformed into Anglo-Saxon, adenoidal 'Eighden', a phonetic semblance of some Kentish village. For the majority of Britons during Aden's final colonial decade the Arabs existed, if at all, on the periphery, insulated from them by a social Bombay mix of banyans and baboos. Ships' passengers were invited to go and look at the cargo coolie they would find taking a nap on deck. 'You'll see a little brown man (probably he won't come up to your shoulder) . . . Often he is quite surprisingly handsome . . . His habitual expression is, I should say, one of sardonic resignation.' The point of contact was tangential, if that.

Increasingly, too, even those who lived and worked in South Arabia and spoke the language kept themselves largely at a remove. Harold Ingrams, an exception to the never-the-twain style of administration, attributes this distancing to the influx of scores of colonial officials from Africa who were used to a totally different social system. Ingrams's belief that the British could penetrate Arabian society and thought was attacked by the Governor of Aden, Sir Charles Johnston: 'I could never follow him in his view that the Englishman in Arabia must try to think as an Arab. It is, I believe, an impossible undertaking, and those who have attempted it usually end up in an esoteric faith based on the incomprehensibility of Arabia and the inherent hopelessness of any Western attempt to influence its development . . . the attitude [is] . . . half rational, half mystical, and wholly oracular.' A photograph in Sir Charles's book, *The View from Steamer Point* (the title is in itself significant), shows him taking tea with the Qu'ayti Sultan in al-Mukalla. The atmosphere in the Delhi-Edwardian sultanic saloon is distinctly uncomfortable: the Sultan, in a curious winged turban, looks like an eisteddfod bard; the Governor frowns into his cup as though he's found a scorpion in the tea-leaves.

Aden is *sui generis*, and in their last decade there the position of the British was in itself increasingly bizarre. Yet Aden is conceptually the closest they and other Westerners of a certain age can get to Yemen. It was surely the Adenis of the 1960s to whom Margaret Thatcher was referring when she advised a British couple about to leave for a posting in San'a: 'You'll have to watch the Yemenis. They're very *fly*, you know.'

Still, early in 1963 something of a calm prevailed. Even if the mercury was rising in the political thermometer, *sang* remained *froid*. The armed forces had not had to exert themselves, except for the aptly named Flight-Lieutenant R. Sweatman who had, for unexplained reasons, made a forty-mile route march across the desert in eighteen hours with only five pints of water; the only violence reported was an attack on a group of RAF men, out climbing in the Western Protectorate, by eight four-foot baboons.

★

Back in my days as a teacher of English, I often knew how the Queen must feel at Buckingham Palace garden parties. Nasir the engineer was number fifteen. For two months, I'd been teaching him the difference between 'How do you do?' and 'What do you do?'; but it was the end-of-course oral test so I had to ask him yet again. 'And what do you do, Nasir?'

'I am an engineer.'

I forced a smile of encouragement, then the prescribed 'Oh, really? What sort of engineer?' He told me he was in cement, which I also knew. I asked about his father; Nasir said he was dead. The past tense was uncharted ground. 'And what did your father do?'

Nasir looked out of the window at the San'a night. Was he struggling with some painful memory? Or with an irregular verb form? Then his eyes turned back to me, their corners creased, and his face broke into a wide grin.

'My father killed the British!'

Nasir's father, Qahtan al-Sha'bi, waged a four-year war against the colonial authorities. His National Liberation Front (NLF) had its first success in Radfan, a mountainous area north of Aden near the border with the fledgeling Yemen Arab Republic. The place is now commemorated in a brand of cigarette; the date, 14 October 1963, remembered as the start of the Revolution in the south. In Radfan snipers tied down two British battalions for six months while the armed uprising spread to Aden, where the hand grenade became the NLF's preferred weapon; in December 1963 they nearly succeeded in assassinating the High Commissioner, Sir Kennedy Trevaskis. A state of emergency was proclaimed which lasted until the British left and Qahtan, recognized as president, shed his *futah* and battledress tunic in favour of the former oppressors' suit. He was the only member of the NLF leadership over forty.

Over these four years the British found themselves under siege: from the NLF; from the unions, who also took up arms and metamorphosed into FLOSY, the Front for the Liberation of Occupied South Yemen; from Arab nationalism in general; and from the UN, which was calling for a proper constitutional state. They had their backs to the Federal wall, and even the wall was to go against them.

A century earlier, in his *Account of the British Settlement of Aden in Arabia*, Captain Hunter had warned that 'long residence [in Aden] impairs the faculties and undermines the constitution of Europeans'. Perhaps, though, it was a siege mentality that caused the final policy meltdown. Under attack from the guerrillas, the British reacted first by firing back at them, then attempting to infiltrate them (using an 'undercover' team led by a gigantic Fijian, Sergeant Labalaba of the SAS), and finally wooing them. Lord Shackleton was dispatched to Aden in April 1967 with the request, 'Would you kindly refrain from shooting us? Then we can talk.' 'Impossible,' the NLF retorted. 'We must be *seen* to be driving you out.'

And drive us out they did. For the military, such a loss of face was unbearable. Lieutenant-Colonel Colin Mitchell of the Argyll and Sutherland Highlanders put it thus: 'Well, you know, purely as a soldier . . . the whole prestige of the Army depended on going back in, obviously. You know, we were thrown out, if the truth be known, and we had to go back in.'

Mitchell was speaking to the television cameras in early July 1967. In the UK he became known as 'Mad Mitch', something of a folk hero. Eyes glinting beneath his glengarry, his clipped

Sandhurst syllables hardly concealed a note of triumph. The Argylls, pipes skirling and kilts frou-frouing in the land of the checked *futah*, had retaken Crater after a thirteen-day rebellion by the previously loyal Armed Police. They had even – an important consideration – saved money by not using the Carl-Gustav anti-tank missile with which they had planned to open the doors of the Chartered Bank, their intended HQ. Someone had the bright idea of ringing the bell, and the caretaker let them in.

'We're a very *mean* lot,' Mad Mitch went on. 'We're very *fair*, you know, but if anyone starts any trouble they'll just get their heads blown orf. They'll get the message in time, you know.' Time, however, had run out. Senior officers put the lid on Mitch, who went on to become a Conservative MP.

The NLF and FLOSY were fighting the British; they were also fighting each other. The third element, the Federation sultans, had at first been backed by a Labour government in Whitehall under pressure from Washington (once in office, Harold Wilson had dropped his lookalike, al-Asnaj); but when in 1966 Whitehall realized how much the place was costing, the decision was made to drop Aden itself, Federation, sultans and all. Bombay had complained in the 1870s of the heavy burden of Aden's cost, £150,000 a year; by 1965 the most conservative estimate of its annual drain on the Whitehall budget was £60 million. The Foreign Secretary George Brown summed things up in September 1967 when he said, 'we want to be out of the whole Middle East as far and as fast as we possibly can'.

We shall never know whether, given more time, the Federation would have collapsed anyway once its ties were cut, or whether it could have survived, Pinocchio-like, without its puppet-master. In the event most of the sultans went on to a life of comfortable ennui in Saudi Arabia; many of their supporters were killed. Whitehall, like a twitchy gambler who loses his nerve and backs a sure winner when the odds are lowest, finally threw in its lot with the NLF. The first UK–NLF talks began on 21 November 1967 at the Geneva YWCA; later that month it was rumoured that RAF planes were being sent to attack FLOSY positions.

The Federation, in the words of its Foreign Minister Muhammad Farid al-Awlaqi, felt 'completely betrayed' by Britain's dishonourable action; for the 'Fidaralis', the phrase *wa'd injlizi*, an Englishman's word, took on a new meaning. According to David Ledger, a political officer in Aden at the time, one of the Federation rulers went further: 'It is far better to be Britain's enemy than Britain's friend. If you are the former there is a possibility of being bought. If you are the latter there is a certainty of being sold.' The British weren't just paranoid – in South Arabia everyone really was against them.

It was three in the afternoon on 30 November 1967. A windmill looked on motionless as the last helicopter clattered into the air. The sun was past its height and heading for the sea behind Little Aden, but a fierce light still glared off the Khur Maksar salt pans. The British had left, in the words of Brigadier Lunt, like thieves in the night.

Publicly, and with masterly understatement, George Brown declared that 'some things which the United Kingdom expected to settle before independence may be left pending'. The last High Commissioner, Sir Humphrey Trevelyan, admitted that 'our period of occupation did the country little permanent good'. Richard Crossman, in the privacy of his diary, confided: 'Chaos will rule after we've gone and there'll be one major commitment out – thank God.'

★

'The problem is the coffins,' said Abdullah the sexton. 'The water rotted them and they collapsed.'

We were drinking clove-flavoured tea in the Christian cemetery of al-Ma'alla. Many of the graves had become gaping holes, as though their occupants had jumped the Doomsday gun and burst out. Aden had just suffered one of its rare but disastrous floods, and even the dead were affected. The surface of the ground was littered with bleached shells and bits of coral – at first I took them for bones, transformed by some sea-change, but then realized that they had been used to decorate the graves. Some of the monuments had been defaced recently. Abdullah shook his head sadly. 'Those who did it are not Muslims,' he said.

In this place of toings and froings, here were the ones who had stayed on. Soldier and civilian, tommy and toff lay side by side; the

younger sons of county families shared the earth with Greek and
Chinese merchants, Italian submariners, a solitary French Baha'i –
one of the small number of post-independence interments – and
Henry Martin Sandbach, who died at sea in December 1896 'as a
result of wounds received attempting to save the life of his shikari
whilst on a lion hunt in Somaliland'. A good number of the graveyard's occupants had expired, their headstones said, 'on entering
Aden'.

The British left much behind beside their dead. Right-hand-
drive Humbers, Rileys and Morris Minor 1,000s chug around the
streets; across from the Sailors' Club a long-stationary Bedford van
sells fish and chips, wrapped these days in the *Straits Times*. Pillar
boxes are still in use, but with the royal cypher chiselled off. A
driver is a *draywal*, a screwdriver – by some obscure semantic quirk
– *dismis*. An old man stopped me on the street and recited 'One,
two, buckle my shoe . . .' Queen Victoria used to sit in the garden
next to the Crescent Hotel; she now lives in the National
Museum's back yard.

Time has picked clean much of what was left by the duty-free
vultures of a generation ago, but the signs are still up at Steamer
Point: shipping companies, chandlers, Stop-and-Shop, the Seamen
Store, the Lax Stores (motto: 'Try us before COMMITTING
yourself'). The latter carries an eclectic stock – stopwatches,
bedpans, defunct petrol lighters, bits of diving gear and so on; but
the main line is in lacquered and mounted sea creatures. A faint
whiff of putrefaction spills out on to the street.

'They never buy anything,' sighed the man behind the counter
as a group of Russian ratings loped out of the shop. 'Well, maybe a
lobster now and then.' He fumbled in the dust under the glass
counter and pressed a pair of cufflinks into my hand. 'Baltic
amber.'

'How much are they?'

'Nothing. I like to give my best customers a little present.' It was
my first visit and I hadn't bought anything. 'Where did you say you
were from? Germany? France? Italy? Belgium?'

Belgium. We were here for 128 years, for heaven's sake. We were
the ones who *understood* the Arabs. We gave them pillar boxes, and
Coventry. 'I'm British.'

'Ah. Then I've got a *special* present for you . . .' He reached down into the lowest shelf of the counter, found whatever it was and added, as he blew the dust off it, 'something we forgot to give you before.' He resurfaced and held out the object.

It was a hand grenade.

'There's nothing in it now,' he said, smiling. The grenade was empty. It would make a fine cigarette lighter. I thanked the shop-keeper and left, still without buying anything.

The eponymous proprietor of Aziz's Bookshop is a better businessman. He knows the value of the period piece, his period being the early 1960s. High glass-fronted bookshelves contain copies of Billy Fury and *Z-Cars* fanzines, '9 Views of Aden – Coloured Real Photographs', and greetings cards from the saucy Barbara Windsor blonde to the beatnik ('Hey, I got so hepped–up about your birthday . . . like I almost combed my hair!').

Aziz exists in a perpetual autumn of disintegrating ephemera; to me, his shop smelt of childhood attics. As he listens to the BBC English Service, his days measured out by *Just a Minute* and *The Vintage Chart Show*, he must be aware that he didn't get his turn-over right. Still, he isn't the first: Aden shopkeepers in the days of the *Periplus*, the later Rasulids, the Turks, all suffered from slumps caused by the vagaries of geopolitics. Small comfort.

★

The history of Aden's earliest trade is a matter of guesswork, but by the tenth century we have a clear picture of the port's position at the hub of international commerce. The Cairo-based Fatimid dynasty had begun to outshine Abbasid Baghdad, and Aden became the entrepôt for its oriental supplies. Al-Muqaddasi, writing at the time, calls it 'the entrance-hall of China and the warehouse of the West'; contemporary sherds of high-quality celadon ware have been found in the region, and the Far Eastern connection lasted – an early fourteenth-century inscribed stone discovered recently in Canton records the building there of a mosque gate and wall by a trader from Abyan, the area immedi-ately east of Aden.

The most detailed account of Aden's medieval trade is provided by Ibn al-Mujawir, who lists the products brought to Aden from

India, Sind, Ethiopia and Egypt, together with the duties paid on them. Detailed ledgers were kept, and on one occasion this caused friction between port officials and merchants. A party of Hadrami cloth traders arrived and were asked for their names. 'Ba Arse, Ba Shit, Ba Slit, Ba Silent Fart, Ba Pubic Hair,' they answered.* The outraged customs officer refused to let the Hadramis through, so they were left waiting while their merchandise was trampled underfoot. By chance the Sultan was passing and asked what was wrong.

'Sire,' said the customs man, 'their names are, . . . *unmentionable*.'

'Well,' answered the Sultan, 'if you cannot bring yourself to mention their names, how can I take duty from them? I absolve them from all payment!'

Security at the port was rigorous. Men were frisked everywhere, including 'between the buttocks'; a crone was employed to examine every crevice of the female arrivals. In the slave market girls were stripped, perfumed and submitted to no less probing an examination.

'Al-Hasan ibn Ali Hazawwar al-Firuzkuhi told me,' Ibn al-

---

* *Ba* is a common prefix of Hadrami family names.

Mujawir recorded, '"I sold an Indian slave-girl to an Alexandrian at Aden. He kept her for seven days, and when he tired of her he alleged that she was defective and had a writ served on me on the grounds of selling poor-quality merchandise. The judge asked, 'What is her defect?' and the buyer said, 'Her vagina is loose and flabby.' So I retorted, 'If your prick is so small that you can't do your best to fill her up, then what use to you is her sleek, white, plucked and scented pussy?' On hearing this the judge cried to those present, '*OUT WITH THEM!*' So out we went. I returned to my work, the girl stayed with the Alexandrian, and I don't know what became of either of them."'

The medieval period was the high point of Aden's trade until 1850, when it was transformed by its new Free Port status. Commerce rose again sharply with the opening of the Suez Canal in 1869, and goods brought to Aden and listed by Hunter in 1877 include feathers, fireworks, fish fins and maws, shells and cowries, tortoiseshell, umbrellas and opium. The drug trade was legal but controlled: opium was not sold to Europeans 'except under a pass', and hashish had to cost at least Rs.100 a *maund* (about £10 for 28lbs) 'in order to prevent abuse'. Trade was not only seaborne – around a quarter of a million camel-loads arrived from the interior annually.

It was during this period that the great trading houses of Aden founded their fortunes. At the forefront were the two Parsee firms of Messrs Cowasjee Dinshaw and Mr Muncherjee Eduljee, the Harrods of Crater where, Hunter says, 'almost anything that could ever be wanted may be purchased'. These emporia, and others like that started by Captain Luke Thomas, were still going strong in the 1960s, when their lists of agencies included transport and irriga- tion equipment, Doulton Sanitary Potteries Ltd., Lea & Perrins Worcestershire Sauce, Babycham, and Walters' Palm Toffee.

Greatest of all was the business founded by the Provençal Antonin Besse. Besse, who inevitably became known as *al-Biss*, the Cat, arrived in Aden in the late 1890s and stayed until his death in 1951, by which time he was able to donate £1.5 million to set up St Antony's College, Oxford. The money came from a vast empire of concerns around the Horn of Africa and along the Arabian coast to Hadramawt. Besse handled 'hides, skins, oilseeds, pulses, black and white cottonseed, incense, myrrh, opoponax, aloes, mother of pearl shells, cuttlefish bones, gum Arabic, and coffee', but the bulk of his fortune derived from monopolies on the distribution of sugar and paraffin. An eccentric, his loves included Nietzsche, Wagner, street football and rambles over Jabal Shamsan; his bugbears were Mussolini and anyone who wore socks with shorts. The latter must have caused friction with the bestockinged British, who prattled about him mercilessly. Perhaps worst of all in their eyes was that he chose to live on the wrong side of Aden, in Crater. But whatever was said about him, Besse was an extremely successful businessman who combined a romantic streak with hard-nosed acumen – something most Anglo-Saxons could only envy. He remains a paradigm for Aden's curious marriage of the exotic and the mundane. John Masefield might have described the arrival in Aden, this city of lists, of a Besse freighter,

> With a cargo of kerosene,
> Car tyres, spare parts,
> Frankincense, lavatories, and Gilbey's gin.

It is all gone. But yet again the tide is on the turn for Aden's trade, heralded by publicity brochures for the resurrected Free Zone; and by that small, insistent voice, pleading from Port Sa'id to Penang and now once more in the late-night hotel lobbies and taxis of al-Tawwahi: 'What you want? I get you anything . . . *anything!*'

★

Alongside more tangible goods, Aden has long had a parallel market in ideas. This century it has been host to anti-imamate Yemenis, Nasserist Arab Nationalists, the labour movement and Marxism.

A photograph taken in 1977 shows the three major personalities of the Marxist period – Salim Rubay' Ali, Abdulfattah Isma'il and Ali Nasir Muhammad. Salim Rubay' looks cuddly, a teddy-bear of a man; Abdulfattah is diminutive and sly; Ali Nasir is thick-set, no great thinker but, in retrospect, a survivor. All three wear regulation safari suits; all are looking to the left as the Independence Day parade rumbles past, out of the picture. They might more usefully have kept their eyes on each other. In less than a year President Salim Rubay' would be deposed, shot, and succeeded by Abdulfattah; in 1986 Abdulfattah was himself killed in a coup against elements unsympathetic to Ali Nasir. In the ideological jostle of PDRY politics, shove all too often turned to *putsch*.

The growth of Marxism in such an outwardly conservative society as that of South Arabia came as a surprise to many; it was largely due to the unique hothouse atmosphere of Aden itself. In the end, differences between the city and its vast hinterland, between the Sons of Haines and the Sons of Qahtan, were never reconciled.

Three factors helped the rise of the Left. First, the British had engaged in a programme of massive social deconstruction. The cash donations handed out by them over the years to Western Protectorate rulers, and which had increased considerably during the 1950s, enabled the sultans to develop standing armies, thereby reducing their need to control or cajole difficult tribesmen. Even more marked was the outcome of this policy in the Eastern Protectorate, where Ingrams was so successful in promoting peace treaties and centralizing authority that in 1953 Sayyid Abu Bakr al-Kaff said of the newly gunless Hadrami tribes, 'They are dead.' At the same time the *sayyids*, the traditional mediating class, were denied the role on which much of their standing in society depended. Some of them became characters in search of parts.

The British, meanwhile, had been rebuilding society in a way that was to have far-reaching consequences. An educational system was set up based on the public-school ethos with an Arab-Islamic overlay. Its beginnings were small: in the Aden Residency School in the 1870s pupils were taught 'the Elementary Histories of England, India and Rome; Euclid as far as the first book; Geography, Arithmetic and Algebra'. The intake was mostly from Adeni Indian families, but at Aden College eighty years later it had widened to encompass the sons of the traditional learned classes. The British brought boys from *sayyid* and other influential families into a milieu where free thought was encouraged. After a millennium of received notions, the colonial rulers took their

Arab protégés and introduced them to 'character training, physical training and literary education' based on the ideas of Plato, Rousseau and Dr Arnold. The sprouting intelligentsia included many members of the traditional élite: Hadrami *sayyids* like Haydar al-Attas and Ali Salim al-Bid were to play an important part in the spread of Marxism.

The third – and decisive – factor in the growth of the Left was the defeat suffered by Egypt in the 1967 war with Israel. The NLF had begun life as the Yemeni branch of Dr George Habash's Arab Nationalist Movement, founded in Beirut in 1954. Thirteen years on, Nasser's rhetoric had begun to ring hollow and Dr Habash embraced Marx and Lenin instead. The NLF followed suit. In the face of Zionist and imperialist might, revolutionary guerrilla struggle was totally alluring and at least partially successful.

Curiously, the doctrine of Scientific Socialism pursued in the south, 'making use of all that is positive and fighting all deviations', was not unlike that of the Zaydi imamate, which enjoined 'commanding all that is suitable and prohibiting that which is disapproved'. To determine what constituted strayings from the Straight Path of Islam, or leftist/rightist swervings from the Socialist path, the northern *sayyids* studied the Book of God, while the books of Marx and Lenin became the major reference for the Socialist Politburo. Chief Politburo exegete was Abdulfattah Isma'il, an expert on Socialist doctrine who was known, wrily, as *al-Faqih* (literally, the scholar of holy writ). Under his guidance, the early caliphs of Islam were classified according to their rightist or leftist tendencies.

According to another Scientific Socialist tenet, 'not all the old and traditional is bad, and not all that is new is good'. But much of the traditional was deemed bad and the post-independence regimes continued the transformation of society begun by the British. Tribal surnames were banned, *qat* restricted, polygamy prohibited. As for the new, housing (except that which was owner-occupied) was nationalized, as were businesses (except BP and Cable and Wireless) and transport (including, it was mooted, bicycles); women were deveiled and encouraged to join the army; a Fine Arts Institute was set up to provide courses in music, painting and sculpture, acrobatics, theatre and ballet; speaking to a non-South Yemeni without permission became a criminal offence.

Within two years of the British departure, President Qahtan al-Sha'bi had been branded a moderate and deposed in a Corrective Move. He was to die after a decade of house arrest. Then, in December 1970, Aden ceased to be a free port. With the remains of Western trade went the fag-end of Western aid, but the PDRY joined another international fraternity and developed close ties with Cuba and East Germany. South Yemen's socialist clubbability was confirmed when the USSR shifted its regional naval base from Somalia to Aden in 1977.

Relations with the neighbours, however, ranged from sullen to violent. There were border clashes with the North well into the 1980s, and the PDRY supported Dhofari resistance to the Sultan of Oman. A singular bone of contention was the tiny Kuria Muria group of islands off the Dhofari coast: Muscat had presented them to Queen Victoria in 1854, Britain had given them back to Oman in 1967 and, although their only natural resource was guano, Aden laid claim to them and incorporated a blue triangle into its flag to symbolize concern for overseas possessions.

Another neighbour, Saudi Arabia, was alarmed by developments within the PDRY – perhaps because, according to a statement from the World Bank, the PDRY had 'among the world's most egalitarian systems for the distribution of domestically earned income'. Nevertheless this income was minute, and by the government's own admission over a million PDRY citizens left home in the decade following independence – somewhere between a quarter and half of the population. Those who stayed were deprived of all but the barest essentials of life. An Italian diplomat, on his way to Nairobi in 1977, said he was going there 'to buy tomatoes'.

Politically, the PDRY was beset throughout its short history by Party squabbles, which reflected splits in the wider Socialist bloc. Salim Rubay' Ali, influenced by the example of Chairman Mao, brought peasants into Aden during the 1970s to demonstrate against bureaucrats and in favour of low wages. Abdulfattah Isma'il, who ousted him in 1978, was pro-Soviet: it was to Moscow that he fled when, two years later, he was himself deposed by the more moderate and pragmatic Ali Nasir Muhammad. In 1985 Abdulfattah was back in Aden and encouraging hardline opposition to Ali Nasir. Events were to reach a bloody climax in January 1986.

★

'So Ali Nasir said, "Yes, but what do I *do* with the opposition?" and Mengistu said, "Oh, it's simple. Kill them." Well, that's what *some* people say . . .'

The man smiled into his tea. The story of the Ethiopian leader's advice to his South Yemeni counterpart may not be entirely apocryphal – Ali Nasir was in Addis Ababa in December 1985, and Mengistu was to support him subsequently; but it is only one of many versions – onion layers which you peel to get to the heart of the matter. Except that, like onions, the stories tend to have no heart, just a final little layer curled in on itself, and the truth is no more than the sum of its different versions. At least, that is how it seemed at the Zaku Café in Crater which, being the centre of Aden's busiest market, the Suq of Rumours, ought to be a place for intrigue and the telling of tales. The Four Martyrs, hardliners killed in the 1986 coup and subsequently beatified by their victorious comrades, smiled avuncularly down as they did all over the former PDRY, and gave nothing away.

The Aden Ministry of Culture's official account, *Aden's Bloody Monday*, was published three months after the events of 13 January 1986, when truth was still at its most malleable. Wherever it stands on the line between fact and fiction, the booklet is compelling reading, a mixture of Marxist rhetoric, British understatement and Damon Runyon. It was 10.20 a.m., the booklet says, and in the Politburo premises Vice-President and Presidium Vice-Chairman Ali Antar, Defence Minister Salih Muslih Qasim, Politburo member Ali Shayi' Hadi and others were preparing for a routine meeting when one of the President's bodyguards walked into the room and shot Ali Antar in the back. As the account comments, 'One can well imagine the moments of total surprise that prevailed.'

While the diehard Marxist dialecticians Salih Muslih and Ali Shayi' were swiftly added to the PDRY role of martyrs others, including the future leader Ali Salim al-Bid, dived for cover and escaped down a rope of curtains. Meanwhile, a gunboat pumped seventy shells into the villa of the Fourth Martyr, Abdulfattah Isma'il. (He was not at home, but may have been canonized presently by an anti-tank missile; *Aden's Bloody Monday* is strangely silent on his fate.) Throughout the city Ali Nasirists moved against other hardliners.

Ali Nasir Muhammad, for nearly six years Party and State leader, was a reformist seeking to broaden dialogue with his neighbours and the West. What he had not allowed for in his drastic solution to problems at home was that, for the most part, the army was loyal to Ali Antar and Salih Muslih.

The fighting lasted ten days, leaving thousands dead – far more than in the struggle for independence. By the end of it 'the so-called Ali Nasir, a cunning opportunist petty bourgoise [*sic*] giving not a hoot to scientific socialism or the class struggle', was out of the country. The hardliners had won.

In their public 'confessions', Ali Nasir's supporters repeated the claim that he had duped them into believing they were fighting a 'rightist' coup *against* him. By the airforce commander's admission, 'there was a great deal of mystery surrounding the situation, which was getting out of hand'. He had put his finger on it: the PDRY had entered an Einsteinian world where the usual co-ordinates of right and left had been reversed, and revolutionaries had become reactionaries.

Much has been made of the fact that the conflict was polarized between regional groups – Ali Nasir's power base was Abyan and Shabwah, that of his opponents Lahj – and commentators have seen the root of it in a centralized 'distributor' state favouring one region over another. At the same time, the more recent history of the former USSR shows how bitter the reformist-traditionalist struggle within Socialist regimes can be.

The waste was appalling, one PDRY diplomat declaring, 'When they see how hard we fight our own brothers, no outsider would ever dare to interfere in our internal affairs.' After the unification of Yemen in 1990, the two sides declared an amnesty, and Ali Nasir stated in Damascus – his home since 1986 – that responsibility for the bloody events was shared. 'The files', he said, 'must be closed.' Memories, however, will last even longer than the rusting and crab-infested hulk of the gunboat in Elephant's Back Bay.

In 1982 it was not outlandishly prophetic to say, as Robert Stookey did in his book on the PDRY, that 'The association [between the PDRY and the Soviet bloc] has, in all likelihood, passed beyond the point where it could be dissolved even in favour of such a major national objective as union with North Yemen.' Unification agreements had been signed by the Yemens in November 1972 and March 1979, both after periods of violent border clashes. Both came to nothing. And then the unthinkable happened: the Soviet bloc crumbled. The PDRY was no longer viable as a state, politically or economically. By 1989, its leaders could see that their own future – like that of their comrades in Eastern Europe – was bleak, and suggested federation with the YAR. At the end of the year YAR President Ali Abdullah Salih made a surprise visit to Aden, and his PDRY counterpart Ali Salim al-Bid agreed to a merger. The Yemenis, a people joined by history, culture, religion and ancestry, had been separated by nineteenth-century empire-building and by Cold War ideology. On 22 May 1990, the two parts of their country reunited and adopted a system of parliamentary democracy with San'a as the capital. And the PDRY, that strange offspring of imperialism and Marxism, ceased to be.

There had already been an intimation of change during the fighting of January 1986, when the British Royal Yacht *Britannia* evacuated the Soviet expatriate community from Aden. Perhaps it was then, in the heat of a South Arabian winter, that the Cold War finally began to thaw. At any rate, those on board, the British and the Russians, might well have reflected as they looked back at the smoking barrack stove of Aden that, between them, they had a lot to answer for.

The Marxist period now seems like a dream that slid in and out of a nightmare. Somewhere back in the ethnographic present of this chapter, in the dying stages of dream-time, I was down in Aden again. Passing by the night-club, I noticed the same desultory scrap going on by the door, and remembered Fidel Castro's comment to the Yemeni Socialist Party leader, Ali Salim al-Bid, following the 1986 bloodbath: 'When are you people going to stop killing each other?'

The answer came, as I shall relate, in 1994. The war of that year, between the pro-unity government and a secessionist faction led by al-Bid, was to bring to an end a quarter century as bizarre, in its own way, as the British era. But, while memorials to the British are

ubiquitous and tangible, the traces of Marxism have all but vanished: the war sent Scientific Socialism the way of the well-devil of Sirah Island. With it went Ali Salim al-Bid, the Four Martyrs and the night-clubs. Husky Havana voices are no longer heard in the Ching Sing, and Arabia has lost its only brewery, dismantled in spite of a last-ditch attempt to convert it to the production of lemonade. Now, work is under way to extend Aden's port facilities; the Crescent Hotel is getting a facelift; Rimbaud's godown in

Crater has become the French Cultural Centre and offers films, good coffee and tasteful décor; and the advance guard of a new imperialism has landed – on Crater sea-front opposite Sirah, at the place where the Portuguese were sent packing, where Sulayman the Eunuch and Captain Haines landed, and plonked down next to the Abdali Sultan's lavatorial green palace, sits a building with a red-tiled roof as unexpected as a Parsee hat: the Aden Pizza Hut.

Looking at it over the water, I had an awful vision: today the Aden Pizza Hut, tomorrow the Marib McDonald's, the Sa'dah Spud-U-Like . . . Yemen subjugated by an empire of fast food, held in bondage by restaurant chains. The vision went. This, after all, was Aden, and here, in this island *manqué*, the finest harbour of the Old World, alien arrivals had come, tied up for a time, then passed on; and so they would until Doomsday.

7

Visiting the Underworld

'There were giants in the earth in those days.'

Genesis 6, v.4

IF ADEN SETS its face longingly seaward, then Hadramawt is a Janus of a place, a land of schizoid tendencies. There is an endless, crab-infested strand looking out to the ocean, where Mombasa and Mangalore, Surabaya and the Celebes, are only a monsoon away. And there is another parallel, interior world, Wadi Hadramawt, Hadramawt proper, introspective, separated from the coast by a five-hour drive across empty country.

The early start for the Wadi turned out to be a waste of time, and it took until mid-afternoon for the taxi to fill up. Did no one ever go there? Or did they all fly? The al-Yemda airline office here in al-Mukalla had been packed with would-be travellers trying to get their names inscribed in hefty ledgers, and by the time I got to the front of the queue the plane was full. In a way I was not disappointed: the calligraphic logos that looped across the walls – *Just as a swimmer needs a lifebelt, the air traveller needs Al-Yemda* – were not reassuring. Al-Yemda, in these post-Marxist times, could do with the services of a decent copywriter.

I had read Freya Stark's account of languishing in Hadrami parlours with measles exacerbated, according to her streams of lady visitors, by washing with *soap*. I had also read Harold Ingrams's story of how he pacified a region where recent history included all the storybook elements of savagery: slaughters at feasts, massacres by slave-soldiers, decade-long sieges where people made their sandals into soup. Ingrams arrived in Hadramawt to find some two thousand *soi-disant* independent political entities. (And the French are supposed to have a hard time governing a country which has 246 different types of cheese.)

After some hours of inactivity I opened the book I had brought, *The History for Those Who Would Perceive Clearly* by Ibn al-Mujawir, at the section on Hadramawt. It was a mistake.

'In the world of coming-to-be and passing-away, there is not a rougher people than the Hadramis, nor a race that exceeds them in evil and lack of goodness. They continually find fault in each other and will offer little protection to those who seek it from them. The blood of the slaughtered is everywhere . . . Because of this, Hadramawt is called The Valley of Ill-Fortune.' He adds that the Hadramis live on nothing but dried sprats, oil and milk, and that they dye their clothes with green vitriol. The women arrange their hair in a crest, like a hoopoe's.

Worse, 'All the women of these parts are witches. If a woman wishes to learn the most complete magic ever witnessed, she takes a human and cooks him until he dissolves and his flesh turns to gravy. When the gravy is cold she drinks it all up, thus becoming pregnant. She gives birth seven months later to a monstrous human called an *afw*. This resembles a cat in length and breadth, but its generative organ is the same size as that of the large *afw*, the foal of a donkey. The witch takes it around with her wherever she goes and trains it until it has grown big and strong. Then, when it is mature, it copulates with its mother . . . [here the text is corrupt]. The *afw* can only see its mother/wife, and is itself visible to none but her.'

Blood, vitriol and priapic-Oedipal familiar spirits. When at last the taxi left, I said farewell to al-Mukalla with a sense of foreboding.

Hadramawt, for outsiders, was harder to reach even than the mountains of north-western Yemen. For information on its coast Hunter, writing in 1877, refers his readers to Ptolemy. The interior was a blank on the map. Probably the first Westerners to see the Wadi itself were Antonio de Montserrat and Pedro Páez, two Jesuits captured in 1590 near the Kuria Muria Islands while on a mission from Goa to the court of the Negus in Abyssinia. The next European visitor did not arrive for another 250 years, when Adolf von Wrede, a Bavarian baron, succeeded in reaching the branch *wadi* of Daw'an; there his baggage was stolen and he turned back for the coast. Von Wrede made many astonishing claims; for example, trying to measure the depth of a patch of quicksand, his 60-fathom plumbline sank without trace. Ridiculed, he emigrated to Texas and later appears to have killed himself. He was followed in the 1890s by Theodore and Mabel Bent,* then from the 1930s onwards by a handful of Arabists, explorers and administrators. During the Marxist period Hadramawt saw some joint Yemeni-Soviet archaeological activity and a few tourists, shepherded closely and at great expense.

The other passengers were silent and showed no interest in the passing landscape. No one spoke to me. Perhaps, in Hadramawt, where in this most conservative of societies the Marxist regime had been most oppressive, they hadn't realized that talking to foreigners had been decriminalized. But then, my fellow travellers hardly spoke to each other. Stranger still, for a people who had colonized everywhere from the Swahili coast to the Philippines, they were not good travellers. As the taxi began to climb the escarpment that overlooks the coastal plain, the man next to me stopped the car to get out and vomit. Shortly afterwards the man on my other side expressed his solidarity, this time into a plastic bag. For the rest of the journey they sat with towels round their heads.

At the top of the pass, a strange landscape unrolled, something like the Yorkshire Moors minus the topsoil. This was the *jawl*. Just as al-Madinah is enlightened and the Aegean wine-dark, the *jawl* has its own epithet in the accounts of all who describe it: barren. It is often called a plateau, hardly the right word as the surface is broken by deep ravines; the road has to follow a winding route from one elevated section to another – perhaps the origin of the name, since the root meaning of *jawl* is to wander or ramble. The

---

* Mrs Bent's book (her husband died shortly after the journey) is one of the most fascinating accounts of Arabian travel. It tells of the couple's wanderings in the region, accompanied by an Indian surveyor who wore a Norfolk jacket and knickerbockers. Among their many discoveries was a new species of scorpion, *Buthia bentii*, which Mrs Bent found inside her glove. The book is, unfortunately, extraordinarily rare.

scene is like a mountain range in negative, its topography the result of attrition. Wind and rain first etch then gouge the surface, depressions become runnels then valleys then gorges. The few people who live here, in isolated stone houses, seem impervious to the *horror vacui* that haunts the place. We went on in silence. The sky blackened and came down to meet the horribly potholed road. At intervals, signposts with numbers pointed into the mist. And then, slowly at first but with increasing gradient, the road started to descend, dropping into the underworld of the Wadi.

The first thing to catch the eye after hours on the naked uplands is the green, of palms, of alfalfa, of *ilb* trees. In the Wadi's palette, houses are secondary and blend into the dun landscape from which they grow. The light was failing, and by the time we left the side-*wadi* of al-Ayn and emerged into the main valley, twilight had swallowed the long vistas of buttresses that confine it. The great city of Shibam was a crouching mass darker than the darkness around it.

★

This glimpse of Hadramawt before nightfall showed that, even if in some ways it is sleepy and insular, one activity continues with irrepressible vitality: building. Everywhere, there are unfinished top floors and herringbone stacks of mud bricks. Many of the older houses and turret-cornered little forts are crumbling – in the last stage of disintegration, the structures look like termite mounds. But new buildings rise all around. It is a cycle of dissolution and rebirth.

The cement block arrived a few years ago, and sometimes there are strange marriages of an ornamental cement porch with a mud house; but the mud brick is still the basic element and the one best suited to Hadramawt's climate. The method of building is deceptively simple. Large flat bricks of mud and chopped straw, dried in the sun, are mortared and then plastered over with the same ingredients. Houses are given a waterproof icing of lime plaster, itself produced by a laborious process: throughout the Wadi you see little shelters where teams of men whack the stuff with long paddles for hours on end. Stone is hardly used, except in supporting columns built of flat stone cylinders like stacks of film canisters.

There are no short cuts in Hadrami building; the more time that is put into its construction, the longer a house will last. An esoteric guarantee of permanence is to have a sheep slaughtered and its blood smeared on the corners of the building.

Inside, Hadrami houses are complex and enigmatic. The sparsely furnished rooms are almost an afterthought to the high, blank-walled corridors and staircases which seem to fill much of the building's volume. Everything seems designed to bewilder, like a maze for laboratory rats, until you realize that the intention is to prevent the meeting of incompatibles – different sexes, different classes. An illusionist would love Hadrami houses, for in them people can be made to appear or disappear.

From the outside, these buildings are sober to an eye used to the baroque plaster frills of San'ani ornament. Façades are unadorned, decoration limited to the wood of shutters and doors. '"Architecture"', Harold Ingrams wrote, 'is the one word which describes the quality which makes Hadramawt different from any other country.' It is an architecture where form, function and mass have won over ornament.

There are exceptions, like the playing-card symbols stencilled in pastel colours over the houses of Daw'an, and the tombs of holy men with their zigzags of green striplights; but it is in Tarim that the mask of sobriety really slips. Alberto Moravia saw San'a as a Venice where dust had replaced water; but then, he hadn't been to Tarim. Here the palazzos of the merchant *sayyids*, founded earlier this century on the wealth of the Orient, are sinking into a lagoon of dust. Extraordinary hybrids of colonial, Classical, Mogul and Far Eastern elements, they are – amazingly – executed entirely in mud. Friezes and flutings are picked out in lapis lazuli, topaz and turquoise, and as the colours fade the structures behind them collapse. Only the mosque of al-Mihdar, its minaret rising like a stretched lighthouse from a sea of dusty palms, is pristine. The pleasure-domes of Tarim are too much for the UNESCO people with their arts and crafts faithfulness to materials, and their owners are too busy making money in Saudi Arabia. Unless someone steps in to champion them, the palaces of Tarim will succumb, though gracefully, it must be said.

★

Earlier this century, Western architectural taste found itself teetering, so to speak, on the cornice of a dilemma: one was told that clean lines, uncluttered volumes, multi-storey living, were good; at the same time, there was a suspicion that buildings constructed according to these criteria might somehow be inhuman, that modernism might turn out to be faddishness. What if Le Corbusier was a charlatan? An innate visual conservatism looked for precedents and found none. Then the pictures of Shibam came out and everyone sighed with relief: skyscrapers had a vernacular pedigree, and a long one. High-rise was OK. It was U to live in a cube.

Shibam, the Manhattan (or Chicago, or, now, almost any other major city in the world) of the Desert, is not in the desert but on a rise in the middle of the Wadi, surrounded by palm groves. Individually the houses are no more remarkable than many others across Yemen; but they stand together and can be framed in an instant by the eye and – more important – by the viewfinder. Shibam, with The Bridge at Shaharah and Dar al-Hajar in Wadi Dahr, has become the ultimate visual cliché of Yemen. It has even appeared in an advertisement for American Express.

Just as the houses of San'a descend from that splendid prototype of Ghumdan, those of Shibam originate in an ancient model best seen in the palace called Shuqur in Shabwah, built when Rome was still an insignificant town. The archaeologists estimate that the palace was around eight storeys high – the same as the tallest houses in Shibam.

Shibam and San'a have much in common. They became prominent at about the same time, both developed the idea of the tower-house, both are situated at central points on trade routes. Today the similarity ends there. San'a is lively, colourful, chaotic; Shibam is hushed. There is little movement in the principal public space, the square behind the main gate. Beyond this on the town's narrow streets, an outsider feels like an intruder. Eyes watch your every movement – the eyes of goats peering down from first-floor windows, of chickens in hutches hung across the street to keep them safe from predators, other eyes behind lattices. A few children wander around, but otherwise there is little human activity. Innate Hadrami reserve is a factor; so is Marxist conditioning. More important is the depopulating effect of emigration – of those Yemenis who were able to stay on in the Gulf States after 1990, many were Hadramis, for they had been best able to blend in with their adopted countries. But I feared also, entering the city for the first time, that the hush of Shibam was also that of a museum.

On the far side of the flood course, on a bluff beneath the city's water tank, an assembly was gathering as it does most afternoons at around five. Today they were mostly French, about twenty-five of them, and as the hour approached chatter diminished and was overtaken by a reverent and suspenseful silence. Marsupial pouches disgorged fittings and filters and macros, film packaging was secreted for later disposal. These were not the sort who dropped litter. Nor did the sun disappoint. For a full ten minutes Shibam turned to gold and the air was filled with Oohs and Aahs and the whirring of zooms.

It would be unfair to criticize Shibam for being photogenic; moreover, they were good tourists, closely shepherded and as unobtrusive as one can be in pistachio-coloured leisurewear. There wasn't even a pair of shorts among them. But I wondered what they *saw*, what the German corporate bonding group who visited Yemen for three days to see Shibam saw, and suspected it was an artwork, an architectural *Mona Lisa*, supremely beautiful but ultimately incomprehensible, preserved by UNESCO yet lifeless, far removed from the world of coming-to-be and passing-away. I longed for a used-car lot, a cement factory, for the erosive effects of wind, rain, sewage and raw economics to disfigure the place. It was a matter of respect for the decency of decay. As the poet-king As'ad al-Kamil said:

> Nothing can last while the fickle sun
> Rises not from where it sets;
> Rises limpid, red,
> And sets saffron.

The churlish moment passed. Now, at 5.45 p.m., the sky to the west was streaked opalescent pink and cobalt in big vertical stripes. It was nauseating, it was *magnifique*, and I wished I had a camera too.

★

In Shibam, I had to deliver a letter to the uncle of a Hadrami living in San'a. Finding the house was not easy, but just when I thought I was irretrievably lost a child materialized and led me to it. I banged on the door and waited. A woman's voice called from a high lattice: 'There's no one at home.' I said I would give the letter to the child, but the door swung open by itself. The child led me up the staircase and into a room, then dematerialized. I sat there not knowing what to do, and was about to leave when I noticed a movement out of the corner of my eye: a tray with a samovar and a tea glass had appeared in the doorway. I poured myself some tea, drank it, put the letter on the tray, and left.

Next day, I managed to get a seat on the little plane from Say'un to al-Mukalla. The aircraft arced over the Wadi, climbing rapidly to hop over its thousand-foot southern escarpment. Suddenly that green and peopled world was far away, the *jawl* below like some grey northern sea. It was not difficult to see how Wadi Hadramawt had kept itself apart.

For me, the Hadrami interior remained – like the insides of its houses – aloof and enigmatic. I felt as though I had been wandering around a painting by de Chirico: a place drenched with light but empty of people.

★

Back on the edge of the ocean I felt a sense of relief. The Wadi walls were confining, more so even than Aden's volcanic mountains. I wondered if all Hadramis were closet claustrophobes, and if this was what made them travel.

From medieval times onwards Hadramis colonized the East African coast. The exodus to what is now Malaysia, Indonesia and the Philippines began not much later, probably in the fifteenth century, and it was in the Far East that Hadrami acumen reaped huge profits. Even after the Japanese occupation, the al-Kaff family in Singapore were still worth around £25 million. Today, the world's reputed richest man, the Sultan of Brunei, is part-Hadrami. Most expatriate Hadramis kept in close contact with their native land, sending their sons home to study and marry. The majority would eventually return for good, some to set up as small traders, the better-off to become gentlemen farmers.

On the Arab of the desert, Jan Morris has written, 'the Bedouin was every Englishman's idea of nature's gentleman. He seemed almost a kind of Englishman himself, translated into another idiom.' In fact the wealthy Hadrami, supervising his model palm groves, poring over manuscripts in his newly built mansion – paid for by money made overseas – was closer to the image of the eighteenth-century English nabob returned from the East. And, sequestered within fine houses, well-to-do Hadrami ladies lived a life of social intrigue, petty squabbles and boredom that Mrs Gaskell would have recognized. Parochialism and far-flung travel blended to produce something curiously familiar to Freya Stark and the Ingramses.

The effects of emigration were noted by von Wrede, who in 1846 stayed with a shaykh of Wadi Daw'an who had lived in India, spoke English, and had a copy of Scott's *Napoleon*. Daw'an, at the western end of the main valley, contains some of the most prosperous houses in Hadramawt. Cliffs of buildings, some painted in harlequin colours like a Battenburg cake, are banked up the base of the canyon. Its wealth derives partly from overseas, but also from a local product – honey. Daw'ani honey is the most expensive in the world.

Entering Daw'an on a later visit to Hadramawt, I was stung on the chin. By the time I reached al-Hajarayn, perched on a cliff above the flood course, my face was swollen into a *qat*-chewer's bulge. Down on a rise in the valley floor was a tent, not a *badw* house of hair but a heavy canvas thing from an army camp. It was surrounded by quadruped hives – earthenware cylinders raised on metal legs. They might, with a little imagination, have been rounded up and driven along the valley. This, in fact, is almost what does happen, since the beekeepers live a semi-nomadic life, travelling around the valley in search of the best pasture for their swarms.

I penetrated the buzzing cordon warily.

'What's wrong with your face?' asked a man in the doorway of the tent.

'I was stung.'

'*Stung?* Where?'

'Here, on the chin.'

'I mean, were you stung here at al-Hajarayn?'

'Oh, I see . . . No, back there down the road.'

'That's what I mean. My bees wouldn't sting anyone. They're the kindest bees in Daw'an. It must have been a foreign bee that stung you. There's a lot of swarm-smuggling these days.' Kind bees. Swarm-smuggling. And a curious wicker object by the tent door turned out to be a hornet-trap. The world of Daw'ani apiculture seemed bizarre.

Over lunch in the tent, the beeherds explained that the quality of their honey was the result of the bees' pasturing only on *ilb* trees – *Zizyphus spina-Christi*. There was a lot of cheating, bumping up yields with sugar-water and mixing different grades, but my hosts would have nothing to do with this. Their *baghiyyah* grade was the finest available – the finest honey in the world. It smelt of butter-scotch. It was the single malt, the unalloyed vintage. The price was commensurate: the equivalent of £40 for a good comb at the honey merchant's in al-Mukalla, and far more by the time it reached the market in Saudi Arabia, where it is believed to firm up sagging sexual potency.* Here at source the prices were cheaper, but still I could only just afford a comb of the inferior winter grade. Even so, testing a fingerful – on the tactile level not unlike eating caviare, bursting through cells to a rich and melting interior – the honey was so strong and fragrant it was hard to imagine it was only the cheap stuff. The Classical geographers mention Arabia Felix as a source of excellent honey, and probably little has changed in production methods since their day, though the queen, or 'father' as she is called here, is now kept in a plastic hair-roller instead of the tiny wooden cage used formerly.

Al-Hajarayn, up above us on the cliff, is the site of Dammun. Here the sixth-century poet-prince Imru al-Qays was banished by his father for excessive drunkenness and fornication. Imru al-Qays's tribe, Kindah, had emigrated long before, and their rise to power in northern Arabia had spun a web of jealousies that resulted in the killing of his father by a rival clan. When the news was brought to Dammun, the prince headed north to lay his father's ghost.

Imru al-Qays the poet was already well known, and his lovesick lingerings at abandoned campsites were quoted all over Arabia. Pursuing the blood feud, he now became the most famous Hadrami traveller, a picaresque and melancholy figure, forced out of his secluded ancestral valley into the harsh world of Byzantine-Sasanian superpower politics. He became known as al-Malik al-

---

* The spiralling price of honey seems to have caused the disappearance of a traditional Hadrami recipe: slaughter a kid and cut the meat into chunks; put these in a large jar and cover them completely with honey; seal the jar tightly and leave for six months. The preserved meat is eaten uncooked. Women should not be allowed to eat this dish, as it is a powerful aphrodisiac.

Dillil, the Wandering King, and posthumously as Dhu al-Quruh, He of the Sores – in reference to his Nessus-like death, caused by a poisoned shirt presented to him by the Byzantine Emperor after he had flirted with an imperial princess. The Prophet, when asked who was the best of poets, said: 'Imru al-Qays will lead the poets on their way to Hell.'*

Imru al-Qays never succeeded in avenging his father's death. Nor did he return to Dammun. Perhaps the fate of the Wandering King, deprived of honour, land and family, is a warning that binds the furthest-flung Hadrami to his place of origin.

★

I said goodbye to the beeherds and carried on along the pebbly track. A short asphalted pass lifts you on to the *jawl*, where the road surface ends as abruptly as it began. I stopped, walked to the edge of the canyon, and looked down. Daw'an was a sunken world, Lyonesse seen through crystal water. Up here, sounds were amplified by the valley sides: a child shouting 'Shoot! Shoot!', the thump of a ball being kicked, a donkey bursting its lungs in an ecstasy of sobbing brays, a dog snarling. A few paces back from the edge you could hear nothing, see nothing. Daw'an had disappeared.

It was a long way to the next stretch of tarmac on the al-Mukalla road. The light faded, more slowly on the uplands than in the *wadi*. Rock darkened from camel to tan to oak-gall like a sepia photograph in a bath of developer, leaving the motor track as the faintest scribble across the *jawl*.

Hours later, a light appeared on the horizon. It turned out to be a truck-stop. I squatted at the edge of the bare room and ate a tray of rice and a hunk of *mindi*, kid half roasted, half smoked over the embers of a lidded fire pit. In the corner of the room a video of American tag-team wrestling was playing; the few customers were too busy with their food to notice. Here too there was a reserve. People kept to their own personal space and the only sounds were the recorded grunts of blond giants trying to pulverize each other.

★

---

* He was not the only Yemeni poet to meet a grisly end. In the seventh century, Waddah, having lost his first love to leprosy, cuckolded the Caliph Walid and was buried alive in a wardrobe.

Three hours into my first *qat* chew in a Hadrami house, I was beginning to think the Hadramis really were a lugubrious lot. There had been none of the playful banter that begins a San'a chew. Salim, our host, who had been brought up in Kenya and was now a trader in Say'un, insisted on speaking a grandiloquent version of Arabic, mostly on the fecundation of date palms. His son, who was in his late teens, sat looking uncomfortable in the middle of the room and speaking only when spoken to.

Now should have been the Hour of Solomon, but I was feeling tetchy and liverish. Until Unification, *qat* had been banned in Hadramawt; the Hadramis still hadn't got into the rhythm of it. A couple of neighbours turned up and talked politics. Salim did not take part in the conversation but sat glancing at his watch. I wondered if we were outstaying our welcome. Suddenly, he bounded up and disappeared. The sunset call to prayer sounded, the others left, and Salim re-entered the room – cheek empty – and began praying.

When he had finished he threw me some *qat* and started chewing again. After a polite pause I said, 'Why don't you carry on chewing and pray the sunset and evening prayers together?' Immediately, I regretted the question. 'Uh, that's what they do in San'a . . .'

'I am perfectly cognizant with the phenomenon. The people of San'a, of course, are notoriously lax in the performance of their obligations. "The best time to pray a prayer is when it is called,"' he intoned sonorously. 'To let what is no more than a pastime interfere with one's duty as a Muslim is, frankly, inexcusable. I have even heard it said that there are some who pray without expelling the *qat* from their mouths, on the pretext that it does not necessarily affect the articulation. To me . . .'

The can of worms was open. I had to stop them wriggling out. 'Perhaps I shouldn't have mentioned it. After all, I'm not even a Muslim.'

'You are not, indeed, a Muslim. But you are a complete San'ani.'

He was grinning. I laughed in relief. The ice, at last, had been broken. As we chatted, Salim's Arabic became less ferociously inflected.

I was keen to find out what Salim knew about one of the geographical curiosities of Hadramawt – the Well of Barhut, a sulphurous and supposedly bottomless pit to the north of the Wadi. 'Have you been to Barhut?' I asked. 'I read somewhere that it's where the souls of the infidels end up.'

'Yes, and they say there is a terrible smell of decomposition, and groans in the night. I haven't been there myself. It's a long way, far off the road that leads to the tomb of the Prophet Hud – peace upon him! But I can tell you the story of the well.' He drew himself up.

'When God created our Father Adam, He commanded the angels to prostrate themselves before him. At first they complained and said, "How can we do this, when he is made from clay and we from light?" But God said, "When Adam is expelled from the Garden, then I shall test him with trials and you shall have your recompense. Now do as I command!"

'So the angels prostrated themselves before Adam – all except Iblis, who was to fall – and events took their turn until Adam was expelled from the Garden, and God began to test Man with trials, as you know. When the angels saw the afflictions Man was suffering, they said, "These are nothing. Any one of us could undergo the sufferings of Man and come out unscathed." "Then," said God, "let it be so. Choose the two strongest ones of your number. I will give them the form of men during the day, and at night they will revert to being angels." So the angels chose two from their number, named Harut and Marut, and God did as He had said.

'Harut and Marut, during their daylight hours as men, soon became respected by all humans on account of their wisdom, and people began to come to them to plead cases. One of those who sought their judgement was a woman named Zahra. She was a beautiful woman, and she fell in love with both Harut and Marut. Of course, being angels, they were exceedingly good-looking themselves. Zahra tried to soften the angels with words; naturally, they resisted her. Moreover, they were shocked to discover that she was married. When she suggested that they kill her husband, the angels were ready to give up being men and return to God's presence for good. "But," they said, "it is easy for us to resist the woman's words and close our ears to the whisperings of Satan."

'One day, Zahra invited Harut and Marut to her house and brought them wine. "This is the easiest of Man's trials to resist," said the angels, "but let us try a little, so that we shall know what to avoid in future. Only a little." Soon, though, they were drunk, and it took only a sign from Zahra for them to kill her husband and sleep with her.

'When God saw this, He called the two angels into His presence and said, "You have sinned and have truly tasted Man's afflictions. I give you a choice: earthly punishment, or that of the world to come." Harut and Marut chose earthly punishment and God cast them into the Well of Barhut, named after a *jinni* of the Prophet Sulayman – peace upon him! – who had dug it. The well was full of snakes and scorpions, and there the two fallen angels are even now. Zahra, who had stolen from them the trick of flight, escaped to the heavens and was turned into a star. And there the story ends.'

I took my leave just before the evening prayer and walked out into the night. It was dead quiet. Rain had fallen, and the earth gave off a rich tobacco-like odour. The air was clear, and the stars were joining Venus, Zahra. I thought of the ending of Salim's story. It all seemed to fit until the bit about Zahra. Why should the woman, this arch-temptress, have become a heavenly body?

Then I realized. The story must be ancient, dating back to the beginning of Islam when the old pagan cults still had a following. Here in Hadramawt, cut off from the rest of Yemen, Christianity, Judaism and the local monotheistic religion of al-Rahman had made few inroads into the ancient astral beliefs in which Venus was a prominent member of the pantheon. The Barhut story was both an attack on a pagan deity, recast as an evil seductress, and a didactic against alcohol, adultery and murder. But perhaps even stranger was that so uncanonical a tale should have been told by someone so apparently orthodox. It seemed to be another case of the Hadrami split personality.

I picked my way along narrow unlit streets, squelching through mud. Palms dripped behind high walls. Say'un is a garden city, *rus in urbe* to Tarim's Venice of dust. In Say'un, I was staying with a Sudanese-American couple, he a Nubian from Dongola and she from the Mid West. Awad and Linda spent most of their time sifting through nineteenth-century land deeds in a turret of the

Kathiri Sultan's palace, a magnificent building like a Carême centrepiece. Its brilliant white plaster threatens snow-blindness. Their own house was a *banqalah* – a 'bungalow' – among the palms; despite the suggestion of colonial or English-suburban images, here the word means a guest-house. It was small but very grand, all blinding white lime-plaster like the Sultan's palace; the upper floor was one large room surrounded by a loggia, the undersides of the arches picked out in the distinctive Hadrami eau-de-Nil. Downstairs was a tiny room in royal blue with a plunge pool, deliciously cold and swirling like a jacuzzi when the pump was started to water the palm grove. The pool is exactly the same as those found in grand Georgian town-houses. One of the last Kathiri rulers was so smitten by the *banqalah* that he requisitioned it.

Linda had spent the afternoon, a Starkian one, with some nouveau-poor unmarried *sharifahs* (*sayyid* ladies) in Tarim. No *sayyid* husbands could be found for them, and marriage into the lower orders was unthinkable; so they spent their straitened spinsterhood in a complex of palaces joined by upper-floor bridges. They hardly ever left their houses.*

Just how frustrating strict endogamy can be is shown by the Hadrami reaction to news of the 1962 Revolution in San'a. While many Hadrami *sayyids* were unnerved, one observer reports that some spinsters of the al-Attas family in Huraydah greeted the expected collapse of the status quo with whoops of excitement: 'We can get married now!' In the event the old order has hardly changed, Marxist attempts to force marriages across social boundaries having met with implacable opposition, and the old proverb holds good: 'The luck of a *sharifah* is blind. If she keeps chickens, the kites come and eat them. If she hangs out the washing, the sky clouds over. And if she loses her husband, she'll never find another.' The belief even used to be current that a non-*sayyid* who married a *sharifah* would be struck by leprosy.

We talked until late about the curious split personality of Hadramawt – parochialism and emigration, stagnation and

---

* *Sharifahs* were, however, credited with the power to promote fertility in others, as Doreen Ingrams discovered: as yet childless, she was made to drink a draught of the Hadrami fertility drug – a *sharifah*'s spittle.

progress, orthodoxy and heterodoxy – and decided that the polarities would never be reconciled. I went to bed and slept the sleep of the dead, as one does in Hadramawt (except in the Well of Barhut), not realizing until the morning that I was sharing my bed with a baby scorpion.

★

I set off early the next day to visit a prophet.

The night before, we had come up with a theory: it was precisely because the Hadramis had been conditioned to present a dour and monumental façade – like their houses – that they needed to let off steam occasionally – hence the festivities connected with Hud, the Prophet of God. Hud, who according to the genealogists was the great-grandson of Sam, is not merely a divinely sent messenger; he is also the father of Qahtan. I felt it only proper to pay my respects to the reputed progenitor of all the southern Arabs.

East of Tarim something changes. You cannot say it is the landscape, although the valley narrows slightly. The *wadi*'s name is different – al-Masilah, the Watercourse – but the same water flows in it. What is different is that civilization, in the sense of ancient

urban culture, has been left behind. Down the great length of al-Masilah there are a few communities, at first quite sizeable, like Aynat, but in no way urban. For the rest of al-Masilah's 150 miles there is nothing bigger than a hamlet. East of the point where the *wadi* meets the coast there are some more fair-sized settlements – Sayhut, Qishn, al-Ghaydah – but they are only overblown villages. Crossing the border into Omani territory, Salalah is a creation of the past two decades; before, it was a collection of small dwellings huddled round a fort. From Salalah all along the southern coast of Arabia there are no major settlements. Only when you turn the corner into the Gulf do you find places with any pretension to being urban; but even Muscat is tiny, a lapis-lazuli palace and a few other houses locked in the jaws of a bay between Portuguese forts, followed by a string of suburbs with no urban heart. Round the tortuous Musandam Peninsula and into the inner Gulf, all the emirates and shaykhdoms that cling to the shore are the recent and monstrous spawn of Western politicking and the Western thirst for oil. It is only at the head of the Gulf that, with al-Basrah and Baghdad, you come again to an ancient urban society. To fill the void, the Arabs built cities of the imagination, the cities of Ad and Thamud which were wiped off the earth for their corruption. Hud was the prophet who foresaw the destruction of Ad, and when urban Hadramis visit him they are reminded of what could happen to them. Leaving Tarim, they are venturing into the margins of an uncivilized world.

Some way past Tarim we turned off the road and headed for a small but dramatic outcrop like an island in the flood course. This was Hisn al-Urr, a castle of great antiquity probably constructed by Imru al-Qays's people, Kindah. Such a site was no doubt in use long before, and long after; the massive walls are still intact. We clambered up and Jay, my travelling companion from San'a, posed in nearly immaculate memsahib white, parasol raised, on the summit of a bastion. The silence was overwhelming.

Suddenly the silence was broken, by a faint rhythm that turned into a clatter then a din. A helicopter came from the east, from nowhere. It circled once and was off up a side *wadi* that first amplified, then swallowed the noise. The silence ebbed back, stronger after its negation.

Unexpectedly, the road improved after al-Urr. Recent patching has made it one of the better ones in the Hadramawt interior, which wasn't saying much. We had just missed the pilgrimage itself, but were benefiting from the annual maintenance of the track to Hud, paid for by the contributions of the pious.

Finally the tomb appeared under the southern escarpment, a gleaming ensemble of dome and prayer hall surrounded by a town. We dipped down across the watercourse, surprisingly deep, and stopped the car at the top of the far bank. Not only the tomb complex but the town itself were freshly plastered, the biscuit-coloured walls of houses finished off with brilliant waterproof *nurah*. And yet the place lacked the element which would have made it truly urban: people. It was empty, totally empty. The town is only inhabited for a few days around the pilgrimage, and wealthier Hadrami families maintain houses here for just this brief season. We had expected some delapidation, some evidence of the decline of the Hud *ziyarah* – the 'visit', or pilgrimage – during Marxist days, but there was none. It was as if a *jinni* had been commanded to build a city but had stopped short of populating it.

If at Hisn al-Urr the silence had been overwhelming, here it was unearthly. I realized that during our first stop there had in fact been sounds, a barely audible wild-track made by the wind and the little sandfalls caused by scuttling lizards. Since the appearance of the helicopter Jay and I had hardly spoken. Now, we tiptoed around. To make a sound would have been blasphemy. And yet, at our feet, was the evidence of mayhem, a litter of packaging from biscuits, cheese spread, fruit juice and, above all, from toys of a warlike and noisy nature: 'Pump Action Shotgun with Dart – for ages 3 and up', 'Cap Gun Hero', 'Dynamic Cap Gun', and 'Mystery Action Wind-Up Helicopter'. Clearly the fairground aspect of the pilgrimage was still alive: Hud could still pull crowds.* I sat on a wall and wondered why.

---

* A prominent local historian, Abdulqadir Muhammad al-Sabban, gives a vivid description of the Hud *ziyarah* and its carnival atmosphere. Alongside the performance of the standard Islamic obligations, pilgrims take part in a series of very uncanonical practices which include giving and taking ritual insults. First-timers are set upon by old hands, who grunt and foam at their victims 'like bull camels in rut', and pilgrims shout lewd nicknames at the villages they pass, sometimes causing fights – all because 'laughter on the Hud pilgrimage is like praising God on others.'

Yemen is littered with the tombs of holy men and prophets, many of them visited at annual festivals. But none enjoys anything like the popularity of Hud; none is honoured by having an entire town built purely to accommodate pilgrims. The motives behind this extraordinary display of reverence had to be connected with Hud himself.

Hud and the Adites make several appearances in the Qur'an. The essence of the story is that the post-diluvian age of innocence had become increasingly flawed. The Adites, who were given wealth such as the world had never seen, refused to thank God for His blessings. Worse, they worshipped idols and tried to imitate Paradise by building fabulous cities like Iram of the Columns. The Prophet Hud warned them against such blasphemy, but was ignored. God therefore destroyed the Adites with a violent wind, a sandstorm of apocalyptic proportions.

A mass of legend has grown around the story. One sub-plot says that before the final catastrophe, the Adites were attacked by a plague of ants. The Adites were giants, and the ants were accordingly scaled up, 'the size of dogs,' one commentator says, 'each one big enough to unseat a rider from his horse and tear him limb from limb.' The cliffs of Hadramawt were built by the Adites as platforms on which they would sit to keep out of the insects' reach. Hud himself was a giant, which accounts in popular belief for the long stone 'tail' extending up the slope behind his tomb. Different writers give different measurements for the tail's length. Like the stone circles in Britain which are said to be uncountable, Hud seems to be immeasurable.*

Another local tradition says that after the destruction of Ad, Hud was chased by some of the remnants of the Adites and cornered at a dead end, the *wadi* wall under which I was sitting. (The

---

* The form can be compared with tombs investigated by Yemeni and Soviet archaeologists above Wadi Rakhyah in Western Hadramawt and tentatively dated to the early second millennium BC. In these, dome-shaped structures containing crouched burials are given tails made of round or oval piles of stones. With the addition of more stones over the years, these would turn into the solid elongated form to be seen in Hud's grave. While there is no obvious reason for the strange form, it may be linked to the shape of a comet, and thus to the ideas of a celestially based religion. A medieval writer, al-Ghazali, says that ringstones made from the rocks of Hud's grave have powerful amuletic properties providing they are set at the conjunction of Venus and Jupiter, a possible survival of these celestial beliefs.

camel races held at pilgrimage time may be a commemoration of the chase.) The moment his pursuers caught up with him, the ground opened and swallowed him and his camel – all but the camel's hump. This was petrified into the huge trapezoidal boulder built into the roof of the prayer hall. Appropriately for a people so attached to their land, their ancestor had been ingested by it.

It was tempting to see the Qur'anic story of Ad's destruction in a sandstorm as an account of the climatic change that altered Arabia between five and seven thousand years ago. It was tempting, too, to see the connection between Hud and the camel as a folk-memory of how the South Arabians were able to overcome the problem of transport in a harsh, dry climate.* And it was even more tempting to think of the Qahtanis as incomers: many of the early historians describe them as *muta'arribah*, 'Arabianized', while the Adites are the aboriginal *arab*. But if Hud, as the Qur'an states, was himself an Adite, how could his son have been an incomer?

Archaeology has confirmed the existence of many of the alleged descendants of Qahtan – Saba, Himyar, Kahlan, Hamdan and so on – at least as groups, if not as individuals. Genealogy – the arrangement of these names in relation to one another and to earlier peoples – tends to be treated with extreme scepticism by modern historians. But it should never be dismissed: as a contemporary Yemeni historian and archaeologist has said, 'While it may not be the voice of history, it is the echo of that voice.'

Whatever their relationship to the present-day Yemenis, a prehistoric people existed. In the sands between Hadramawt and Marib, and further east into Omani territory, they left traces of their passing in the form of thousands of finely worked stone arrowheads. These can be picked up around the shallow depressions which were once waterholes, where hunter-gatherers would shoot the rich herds of game that disappeared with desertification. Until someone stumbles across one of those gem-studded cities, it is these arrowheads that are the true memorials of Ad.

My visit to Hud had begun as a personal pilgrimage. I was going to pay my respects to the ancestor – at least in a symbolic sense – of

---

* All available evidence points to this part of Arabia as the place where the camel was domesticated, possibly as early as the third millennium BC (see Bulliet, *The Camel and the Wheel*).

the people to whom I had grown so close. My own ancestors were lost in a welter of Celts, a muddle of Angles; Hud was, for me, almost an adoptive grandfather figure. But the more I considered the few tantalizing facts about him given by the Qur'an, and the body of fable with which the Yemenis had fleshed him out, the further Hud the father of Qahtan receded into the mists – no, the impenetrable fog – of time.

The sun, and the whiteness of the buildings, seemed more intense. Jay had wandered off to explore the ghost-town. In front of me was a sort of triumphal staircase, its two wings joining above the prayer hall then rising like the climactic approach to the *piano nobile* of a Palladian mansion. I climbed slowly. The only sound was the throb of blood in my inner ear, which beat faster as I neared the top of the staircase. Everything was saturated with light; blinded, I had to feel my way past the pillars that supported the dome.

At last, I was at the holiest spot in Yemen.

When my eyes adjusted to the shade, I saw that the tomb was empty. There was no grave; not even a cenotaph. Just a few gim-crack incense-burners and empty 'Chef' ghee tins on a shelf, and a cleft in the rock where, they say, the ground failed to close completely. The lips of the cleft were smooth and slightly damp.

A seventh-century visitor said: 'And there we saw two rocks next to one another, with a space in between big enough for someone thin to squeeze through. So I squeezed through. And there I saw a man upon a couch, very brown, with a long face and a thick beard. He had dried out on his couch. I felt part of his body and found it to be firm and uncorrupted. At his head I saw an inscription in Arabic: "I am Hud who believed in God. I sorrowed for the impiety of Ad and their refusal of God's command."'

I had come in search of a corporeal Hud. It was a long way to his resting place here in the margins of Yemen, but the last stage, via the crack in the rock, was the longest. Hud the Prophet is there in the Qur'an. Hud the Progenitor, the grandfather of Yemen, is harder to reach; squeezing through to him would need a lot of faith.

The idea of a single ancestor is almost certainly a simplification; but if by personifying their origins in Hud and Qahtan the

Yemenis have rationalized their own history, they have done no more than most other peoples. And while the roots of the family tree may be more complex, they are – for the moment – as deeply hidden as Hud.

★

East of Hud along al-Masilah there is another change, this time in the place names. The list of settlements, as given by Ingrams, runs: Qoz Adubi, Taburkum, Marakhai, Bat-ha, Dhahoma, Buzun, Semarma. Still physically in Arabia, you have fallen off the Arabic map, a map on which the toponyms are comfortingly familiar as far away as the north of Syria or the Atlantic coast of Morocco. It is like driving out of Newtown in the Welsh borders and suddenly seeing a sign for Llanwyddelan. A parallel with Welsh, or Gaelic, or Provençal, is not far-fetched. Here is a remnant of the days before what we know as Arabic took over Southern Arabia, still a Semitic language but one more closely related to that of the ancient epigraphic texts, pushed into a backwater of the peninsula. It is not that the Mahris who live here are a race distinct from other Yemenis; rather, being so isolated from contact with the North Arabian world where Arabic came from, they have held on to the old speech by a quirk of geography.

The Mahris also preserved until recently some characteristics of ancient South Arabian social organization, like the alternative matrilineal descent system. In this, for example, a child born out of wedlock was brought up by his maternal uncle: no stigma attached to him, and he enjoyed full rights in his mother's clan. Other customs throw light on practices criticized by early Islam. Until recently, for instance, the women of Mahri Dhofar used to knot pieces of twine while heaping anathemas on the tribe's enemies – an illustration of what the Qur'an refers to as 'the women who blow upon knots'.*

In the whole vast expanse of more or less empty country where

---

* See Johnstone's 'Knots and Curses'. Such spells have also prevented the consummation of marriages. Knotting, however, can be used in white magic. On the isolated mountain of Razih, north-west of Sa'dah, lives a woman physician of repute who diagnoses illnesses by smelling the patient's clothes, and then prescribes a remedy in the form of an amulet of knotted string.

Hadramawt Governorate ends and al-Mahrah begins, al-Masilah is the prominent topographical feature. It is that rare thing in the Arabian Peninsula, a real river with hidden fishy pools, overhung with trees. The desiccated right angles of Wadi Hadramawt have been replaced by a softer landscape where you can lie on grass – grass! – and dangle your toes in a burbling stream that smells faintly musty, like last Christmas's brazil nuts.

Down near the seaward end of al-Masilah, on featureless heights above a bend in the river, is the grave of another giant, Mawla al-Ayn. Unlike Hud, al-Ayn does not appear in the Islamic canon.

We bumped up a rough track and climbed out of the pick-up. The tomb was a barrow about eighteen feet long, and the ground around it was scattered with objects – a pierced lead seal, an ancient .303 cartridge case, a little package of sewn cloth – all half-embedded in the dust. The barrow itself was adorned with a few very rusted tin cans and an old hinge. My companions stood next to one another at the foot of the grave and recited the Fatihah – the opening chapter of the Qur'an – as one does when visiting the departed. Then they bent down, scrabbled up some dust from between the rocks of the tomb, and rubbed it into their hair and headscarves. One of them gave me some dust and told me to do the same. '*Barakah*,' he said, 'a blessing.'

Later, in a teahouse in Sayhut, I asked a venerable-looking man, the sort who would know about such things, about Mawla al-Ayn. He could not add anything to what I had already been told, but suggested that I visit Ba Abduh of Qishn, the local authority on *walis*. 'And on the way you could visit Asma al-Gharibah – she is a *waliyyah*, a holy woman. They say she was out at sea in a boat when she suddenly felt she was going to die. She told the crew and instructed them to throw her body into the waves. The men were shocked – she was a great *waliyyah* and should be given an honourable burial. But Asma said, "Do not be afraid. My body will find its own grave." And it was as she said. Her body found its way to Itab, between here and Qishn. People still visit the spot by boat, and they leave coffee, sugar, flour and ghee there in case travellers pass by who are hungry or lost. And the strange thing is that by her grave a well of sweet water rises from the sea, from out of the salt.'

There was no time to visit Ba Abduh of Qishn, but I began to think about the story of the *waliyah* and her miraculous well. The name of al-Ayn, the holy giant of al-Masilah, can mean 'a spring of sweet water'. Further west, between Wadi Hadramawt and the sea, is the tomb of another holy man, Mawla Matar; Matar is an ancient personal name, but it is also 'rain'. Then, in the Hadrami interior, is a fourth ancient grave, of the Prophet Sadif. Ingrams was told that he was another prophet of Ad, but he makes no appearance in the standard Islamic literature. There is still a tribe of the same name in Hadramawt, but the name of Sadif, the eponymous holy man, is yet another connection with water: *sdf* (the vowelling is uncertain) is the ancient technical term for a sluice gate controlling irrigation.

The four ancient holy people all share a link with water. The Islamic association of water with divine mercy is strong. Here, though, is a group of saints, clearly revered from ancient times, who seem in themselves to embody what, in a generally poor and parched land, is this most vital aspect of divine bounty.

Johnstone has pointed to a belief among the Mahrah and related groups in earth-spirits, a belief that their Arabic-speaking neighbours do not share, or have lost. It may be that in al-Ayn, Matar, Sadif and Asma al-Gharibah there is a faint and only sketchily Islamized memory of a chthonic cult connected with irrigation, a cult which goes back far beyond monotheism, beyond even the celestial religions of Hadramawt and Saba – to the very dawn of tillage, when the desert had smothered much of Arabia, the last hippopotamus was dust, and the Qahtani family tree was still struggling to take root.

★

Back in Say'un after the visit to Hud, I noticed a pungent and disagreeable smell. Awad saw me wrinkling my nose. 'It's this carpet. We found it in the old animal shed and . . . well, you can guess the state it was in. So I washed it and it got worse.'

I went and looked at the carpet, a magnificent Tabriz rug that had probably come via the Mecca pilgrimage. It was good enough to date to the time the Sultan requisitioned the house, but it was ripe with the stink of mildew and other odours.

Next day, equipped with brushes and half a dozen packets of

soap powder, we set off for Tarim and the irrigation tank outside Qasr al-Qubbah, the Palace of the Dome, the 'perfect Riviera villa' where Ingrams stayed in the 1930s. Now it is a hotel, a little over-enthusiastically painted but, unlike most of the Tarim palaces, still in one piece.

I scrubbed away, up to my neck in grey and soapy water. Awad sat on the cement lip of the pool, giving the rug an occasional brush and frowning in concentration so that the lines on his brow echoed those on his cheeks – the deep parallel scars that identify a Nubian's tribal origin. He was so much at home in Hadramawt that I was convinced he had Hadrami blood. It was not a far-fetched idea, since among the conquering armies of Islam there were many Hadramis, and some of them had penetrated as far as Awad's town of Dongola. But then, Awad is said to look at home in Texas, wearing cowboy boots and a stetson. So much for genealogy.

When the carpet was as clean as it would get, we hung it on an overflow pipe where it glistened in the sunlight filtering through the palms. I joined Awad on the edge of the pool and sat drying off. With the light and shade, and the pink and yellow cupola of Qasr al-Qubbah emerging from a sea of green with the tawny cliffs behind, it was like sitting in a Persian miniature.

The reverie was shattered by a high-pitched buzzing from along the track. It got louder until the source of the sound appeared: two very suntanned Westerners in shorts, riding four-wheeled motor cycles. They slewed round the corner, stopped in a cloud of dust, and dismounted next to us. The first one, who had a grey beard and a body like a grizzly, grunted a 'Hi'; then, as his eye caught Awad's tribal scars, a look of childlike wonderment came over his features. 'Hey, what's wrong with your face? You . . . you been in a fight with a tiger or something?'

Awad patiently explained the history and significance of tribal markings. The two quad riders listened with raised eyebrows. Outside the exchange, I considered the elements of the scene: a nearly naked and very white Brit; a ritually cicatrized Nubian who sounded like a Texan; two Texans working for a drilling contractor up on the *jawl*; a lemon and lime and raspberry mud palace. There was no question that the Americans were the most exotic.

Later, waiting for the Aden plane at al-Mukalla Airport, I was able to observe *Homo petrolensis* in his natural environment. The airport used to be deserted. Now, daily, it echoed with the voices of half a dozen nationalities, Egyptian, Palestinian, Lebanese, French, British, American. But it didn't really matter where they came from. They all had the same steak-fed physiques, ballgame voices and expensive wrist accoutrements. Whatever the nationality, oil smooths over national differences and lubricates communication.

These two, though, had been temporarily displaced. I tried to picture where they had just come from. Somewhere, I suppose, up on the *jawl* where signposts with numbers point into the mist.

★

The pipeline which carries oil from the Hadramawt fields to the coast, opened in September 1993, arrives at the sea east of Shuhayr. Here, men in boiler suits and hard hats do unfathomable jobs on a desolate bluff, surrounded by a high fence and permanently blazing arc lights. It all looks like one of those evil-empire training camps that get blown up at the end of James Bond films. Most of its inmates are unaware of their place in the continuum of South Arabian trading history of which al-Shihr, a short distance further east, is a reminder.

The once-great city exported, according to a Chinese visitor of the twelfth century, frankincense, ambergris, pearls, opaque glass, rhino horn, ivory, coral, putchuk, myrrh, dragon's blood, asafoetida, liquid storax, galls and rosewater. Al-Shihr, however, having like Aden 'a great trade . . . with the Moors of Malabar and Cambaya', caught the eye of the early sixteenth-century Portuguese, who raided it several times. At a spot by the shore, the tombs of the Seven Martyrs killed by the Franks in 1522 are still to be seen. They were resurrected in recent years, to become the first entries in the PDRY anti-imperialist role of honour. Ninety years on a Dutchman, van der Broeke, followed the Portuguese. His intentions were more peaceful, and he set up a trade mission and left behind three of his colleagues to learn Arabic by what would now be called the total immersion method. He did not call again until three years later.

But al-Shihr's fortunes declined. Not long afterwards a Venetian described it, with Johnsonian disdain, as 'a desert place where both Men and Cattle are forced to live on Fish'. It was overtaken as the main port of Hadramawt by al-Mukalla, although there are still a few memories of its greatness. You enter the town past a white-washed gateway flanked by little cannon; bereft of its walls, the gate stands shut on a traffic island, a miniature Arc de Triomphe. Inside the town, carved doors and crumbling plaster speak of links with Goa, Lamu and Zanzibar, while a figure of astonishing sculptural ineptitude – it could represent Hiawatha or Hereward the Wake – rises above a fishy miasma to commemorate, presumably, more recent events.

Down on the beach the remains of another part of Arabian maritime tradition can be seen in a few small abandoned craft, the last of the sewn boats. Coir was brought from the Maldives – ruled in the Middle Ages by Yemenis – to bind together the vessels' planks with enormous cross-stitches. Sewn boats are mentioned in Classical sources, and later writers attempted to explain the reasons behind this method of construction: the medieval scholar al-Mas'udi said that, unlike the Sea of al-Rum (the Mediterranean), the Ethiopian Sea (the Indian Ocean) dissolves nails; the traveller Ibn Battutah thought that sewn vessels withstood collisions better than nailed ones; while the late fifteenth-century Rhinelander Arnold von Harff believed that the Arabian Sea contained magnetic rocks which would suck all iron out of a boat's timbers. Now, in al-Shihr, the beached hulls are dumps for hundreds of rotting fish heads.

Of all the travellers' tales emanating from Yemen, one of the strangest collections comes under the entry for al-Shihr in Yaqut's great geographical encyclopaedia. It concerns the *nisnas*, whom we have already encountered as a race of men whose faces grow out of their chests, brought to Yemen by the Himyari ruler He of the Frights. Yaqut's *nisnas* are different: they have only one of each member – one ear, one eye, one arm, one leg, and so on – and pogo at tremendous speed around the al-Shihr hinterland. One story tells of their stupidity.

Some people of the area went out hunting *nisnas* and captured one – on the hop, so to speak. They roasted and ate him under a tree where two of his companions were hiding. When one of these said to the other, 'Look! They're eating him!', the hunters heard the voice and netted him as well. 'You should have kept your mouth shut!' they laughed, at which the third *nisnas* blurted out, 'Well, *I* haven't said anything . . .' They caught him and butchered him too. Another tale reveals that the *nisnas*, although stupid, are accomplished versifiers. Some Shihris were joined on a hunt by an outsider, and when they caught a *nisnas* the victim extemporized a lament for himself:

> Perforce, oft have I fled from evil men
> In times long past when I was strong of limb.
> But now my youthful days are gone,
> And I am old and weak and thin.

The visitor was shocked that his hosts intended to eat the *nisnas*. 'Surely', he said, 'it is forbidden to eat creatures that can recite poetry.' 'On the contrary,' the Shihris answered, 'it lives by grazing and has the digestive tract of a ruminant, so it is perfectly *halal*.'* Yaqut adds an apologia: 'I admit that these stories are extraordinary, but I have merely quoted them from the books of learned men. If the information is at fault then I personally am not responsible.' One can only echo the disclaimer.

Al-Shihr has always been associated with one of the strangest, and costliest, of all the sea's products: ambergris. Despite its origin in the bowels of the sperm whale, it became part of the poet's stock-in-trade of amatory metaphors: 'and if you, my beloved, are perfume,/ You are ambergris of al-Shihr'. As well as being a constituent of cosmetics, in other more hedonistic lands it is mixed with tobacco for a voluptuous smoke. Ambergris also has a place in the traditional Arab pharmacopoeia: I have taken a course of 'beef ambergris', a concoction of the stuff with honey and herbs, in an attempt to improve my puny-looking physique. There were no visible results. Aphrodisiac properties are also claimed for it. I once bought a lump on the street in San'a as a wedding present for a friend. It smelt of the real thing, somewhere between truffles and BO, but turned out to be mostly candlewax.

---

* The story recalls the debate that raged over the permissibility of eating mermaids.

Ambergris has always been a great rarity. Ibn al-Mujawir, who calls it 'sea hashish', ascribes its scarcity to 'the wickedness of our opinions and the ugliness of our deeds'. Today, a fist-sized lump is worth at least the equivalent of £100. Down on the shore at al-Shihr, I decided to do some beachcombing. The problem was that I didn't know what to look for. I walked over to an old man, who was painting the hull of a boat with an evil-smelling substance. He might be able to help.

'*Ambar?*' He grinned. 'When you find it, it smells of shit. It even looks like shit. It's only when it begins to dry out that the smell changes. And if you do find some, you must cut your finger and let the blood drip on to it. Then you must pray two prostrations and give a third of it away as alms. Finding *ambar*, you see, should be what they call "a discovery where joy is mixed with pain."'

I scanned the beach, which seemed an allegory for the ugliness of men's deeds: it was used as a rubbish-tip and public lavatory. 'So how do you tell the difference, I mean between *ambar* and shit?'

The man looked at the ocean. 'Ah . . .', he said, and smiled. I thanked him for his advice and left.

★

The coast of Yemen – all 1,200-odd miles of it excluding the kinks – is, for me, a tacked-on sort of place. The essence of Yemen is here diluted in the ebb and flood of outsiders. If I treat the coast as an afterthought, I admit to prejudice. It is the view from the tower-house in the mountains where I live.

With few exceptions, the coast is visually unexciting. But for this reason, other sense-impressions are heightened, and none more so than those created by smell. For someone used to dry mountain air, the increased humidity acts as a fixative for smells; at times they seem almost solid, trapped in a matrix of moisture. The Greek geographer Agatharchides, writing of the Yemeni coast, notes 'an indescribably heavenly exhalation which excites the senses, even for those out at sea; and in the spring, whenever a breeze blows off the land, it comes redolent with the scent of myrrh and other trees'. As a sensual *idée fixe* it is remarkably persistent, occurring in the Bible, in the Latin poets, and in Milton:

201

When to them who sail
Beyond the Cape of Hope, and now are past
Mozambic, off at sea north-east winds blow
Sabaean odours from the spicy shore
Of Araby the Blest, with such delay
Well pleased they slack their course.

It was only when a new generation of Western romantics began
to extol the antiseptic and odourless virtues of the desert that the
cliché turned stale. Jeddah, T.E. Lawrence wrote, 'held a moisture
and sense of great age and exhaustion such as seemed to belong to
no other place . . . a feeling of long use, of the exhalations of many
people, of continued bath-heat and sweat'. He has a point: the
Red Sea is an armpit of a place, where the perspiring proximity of
Arabia and Africa generates heat, passion, magic. Hence the practice of infibulation, supposed to reduce the feminine libido; hence
the *zar*, the exorcism by wild dancing and drumming of a jealous
spirit, implanted by a rebuffed woman in the object of her desire
by making him smell basil.

One could compile an olfactory gazetteer of the Yemeni coast,
in the tradition of the founder of Zabid. He was said to have trav-

elled down Tihamah, sniffing handfuls of earth as he went, until he came to a spot where he found 'the butter, *zubdah*, of the land'; *zubdah* gave the city its name. Similarly, Awad ibn Ahmad ibn Urwah, a blind pilot of al-Shihr, was famous for his ability to tell a vessel's position by smelling the mud on the ship's plumbline. Once, while his ship was in the Gulf, the crew tried to catch him out by giving him mud from al-Hami, a few miles east of al-Shihr. 'All this time,' Awad said, 'and we've only got as far as al-Hami?'

The Sabaean odours of Milton and Agatharchides are now faint. Frankincense has never recovered from the blow dealt it by the early Christian Fathers although, in a sense, it still contributes to Yemen's hard-currency earnings in the form of tourism: roads (the Incense Road, the Silk Road, the Road to Samarkand) are marketable. And no more striking a setting could be desired for the Incense Road's southern coastal terminus, Bir Ali, the ancient Qana. Here, at the end of a long sickle bay of white sand, is the sheer black bulk of an extinct volcano. On top are a few fragments of wall; below, the basalt outlines of port buildings where, occasionally, you can pick up a lump of frankincense that was intended for the nostrils of Capitoline Jupiter or many-bosomed Diana of the Ephesians.

Even if the shores of Yemen are no longer as spicy as they were, Tihamah at least is still redolent with the scent of *full*, a kind of jasmine, and of *kadhdhi*, *Pandanus odoratissimus*, a long spiky flower used to scent clothes. It is said only to bloom when lightning strikes its buds. *Full*, *kadhdhi*, civet, musk, ambergris and numerous other ingredients are combined to make the perfumes used today by Yemeni women.* The reason for their fondness for scent is in part a practical one, Ibn al-Mujawir says: the women of Yemen are 'pretty of face, fond of chattering and loose of trouser-band', which proves that their sexual appetite far outweighs that of men; consequently women have to 'resort to using much scent in order to excite lust . . .'

And then there are the odours that accompany change and

---

* The eighteenth-century traveller James Bruce noted the use of 'a composition of musk, amber-grease, incense and benjoin, which they mix with the sharp horny nails that are at the extremity of the fish surumbac'.

decay. The once-great coral-stone merchants' houses of al-Luhayyah, where Niebuhr landed and played violin duets with the artist Baurenfeind to a people 'curious, intelligent and polished in their manners', fill with the reek of bats, then, giving up the ghost, collapse into dust, verandas, painted ceilings and all. Dust is everywhere. The cruel afternoon wind whips it up, turning the sun into a liver-spotted ball of yellow bile, then blotting it out. Caught in this recurring apocalypse, this death of air, there is nothing to do but assume a foetal position and wait for the redistribution of defunct earth, houses, creatures, to come to an end. Yet, by the grace of God, the sky opens most years and the coast gives off that most magical scent of all: rain on dust. It is the smell of life in death, and for a time the dunes sway with millet as far as the eye can see.

★

I have left out much material on the coasts of Yemen (much of it dashed, as Niebuhr said of Arab tales, with a little of the marvellous: a recent Sultan of al-Mukalla who would catch his serving-girls as they flew off a water-chute by the dozen; his neighbour of Balhaf who would throw enemies into the sea in perforated tea-chests –

the more hated the enemy, the smaller the holes; a tribe descended from a mermaid; another whose young men rugby-tackle gazelles and play leap-frog with camels; two villages whose people, about their usual business one day in the year 1169, rose into the air, never to be seen again; Sufi adepts who stab themselves and hang by the neck from buttered poles; brides who train their pubic hair in plaits which their husbands rip out on the wedding night; a woman who spent her life standing on her head and was cured by a meteor shower; and so on). But then, I am not Scheherazade.

8

True Ancient Naturals

'Stories of old . . .
Of dire chimeras and enchanted isles,
And rifted rocks whose entrance leads to hell,
For such there be, but unbelief is blind.'

Milton, *Comus*

THIS WAS TO HAVE BEEN a footnote on a place I would never see, but it grew, inexorably, into a chapter. Mine has been a digressive account; the Island of Suqutra, with the clarity of its light, the grotesqueries of its landscape, with its almost palpable *genius loci* – the spirit of old South Arabia now fading away on the mainland – is the last great sidetrack. To end there is, in a sense, to end at the beginning.

Suqutra had always been unattainable. Waq Waq, the Arab Ultima Thule at the far end of Mozambique, and sometimes beyond China, seemed hardly more distant. There it was on the map, somewhat larger than Skye, butted off the Horn of Africa, nearer to Somalia than to Yemen. But to get there . . . It might as well have been a place in a dream.

The origin of the island's name is in itself obscure. Arab writers have glossed it as *suq qatr*, the Emporium of Resin, but it probably derives from the Sanskrit *dvipa sakhadara*, the Island of Bliss. This in turn may be a version of Dh Skrd, which appears in South Arabian inscriptions and seems to have given the Greek geographers their home-grown sounding name for the island, Dioskurida. The etymological enigma is compounded by questions about the racial origins of the Suqutris, whose veins are thought to flow with South Arabian, Greek and Indian blood, with perhaps a dash of Portuguese.

Medieval writers did their best to shroud the island in a mist of dubious or downright incredible facts. Ibn al-Mujawir says that for six months of the year the Suqutris were forced to play host to pirates, who would make free with the Suqutri girls. The pirates seem to have worked *en famille*: 'They are a mean bunch, and their old women are meaner than their men.' For defensive reasons, the islanders took to sorcery, and when the late twelfth-century Ayyubids sailed for Suqutra with five warships the Suqutris magicked their island out of sight. For five days and nights the Ayyubid fleet quartered the seas, but found no trace of it. A century later, Marco Polo reported that the Suqutris were the best enchanters in the world and could, Aeolus-like, summon winds at will. The archbishop in Baghdad, to whom they were subject, disapproved strongly. Moreover, the Venetian goes on, the islanders 'know many other extraordinary sorceries, but I do not wish to speak of them . . .'

Eight centuries on, Suqutra occupies an apparently stable position 12½ degrees north of the Equator. It is home to a breed of dwarf cattle, to wild goats and donkeys, and to civet cats, which lurk in an eccentric arboretum where a third of the flora is unique to the island. The only pictures I had seen were of trees like yuccas and other pot plants but bizarrely mutated and enlarged; a few illustrating a British colonial official's visit to the Sultan in 1961; and Wellsted's drawing, done in the 1830s, of a scene near the capital Hadibu, which owed more to the Picturesque than to observation – a vista of craggy peaks with a foreground of artfully positioned swains, in which the artist himself surveys the view in a peaked cap, like a commissionaire lost in a willow-pattern plate. As for the written sources, my scant knowledge of the place was founded on rumour and travellers' tales. There were whispers of witch trials as late as the 1960s; Cold War demonologists of the 1980s suspected the existence of a 'massive' Soviet naval base with nuclear submarine pens. Cartographers should, by nature, be more down to earth; but a look at the toponyms they had collected included Buz and Berk, Gobhill and Yobhill . . . *Dinkidonkin.*

Clearly the only way of proving the place actually existed, was not some elaborate fiction, would be to go there. But how?

For half the year, Suqutra is cut off from the rest of the world by violent storms; for the other half, a small plane is supposed to go there twice a week but flights are often cancelled or booked out. The islanders number around 40,000, but I had never met a Suqutri and knew no one who had. San'anis, if they had heard of the place, thought of it as the very margin of the world. (The problems of getting there are not new. Many years ago, it is said, a mainland woman whose husband had been on Suqutra for seven years could only get to the island on the back of a phoenix. The bird was meant to touch down on the al-Mahrah coast during the first ten days of the lunar month Muharram.)

And then, unexpectedly, the door to Suqutra opened. I was on my way to see Linda and Awad, waiting in Crater for the Aden-al-Mukalla taxi to fill up. It was two passengers short, and had been for most of the morning. Everyone was ratty, with lunchtime approaching and an eleven-hour journey ahead. Hadramis with plastic briefcases and new starchy *futahs*, worn ankle-length with the labels still attached, were trying to get each other to shell out for the empty seats. I had refused to part with a *shilin* more. If anyone was pressed for time then let him pay up. I was in no hurry. And since no Hadrami will countenance publicly spending more than the next one, we waited.

Another debate began, on whether to have lunch here or on the road. The driver knew that no more passengers would arrive in the dead small hours between the noon and *asr* prayers, and lay down to sleep on the desk of the Controller of Taxis, who had nothing to control. The Hadramis went off for lunch. Two passengers appeared. In an instant the driver was out of a deep slumber and running after the lunch party, and soon afterwards we were bowling north-east along the Abyan shore.

My fellow passengers were silent until we had eaten in Zinjibar. Conversations started, I unwrapped my *qat*. Then I heard something that made me sit up: it cut through the low hum of talk, audible as a stage-whisper. It was that phonemic phantom of

South Arabia, the lateral sibillant which is a *sh* hissed through the corners of the mouth. I turned to the latecomers. 'You must be Mahris.'

'No, we're from Suqutra – if you've heard of it.'

I must have stared at them longer than was polite. One of them said something incomprehensible and they both laughed. Still, they *did* look different. For a start, they were darker and much wirier than the Hadramis; then, there was something about the eyes, a slight upward flare to the outer corners, something feline. *The best enchanters in the world.*

They brushed off my apologies and we started chatting. Sa'd and Muhammad had finished secondary school in Aden. They were going home to be teachers. 'And you're flying from al-Mukalla?' I asked them.

'We wanted to, but the plane's full and will be for weeks. You see, it's the end of *al-kaws*, the season of storms, and everyone's going home. We're travelling by sea.'

I cut short my Hadramawt visit and returned to San'a. Less than a month after the meeting with Sa'd and Muhammad, I bade an emotional farewell to my San'ani friends. For them, the great and wide sea teems with leviathans and other terrors. 'You'll end up', they said, and in all seriousness, 'in the belly of a whale. And you're a *nasrani*, so praying won't do you any good.' At their insistence I had written my will. With me was Kevin, recently returned from four years in Kuala Lumpur, Georgetown and Chiang Mai. In the Far East he had suffered from breakbone fever and from not being in Yemen.

We left a San'a strangely transformed. The authorities were running a clean-up campaign to rid the city of its rubbish, and even the Prime Minister took to the alleys with a broom. Street traders were also swept away, and without its second-hand clothes, tobacco, alfalfa and impromptu poets the *suq* outside my house was eerily quiet for the first time in centuries. There was no longer a smell of basil on the stairs. The transformation of San'a into a museum had begun, and I was glad not to be watching it.

Three days later we arrived in the small town on the Hadramawt coast which Sa'd and Muhammad had said was the main port for Suqutra. It was late afternoon and the sun slanted, mellifluous, across a broad bay. The only craft were a few *hawris*, slender, sharp-nosed fishing boats. They hardly moved, so calm was the ocean.

At a tea-house that smelt of fish we asked about a boat to Suqutra.

'You're in luck. There's a *sambuq* leaving tonight.'

Kevin and I looked at each other. It couldn't be this easy.

A tuna appeared in the doorway. 'It's going to Abdulkuri, not Suqutra,' said the boy who was carrying it. Abdulkuri is a small island in the Suqutra group but more than 60 miles closer to Africa. Some 250 people live on its volcanic coast in, I had read, 'extreme poverty, cut off from the world, and suffering great distress'. It was the sort of place where you could get stuck for a long time. Tempting as that sounded, we shook our heads.

'I'll take you to Salim bin Sayf,' the boy said. 'I think he's going to Suqutra soon. And he's the best *nakhudhah* anywhere.' *Nakhudhah!* That was a word with resonances! Persian for a ship's captain and used in Arabic since the time of Sindbad, it recalls the days before the sextant, before even the lodestone, when 'the Junk and the Dhow, though they looked like anyhow,/ Were the Mother and the Father of all ships . . .'

The boy took us to the far end of the street, past the school and up an alley where we knocked on a plywood door. Goats wandered past masticating nonchalantly; there was that rich Hadrami dung-and-tobacco smell and a pinch of salt-sea shark. Salim bin Sayf stuck his head through the door, bushy bearded, rheumy in the eye, the very picture of the best *nakhudhah* anywhere. He was sailing for Suqutra on the eve of Wednesday. At first suspicious of why we should want to go by sea, he softened when we explained that as foreigners we'd have to pay for the plane tickets in dollars, which meant they would cost us five times what they cost Yemenis. Anyway, the plane was full.

We asked how much he charged. Salim tugged his beard, the gesture that means 'Shame on you!', and named a price less than the cost of a couple of afternoons' *qat*.

'And what about food?'

He looked us up and down. 'Can you eat what we eat?'

I tugged an imaginary beard. Salim chuckled and we said goodbye, until Wednesday evening.

★

On our way back to the port we shared maritime experiences. I had pottered around the cliffs of Donegal in a skiff and had spent a pleasant weekend pub-crawling the East Anglian coast on a Cornish crabber. In the East Indies, Kevin had sailed in a Bugis craft of immaculately polished teak with a prow like a stiletto and a cushion-strewn poop. I could picture him, lolling on a burnished throne, a pipe, perhaps, of opium in his hand.

'Don't expect anything too smart,' I warned. In the early seventeenth century the Sultan of Suqutra had 'a handsome Gally and Junk of Suratt'. But that was in the golden age of Arab seafaring. I felt Kevin might be harbouring grand hopes. 'And the loo will be a tea-chest with a shitty hole, lashed over the back end.'

Down on the beach once more, we scanned the water. There was no sign of an ocean-going vessel. Perhaps we'd got the day wrong. 'He did say *Tuesday* evening, didn't he?' Kevin asked.

'No. He said Wednesday evening. But that means the eve of Wednesday, which is Tuesday evening. I checked with him and he said, "Yes, I mean Tuesday."'

'You don't think he meant the eve of Tuesday? If he did, then we've missed the boat . . .'

A child was standing in the shallows, lazily casting a weighted net into the water again and again. We walked over to him, fearing the worst. 'Where's the *nakhudhah* Salim bin Sayf?' I asked.

'I don't know.' He cast the net again. 'But that's his *sambuq* out there.' The boy pointed to a boat that seemed little bigger than a *hawri*. The only difference was that it has a single forward-raking mast. The hull was painted red and yellow.

'*That's* the one that goes to Suqutra?'

The boy stopped in mid-cast, looked at us strangely, and nodded.

The seas around Suqutra are notorious for their unpredictable winds and mountainous swell. I remembered reading an old verse, in a book of cautionary tales for sea captains, which spoke of the perils of navigating between the island and Cape Hafun – the tip of the Horn of Africa:

Between Suqutra and Hafun's head,
Pray your course be never set . . .

Somewhere out in the 260 miles of open ocean that separated us
from Suqutra, Leviathan was licking his many pairs of lips.

We tracked down Salim bin Sayf at a wedding party. The whole
town was invited and the main street had been turned into a
concert-hall. The band sat on a stage in front of a painted backdrop showing an idyllic bay. Not far behind that there was an
idyllic bay, not that you could see it in the dark. The music had a
hillbilly beat, and young men came to the front in twos and threes
to perform a hip- and shoulder-wiggling shuffle.

Kevin and I watched for a while then strolled back to the beach.
The sea was black, but in the glow from the town slender forms of
beached *hawris* could just be made out. Knots of men sat in the
sand, chatting and smoking; others had wrapped themselves in
sheets and were sleeping. We were joined by a middle-aged man

who introduced himself as Muhammad Ba Abbad. Muhammad worked as a surveyor in the Emirates but was a native of the town who knew the sea as well as anyone. We told him we thought the *sambuq* was a bit on the small side.

He laughed. 'Actually it's one of the bigger ones. But don't worry, the dangerous season's over. It begins with the star of al-Nat'h in the horn of Aries, and ends with al-Ramih, Arcturus. They say *idha ma natahsh, ramah*, "If it hasn't butted, it'll kick." This year the sea kicked – the storms came at the back end of the dangerous period. It will be calm for you, *in sha Allah.*' Now, at least, it was calm, the sea susurrating almost inaudibly on the strand. 'But you'll still be puking from the smell of *sif.*' *Sif*, used for protecting wooden hulls against rot, is made from 'the innards of sharks, simmered in earthen pots until the flesh dissolves and turns to oil', according to a medieval Adeni recipe. Eventually, the crew arrived and Muhammad wished us a safe voyage. We boarded a rocking *hawri* and set out into the black, the sounds of the wedding fading behind us.

On board the *sambuq*, which rolled even in this calm sea, a paraffin lamp was lit. A smear of light revealed a deck crowded with boxes, oildrums, ropes, anchors and bodies. There were fifteen other passengers, already embarked and asleep. That made twenty-three of us in an open thirty-five-foot boat, and the voyage would last two nights and a day.

The *nakhudhah* Salim was last on board. Bare-chested, issuing orders, he had somehow grown bigger and younger. A crew-man skipped below deck and cranked the engine to life; Salim produced a compass sitting on a bed of woodshavings in a twine-bound box. He lined the box up with the mast and secured it with a few nails banged into the deck. At one in the morning we weighed anchor and headed, on a course of 110 degrees, for the ocean.

Gradually, activity subsided. The crewmen joined the rest of the sleeping bundles. Kevin stretched out too, his head cushioned on a tin of Telephone Brand ghee. Only a small space was left, next to the *nakhudhah*, and I propped myself on the gunwale and watched the lights of the town grow more distant.

Salim told me about his family. His father and his ancestors had been skippers here for as long as anyone could remember. His mother was a Suqutri from Nujad on the island's south coast. The lamp was turned low. Salim kept his eyes on the stars. A cord, looped round the hewn tiller, tightened and then slackened in his fingers.

'Nujad is where they come down the mountains to pasture the flocks. *Lubnan*, my father calls it.' Lebanon, the land rich in milk. He refolded the tarpaulin he was sitting on and wrapped himself in a large striped blanket. 'They make these in Suqutra. You see, everything comes from their flocks – milk, butter, cheese, wool, meat.'

'What about fishing?'

'There's some. The real Suqutris are bad sailors.'

I looked back to where the town had been, and gone. Three in the morning. The painted backdrop of sea would be lying rolled up. The real sea under us was more jelly than liquid. Blackcurrant jelly. The bride would be lying, deflowered. Tenderly, I wondered, or mechanically? Beneath me the diesel thumped yet, somehow, did not disturb the calm.

'That's why we Hadramis marry Suqutri girls. It puts some salt in their blood. I've got a wife on the mainland and a wife in Nujad.'

I stretched out, feet hanging over the engine, head next to the compass.

'Look!' Salim whispered.

There, to starboard, a pair of porpoises were shadowing the *sambuq*. They leapt, silent and ghostly in the starlight, disappearing with a flicker of phosphorescence at the end of each parabola.

Salim tapped my shoulder. 'Listen: my father, when he was young, was out fishing with a friend. They were in a *hawri*, a long way out from the shore. Suddenly the boat turned over. It was a dolphin that did it, a big one. Anyway, the boat was sinking and it was too far to swim.' He tightened the cord on the tiller. 'But the dolphin saw what he'd done and came to them. He took them on his back and stayed by the boat until they'd baled it out. Then they got back in and returned to land. Glory be to the Creator!'

The porpoises had gone. Again I stretched out and began slipping away from consciousness.

'When you go to sea,' I heard Salim say, 'the Angel of Death follows you.'

★

Salim was still at the helm when I awoke. Kevin was sitting upright, rubbing his eyes. 'I'm bursting for a piss,' he said. 'What are you supposed to do? I can't see one of those boxes.' One of the crew, on cue, showed how it was done. Kevin changed into a *futah*. 'Keep an eye on me.'

He picked his way across the sleepers towards the prow, squatted on a greasy gunwale and, gripping a stanchion, hitched up his *futah*. It took a long time. 'God!' he hissed, when he got back, 'What do you do when it's rough?'

But it was as calm as ever. The sea curdled where the prow cut through it, then recongealed in the *sambuq*'s wake. An odd flying fish shot out of the water like a spat pip. In such a sea, 'without a stir, without a ripple, without a wrinkle – viscous, stagnant, dead', perhaps at this very spot, Conrad's Lord Jim had abandoned the doomed *Patna* and her eight hundred pilgrims.

Over to port a ship was approaching, a phantom, silvery in the rising sun. Salim steered across her course. No sound came from her, though the decks and companionways were packed with people, standing silent and immobile as statuary: 'there were people perched all along the rails, jammed on the bridge in a solid mass; hundreds of eyes stared, and not a sound was heard . . . as if all that multitude of lips had been sealed by a spell'. God knows, it was the *Patna* herself. It was the only other vessel we were to see.

Our six-ton *sambuq*, the *Kanafah* (no one ever used the name, and even Salim had to think before he remembered it), had been built a few years ago in al-Shihr. Below the waterline the hull was of teak. For the rest a cheaper hardwood, *jawi*, 'Javan', was used, with pine planking for the deck. Powered by a 33-horsepower Japanese engine, she was also lateen-rigged like all Arab craft but her sail would only be used in emergencies. 'Diesel engines started coming in in the mid-fifties,' Salim said. 'By about twenty years ago they'd taken over completely. If we were under sail it would usually take about five days to reach Suqutra. In weather like this, much longer.' I remembered reading about the leisurely pre-diesel voyages of the great ocean-going *baghlahs* of the Arabian Gulf, when the ship's carpenter would have enough time to build a smaller vessel on the main deck, to sell when the *baghlah* reached her destination; and I had a vision of a series of ever-diminishing carpenters building ever-diminishing boats, each on the deck of the other, and so on *ad infinitum* in a windless sea.

Ten feet below the surface, red-shelled crabs, dozens of them, were heading towards the mainland, slowly, as if through aspic. They had a long way to go.

The cook, a pudgy boy, appeared from a hatch towards the fore with a pile of pancake bread and a thermos of milky tea. Most of the passengers who had not already risen surfaced at the smell of cooking, and a queue formed to pray in the single free bit of deck. A couple of others slept on. One, I was sure, I saw for the first time only when we dropped anchor off Suqutra.

The passengers fell into two groups. There were the outsiders and semi-outsiders, like Hadid bin Bakhit bin Ambar, another Hadrami with a Suqutri mother. Most Arabic personal names have a meaning, like 'Handsome' or 'Faith'. Hadid's meant 'Iron son of Lucky son of Ambergris'.* Hadid had lived in Kuwait and was going to spend a month in Suqutra, his first visit in seven years. Of the other non-Suqutris, one was a crabby old Mahri trader with jug-handle ears that stuck out from under a white crocheted cap. He had a store on the island and most of the cargo below deck, sacks of flour and sugar, was his.

The Suqutri passengers were silent men with wild, auburn-tinted hair, wrapped in huge Kashmir shawls and looking queasy. If they did speak, it was in undertones, all aspirants and sibillants like the soughing of the wind in treetops. It reminded me of Hebridean Gaelic. To a speaker of Arabic, the Suqutri language sounds like a distant and dyslexic cousin. But occasional words are familiar and, in time, I realized that it shares with the Raymi and Yafi'i dialects of Yemeni Arabic the past-tense *k*-ending, another revenant from the ancient languages. Island and mountains, cut-off places: the Celtic fringe of Arabia. 'There are still some Suqutris in

---

* The choice of name rarely has any significance. However, I have seen a boy with six toes on each foot who was called Zayid, 'Extra'.

the interior', said Hadid, 'who can't speak Arabic. Thirty years ago, perhaps ninety per cent knew hardly any.'

One of the Suqutris spent most of his time as the *sambuq's* figurehead, his legs wrapped around the bowsprit, singing. It was a four-bar melody, full of quarter-tones and flicked grace-notes, repeated, *da capo*, without let-up, to the rhythmic chug of the diesel. Salim said it was poetry. With a wavy mane of hair, a high forehead joining his nose in a single arc, and flaring nostrils, he looked like one of the Trafalgar Square lions. There was, too, something archaic in the profile, an eerie resemblance to the early Sabaean bronzes.

'There are some strange-looking people in Suqutra,' Salim told us. 'The mountain tribes don't mix much with outsiders.' I remembered the people described by Sir Thomas Roe, who anchored off Suqutra in 1615 with his ships the *Dragon*, the *Lion* and the *Peppercorn* on his way to visit the Mogul Emperor of India. The Suqutris, he said, were divided into three groups, Arabs, slaves and 'savage people, poor, leane, naked, with long haire, eating nothing but Rootes, hiding in bushes, conversing with none, afraid of all, without houses, and almost as savage as beasts, and by conjecture the true ancient Naturals of this Iland'.

Hadid didn't agree that all the mountain people were shy of strangers. 'There's a place in the east called Shilhal', he said, 'where they've got fair skin and blue eyes. Just like you *nasranis*. You tell me where they got them from.'

'Greeks?' I suggested, 'Shipwrecked mariners, Portuguese?'

'Oh, they're probably Crusaders,' Kevin said ironically. 'They seem to have got everywhere else.'

We made a mental note to visit the *nasrani*-like clan of Shilhal.

The sun crossed the sky, planishing the surface of the ocean like a coppersmith's hammer. The *Kanafah* seemed over-crewed. One of the seamen put out a line, but nothing bit all day. Another, whose father had been a *nakhudhah* running paraffin to al-Mukalla for the Provençal-Adeni merchant Besse, lashed his shirt to another line and threw it over the side for the sea to wash. The only one who seemed fully occupied was the cook, who popped up again from below deck, like a pantomime genie through a trap-door, bearing a great plate of rice and something he'd cut off an object hanging from the mast. If the object looked like anything it was a bit of old tractor tyre, but it turned out to be dried shark. After lunch I curled up in the bows and fell asleep to the song of the figurehead.

Sleeping was the main occupation on board. Kevin had fallen in with the rhythm and settled down for the night soon after evening prayers. Salim was at the helm again and I joined him, curious to learn more about techniques of navigation and whether much knowledge had been passed down from its heyday among the Arabs, the fifteenth and sixteenth centuries. During this period, the celebrated pilot Ahmad ibn Majid led the field in a science in which mnemonic verses played the part of charts, and *nakhudhahs* held international conferences to discuss abstruse points on winds and stars.

'We all know Ibn Majid,' Salim explained. '*Nakhudhahs* consider him their ancestor. But now we rely on the compass. See, we started on a course of 110 degrees. Now it's 135 degrees. By the time we reach Suqutra we'll be following a course of 150 degrees. If we went in a straight line, the current would take us into the ocean.'

'And if there were no compass?' To describe, without one, this huge westward-curving trajectory and arrive at a particular spot on a small land-mass in a vast ocean seemed an impossibility, like shooting an arrow at a tiny and invisible target. The *sambuq* had no radar or radio, and I imagined us overshooting Suqutra, ending up in Madagascar, or wandering the Indian Ocean far from the ship-ping lanes until the fuel ran out and we were carried past Réunion and the Prince Edward Islands, on and on, towards the ice floes of Antarctica.

'Ah, every *nakhudhah* knows the stars. Those two point to Mirbat in Oman; those, to Qishn; then', he went on, running his finger across the sky, 'Sayhut, Qusay'ir, al-Shihr, al-Mukalla, Aden, Djibouti, Berbera, Abdulkuri, Qalansiyah, Hadibu. Every three hours you must change to a new pair of stars as the old ones fall away.'

I lay back, leaving Salim at the tiller, wrapped in his woollen *shamlah*. The old familiar constellations above me were rearrang-ing themselves. Where the Plough, Orion and the Little Bear had been, there was now an array of new signs above like the overhead gantries at a motorway interchange, but on a cosmic scale.

I was awakened by the dawn call to prayer, which Hadid chanted before the mast in a thin voice as penetrating as an alarm clock's bleep. A change had come over the sea. The dead, viscous surface was now alive. We were still six or seven hours off Suqutra, but even this far away the invisible island was loosing its aeolian forces on the water. One by one passengers and crew relieved themselves, abluted and prayed. Kevin and I were both unnerved by the business of urinating. Over breakfast Hadid told us that the sea off Suqutra was always *za'lan*, angry (the dictionary definition is 'Lively. Writhing in hunger'). 'This is nothing. Often the waves come over the deck. I've done this journey many times, and I've usually been soaked from start to finish.'

Throughout the morning the unseen presence before us made itself known by great banks of clouds and a headwind that brought boobies and terns with it. I imagined we might scent Suqutra before we saw it. Hadid laughed at the idea. 'If you smell anything, it'll be goats. There's still a bit of frankincense-collecting, but the trade's almost disappeared.'

'What about ambergris?' Kevin asked.

'I've never found any,' said Hadid, 'but they say that about twenty years ago a Suqutri came across a huge lump on the beach. He thought it was tar from a steamer and used it to waterproof the roof of his hut.' He shook his head slowly, looking towards the queasy men in their shawls. Suqutra was beginning to seem a sort of paradise on earth, I said, a land abounding in milk and meat where precious gums dripped from trees and the sea cast up costly unguents unbidden.

'Paradise . . .', said Hadid, smiling at the clouds, 'paradise without doctors or medicines, without communications for half the year. It's only you *nasranis* who find paradise in this world.'

And then it appeared. First just a smudge on the horizon, it resolved into a line of cliffs with a streak of white sand at their base. We headed for a spot where the line dipped. The dip became a broad strath carpeted in seamless green, its sides framing a fore-ground of palms and the low cuboid houses of Qalansiyah. Hadid hoisted his red-checked headcloth as an ensign and we dropped anchor in water of incredible clarity. A couple of *sambuqs* and a few *hawris* bobbed around us; shoals of fish darted under the hull. A *hawri* came and took us to the shore, where Egyptian vultures the colour of an octogenarian smoker's hair stood among green weed, unfazed by a crowd of children who gathered to study the new arrivals. Sa'd, the high-school graduate with the enchanter's eyes, was there too with a notebook to list the incoming goods. Salim, Hadid and the others were greeted with a gracefully choreographed double nose-touch accompanied by little sniffs. Sa'd and I shook hands.

On board, Kevin and I had felt no discomfort from the boat's motion but now, on dry land, we were both hit by the effect of thirty-six hours on the ocean. My brain seemed to swivel on gimbals inside my skull. Ali bin Khamis bin Murjan (Ali son of Thursday son of Coral), one of the passengers and a native of Qalansiyah, took pity on us and invited us home. He led us along narrow alleyways where the ground quivered and the walls throbbed. When we arrived at his house, the only two-storey building in the town, he took us to an airy upstairs room with yellow walls and a repeating calligraphic frieze, the Islamic creed stencilled in pink. It just wouldn't stay still. We were ordered to lie down.

Half an hour later I woke to the sound of low voices. A woman who must have been Ali's mother was talking to him in a stream of Suqutri and Arabic. In early middle age, she was unveiled and handsome in a strikingly Iberian way – the sort of woman you might run into in a smart Lisbon department store, I thought, remembering the Portuguese connection.

Kevin was stirring. *There is no god but God* still undulated slightly above him; however, the worst of the delayed motion-sickness had worn off. It was then that I realized something was different: there had been no interrogation. Usually in Yemen a newcomer, and particularly a foreigner who speaks Arabic, is subjected within moments of arrival to intensive questioning on every subject from the Resurrection of Christ to the Duke of Edinburgh's precise constitutional status. There is rarely any other motive than a wish to break the ice, and to this end the interrogation is very effective, preferable by far to an embarrassed Anglo-Saxon silence. It is a small price to pay for often bewilderingly generous hospitality but, if all you want to do is sleep, the need to perform can be exhausting. Here, though, no demands had been made on us. Writing of his visit to the island 160 years before, Wellsted said of the Suqutris that 'the most distinguishing trait of their character is their hospitality'. Nothing has changed.

The only losers in the hospitality stakes are the goats. That evening Ali slaughtered one for the *Kanafah's* crew and the two *nasranis*. It was a skull-smashing, cartilage-wrenching occasion, a hands-on lesson in caprine anatomy. An hors-d'oeuvre of bones was served on a palm-frond mat by Salim, who cracked the head with a mighty double-fisted blow and shared out creamy morsels of brain. Then followed the meat itself and intestines stuffed with fat. The flesh was delicious, almost gamey, and an improvement on the days of Captain John Saris, who wrote of the goats of Suqutra after a visit in 1611 that 'most of them are not man's meat, being so vilely and more than beastly buggered and abused by the people, so that it was loathesome to see when they were opened'. (The comment is strange – the Suqutris are indulgently gentle with their animals.) Ours was a Homeric feast, its victim the first of a hecatomb which was to fall as Kevin and I wandered the island.*

Salim said it was time for bed. After all, for the last two nights he had, Odysseus-like, 'never closed his eyes in sleep but kept them on the Pleiads'. Before turning in he spoke to Kevin and me. 'Come with us tomorrow. We're going round the island to Sitayruh, my mother's village in Nujad.' We agreed eagerly. 'It's a ten-hour journey so we must be up before dawn. Sleep now.' We bedded down with the crew in Ali's courtyard. With no diesel thumping beneath me, the silence was as profound as the ocean. There was only a single heroic belch answered by a hushed '*Hani'an!*' – *bon appétit* in reverse.

At 4.30 in the morning the cold was bitter. The sun rose as we weighed anchor and headed west. Far off to starboard a pair of rocks jutted out of the sea, fondled by rosy-fingered Dawn. Salim

---

* Unfortunately, we missed out on a delicacy of the Hajhir Mountains eaten by Vitaly Naumkin, the Russian scholar of all things Suqutri – the stomach of a goat cooked complete with its undigested contents, a sort of Suqutri haggis.

said they were called Sayyal, but I later came across their more poetic name in an early nineteenth-century rhyming pilot's guide: Ki'al Fir'awn, The Pharaoh's Bollocks. We passed the headland of Ra's Biduh and crossed the broad bay of Shurubrum, backed by steep green hills.

Here a gurgle from the prow marked the slaughter of another goat, a present from Ali Khamis. When I went to investigate, its skin was almost peeled off and the deck was running in blood. Its dismembered carcass disappeared below with the cook while the skin was draped, Argonaut-fashion, over the bowsprit in front of the singing figurehead. By the time we rounded Shu'ub, the island's westernmost point, the meat was cooked and we break-fasted at the captain's table – again, a palm mat – on pancakes, tripe wrapped in small intestines, and liver. Salim, with the help of a spanner, extracted a single quivering column of marrow from a femur and then presented it to Kevin and me, performing the operation with his usual combination of brute force and fastidious delicacy.

Our course took us under the lee of the cliffs, disturbing the cormorants that nested in the rock-face. Over to the south-west Salim pointed out two distant islands, the Brothers, rising from the sea like plinths waiting for statues. 'That's where I go shark-fishing. One of them, Samhah, has a few people but Darzah, the other one, is covered in rats.' A British expedition in the 1960s was unwise enough to camp on the second island; they spent the whole night fighting off its inhabitants.

At the village of Nayt, a few huts on the beach, we dropped an oildrum of salt into the sea; a boy swam out and pushed it back to the beach. Further on at Hizalah, where half a dozen tiny stone cabins clung like barnacles to a cleft in the rocks, we shouted for twenty minutes before anyone answered. Eventually, another boy swam out and climbed into the *sambuq*. He stood on the deck, dripping, like the half-seal half-man amphibians of Norse legend. After a panted exchange in Suqutri he plunged back into the aqua-marine water and fetched a *hawri*, in which we deposited a spare anchor.

Soon after Ra's Qutaynahan the cliffs rose again, 1,600-foot walls striated horizontally and falling sheer into the sea. Here and there, high up, there was an inaccessible cave, curtained by creepers. The noise of the diesel bounced, amplified, off the rock; there were no birds. The crew ceased talking and stared up at the caves, as if half-expecting an Arabian Scylla to pop out.

At last, where a tiny settlement called Subraha appeared at the foot of the cliff wall, Salim broke the spell of silence. 'This is the start of the Nujad Plain, where people bring their flocks down from the mountains.'

Kevin pointed out that there didn't seem to be any way down. Ahead, the cliffs marched beyond the horizon, sheer and uninterrupted. It was now midday and the bloated shapes of clouds, tethered like balloons in the windless air, were projected on to the escarpment.

'Oh, there are paths, not that you'd call them that,' Salim said. 'The ledges are sometimes only this wide.' He showed a span. 'In some places they use ropes. And their flocks can be several hundred head.'

Slowly, the plain broadened, and at Bi Zidiq, another minute hamlet, the figurehead jumped over the side and struck off for a shore of hound's-tooth rocks. We watched him drag himself out – with difficulty, as a wind had begun to stir up the swell. Soon he was back in a *hawri* and the last few passengers left. Lunch was rice and the remains of the goat. This time, Salim produced a hatchet from his toolkit-cum-*batterie de cuisine* to get inside the skull.

The *sambuq*'s shadow began to lengthen on the sea bed, crossing white sand and black rock beneath water so transparent we seemed to be in levitation. Kevin hung over the matting sides trying to photograph a school of porpoises. A couple of pale, yard-long turtles glided beneath the hull with indolent flicks of their flippers, descendants of the 'true sea-tortoise' for which Suqutra was famous in the days of the *Periplus*.

We arrived at Sitayruh an hour before sundown. The shoreline was busy, a metropolis after so many hours of near-empty coastline. Men staggered under unidentifiable loads, draped across their backs like huge rubbery cloaks, which they tossed into a beached *hawri* before returning to reload at the little headland that formed the bay's eastern arm. Landing was precarious and we had to jump, between breakers, from the boat which took us ashore.

Kevin went to investigate the loads. They turned out to be sharks, split kipperwise, salted and dried. I found him examining a pile of fins, which they call *rish*, feathers. Some were enormous and had been cut off the hammerheads and maicos whose flesh was stacked nearby. While this is exported to Hadramawt, the Suqutris themselves are said to be fond of the shark's liver, salted and preserved in its stomach. The fins were sold on the mainland for 1,200 *shilins* a kilo, around $30 at the time. 'We know they go to the Far East,' said a voice from beneath one of the sharks, 'but what do they do with them? They must be crazy to pay that much. Praise God!'

I explained that the fins were made into soup. 'And they pay even more for birds' nests.'

'*Birds' nests?* The cliffs here are full of them!' the man exclaimed. Kevin described the collection and auctioning of nests which he had witnessed in a Sarawak cave. The Suqutri listened, then staggered off under his gruesome mantle, muttering the only possible response: *There is no strength and no power save in God.*

Hadid, who like Salim also had a wife here, appeared and led us over the dunes to the village. The houses were compounds of single stone rooms, bewigged with palm-frond thatch and surrounded by fences of the same material. We sat in Hadid's yard, eating dates and drinking coffee, until the evening prayer. A bowl of *rawbah* was passed round. *Rawbah* is milk after the fat has been removed to make ghee; it is poured into a goatskin, which is inflated with a lungful of air and sealed, and then left to turn sour. Slightly *pétillant* like a Lambrusco, the Suqutris are addicted to it. At first we found it delicious; a fortnight later we were sick of the taste.

Hadid, Kevin and I went that night to Salim's house, where the crew and most of Sitayruh's adult male population sat waiting for more goat. The large compound was mostly in darkness, with a couple of lanterns making feeble pools of light. When the food arrived, we ate in silence while Salim carved bite-sized chunks of meat with which he constantly replenished a pile on top of the huge plate of *rawbah*-soaked rice. After supper, we talked about magic. The subject seemed appropriate: Sitayruh was the sort of place that would breed spells.

'There's a man in al-Shihr', pronounced Hasan, one of the *Kanafah*'s crew, 'who writes charms. He can do one that guarantees you a forty-ton catch of shark!'

Salim scoffed. 'I suppose you'd believe what they used to say about Ali Salim al-Bid's father, that he could sell you a charm that made girls think they were walking in water so they'd lift their skirts.' (The idea, at least, had a Qur'anic basis in the account of the Queen of Sheba's visit to Solomon, when the prophet made her walk across a mirror-like floor and she bared her legs.)

I asked about witch trials. Snell, a colonial official, gave an account of the procedure in the mid-1950s: a suspect was first sub-jected to an oral inquisition by the Sultan then, if he decided there was a case against her, she was tied and weighted with 8lbs of stones; if she sank three times in three fathoms of water – the inquisitors pulling her up with a rope each time – she was inno-cent; if she was seen to be floating in an upright position, she was held to be a witch and exiled to the mainland. Not so long ago she would have been hurled from the cliffs. At another trial, in 1967, a guilty woman is said literally to have sprung out of the waves. Salim's guests confirmed that the trials had continued until recently. Nowadays witches go about their business more or less unmolested.*

'It's since Unification that the old customs have really been dying out,' Salim said. 'People come from the mainland to teach the Suqutris about Islam. Take circumcision, for instance. Do you remember the boy who got off first at Bi Zidiq? I saw him circum-cised a few years ago. He was about ten at the time but, in the past, they used to circumcise young men not long before their wedding night. Well, long enough for the cut to heal.

'This is what I saw: three boys were brought, as naked as when they were born, before all the people of the area – hundreds of them, men and women. These guests had brought over a hundred

---

* The Moroccan traveller Ibn Battutah witnessed a witch trial in fourteenth-century Delhi, exactly the same as the Suqutri version except for the substitution of water-filled jars for stones. Naumkin suggests that Suqutri anti-witch campaigns could be connected with a subconscious fear of the island's ancient matriarchal system reasserting itself. The term he gives for a witch, *zahra*, may be the same as the name of the seductress in the Bir Barhut story (see pp. 185–6). We also heard of an ancient Suqutri female ruler called al-Zahra.

head of sheep and goats, just as they would at a wedding. The boys' hair was cut very short and their heads were covered with butter – I'll tell you why in a minute. They were seated on a special stone while the circumciser, whom the Suqutris call *mazadhar*, did his job. Each boy concentrated on the *mazadhar's* chest, or on some distant object, and I swear that not one of them flinched while he was cut. Not even a blink. Any sign of pain, any reaction at all, is a big disgrace to the boy and his people. That's why they crop their hair and butter it, because if it were to stand up people would see that the boy felt fear. Anyway, immediately after each one was cut he jumped into the air three times, higher and higher until he jumped as high as himself. Then the boys ran together, with their blood still flowing, to a special hut a couple of miles away. Here they have to stay until the cut is better. They heal it with plants and hang bags containing a strong smelling substance – I don't know what it is – under the boys' noses. No woman may visit them there. This is what I saw; this is how it was with the Suqutris until not long ago. *Wallah!* Now, the religious leaders have stopped it because it is unIslamic.'

Public pre-marital circumcision, it seems, is another feature of the old South Arabian fringe. Wellsted noted it among the Mahris, and Thesiger records that the notorious 'flaying' version – removal of the entire skin down to the thighs – was practised in Asir. Now, for better or worse, it seems to have disappeared.

We talked of *makólis*, the traditional Suqutri magic-makers, and of *sayyids*, the incomers who had usurped many of their super-natural powers. The *sayyid* who built the main mosque in Hadibu, they said, woke up one day to find its roof miraculously completed overnight, and Johnstone reports that *sayyids* had taken over from *makólis* the power to control the wind. One of the villagers told us of the female *jinn* who roam the mountains at night. 'And if you meet one,' he said, 'she sings to you.' He sang, very softly, in falsetto. The tune had a lilt to it, something like 'Girls and boys come out to play', and it made the hairs on my neck stand up. I asked him what the words meant.

'They mean', he said, smiling, '"I've been waiting for you so long. Now God has brought you to me, and I'll have your flesh . . ."'

The evening went on. Riddles were told, tongue-twisters recited in Suqutri, English and San'ani Arabic, everyone laughing at my attempts to produce a lateral sibillant. Gradually, conversation changed to Suqutri, then subsided, until you could hear the beating of moths' wings against the lamp-glass.

★

Kevin edged closer to the bush, camera poised. The snake lay coiled and motionless, its grey and orange stripes camouflaging it against the twig shadows and sand. The lens was inches from it. 'They did say there weren't any poisonous snakes in Suqutra . . . ,' he whispered, without turning his head, '. . . didn't they?'

'Yes, but I'm taking no responsibility for . . .'

The shutter clicked, the snake reared, swayed, then looped off. We found out later that it was a harmless desert boa, probably of the type called *Eryx jayakeri*.

So this was the Nujad Plain, Salim's land of rich pastures: a dry waste of dunes and low bushes.

We had set off early along the beach, then struck inland for Mahattat Nujad. 'It's an hour and a half if you take it easy. And Mahattat Nujad is *full* of shops. And cars. You'll have no problems getting a ride to Hadibu,' Salim told us. Five hot hours later we arrived at Mahattat Nujad. We had lunch – *rawbah*-soaked rice and dates followed by tea in old bean tins – in the police station, a room with half a dozen iron beds and a few well-gnawed foam mattresses. After the meal, we asked the policemen if there was a car to Hadibu.

'There may be one.' The 'may' was ominous. 'In a couple of days.' And shops?

One of the policemen sprang to attention. 'What would you like?'

'What is there?'

'Biscuits.'

'Anything else?'

'No. Just biscuits.'

The policemen directed us to Halmah, another three hours to the east, which they said was *full* of cars and shops.

We passed the great palmeries of al-Qa'r, then re-entered scrub and dune country. Not long after the snake encounter, we saw a large settlement and headed straight for it, abandoning attempts to follow the track. At last, nine hours after leaving Sitayruh, we arrived in the village of Halmah. Some children were playing in a dry *wadi* bed; when they saw us they ran, blubbing, for the village. We followed them and found a pick-up. One of its wheels was off and a man was belabouring the hub with a spanner. Yes, he was going to Hadibu in the morning, if he could fix the wheel; we should stay the night with him.

Ali Shayif was a Dali'i from north of Aden who had come to Suqutra on military service, married a local girl, and stayed. He was part-owner of a fishing-*hawri* but now most of his income came from trucking. His sole reason for settling here was that he liked the place; in this he probably resembled generations of outsiders who, like Salim, Hadid and their forebears, have been enchanted by the island and have intermingled with the coastal population. 'The real Suqutris', Ali said, 'are the mountain *badw*.' He went on to repeat the story about the blue-eyed tribe of Shilhal. Hadibu, he said, was full of slaves.

That evening Kevin and I bathed at a well just outside the village, drawing the water in a bucket made from an old inner tube and decanting it into hollowed-out boulders. Goats came and drank our bathwater, then some men joined us and the village idiot crept up and poured a bucketful over me from behind, just after I'd dressed. They went off, laughing, to pray. Back at Ali's I hung my sodden shirt and *futah* on the palm-frond enclosure fence and we stretched out in the guest room. Ali caught a tiny bird and evicted it; it was back immediately. I fell asleep listening to it fluttering in the roof beams.

★

The crossing of Suqutra to Hadibu, a direct distance of around 24 miles, took four hours. It could have been quicker, but Ali had to stop time and again to unblock his petrol filter or beef up the truck's sagging springs with wooden wedges, banged in with stones. The steering had an alarming leftward bias but no one else seemed worried. Our fellow passengers included an old man with a beard; it was patriarchally long and brightly hennaed, and with his tawny face and green crocheted cap he looked like an upside-down traffic light. A slightly younger old man had a thorn deep in his foot, and whenever we stopped he tried to excavate it, groaning, with an iron spike. There was also a young man in cool-dude denims and shades who had a Nujad mother and an Adeni father. The cargo included several engorged goatskins. These, Ali explained, contained dates which had been stoned, left in the sun for a fortnight, then trodden underfoot. The necks of the skins oozed slightly and attracted flies, as did the younger old man's foot.

We crossed the plain, heading for a break in the cliffs. Once through this, the scenery changed abruptly. The road followed a perennial stream lined with little date palms, while ranks of bottle trees marched across the slopes above. The place was full of dragonflies and pink-breasted pigeons; at intervals, herons stood staring into the water.

A series of steep switchbacks took us to a high plateau beneath the watershed. Here, there was another sudden change of scenery. The background was dominated by great humps of mountains, covered in green except where granite outcrops thrust through a scanty topsoil. Look upwards and you were in the Scottish Highlands, the Cairngorms, say, complete with shielings and thatched stone croft houses. Lower your gaze, and the vision was broken: the burns below were filled not with rowan and ash but with palms, and the foreground was a gravelly plain studded with euphorbia. It was like being in two places at once; or in Dictionary Land.

We followed another watercourse down to the eastern end of the Hadibu Plain, a great theatre crossed by *wadis* and backed on the south by a wall of gigantic granite spires, the 'raggie mountains' noted by Sir Thomas Roe. I remembered Wellsted's drawing: it had not been fanciful. Two of the spires appeared to be joined by a bridge. Altogether, it was a most unlikely skyline.

Hadibu itself is a functional place. Its buildings are uniformly cuboid, except for the Communications Office, an edifice in late twentieth-century quasi-San'ani style with coloured glass fanlights. It was a reminder of where central power resides; architecturally, it was wholly out of place, and at the time it wasn't even working as there was no fuel to power the generator. We cadged our way into the government rest-house. Some of its fittings had come from a wrecked German freighter. It had all the charm of a reform-school dormitory, and little of the hygiene. Goats wandered, farting, along the dark corridors.

'That's funny,' said Kevin. 'I'm sure I can hear a circular saw.' Then we realized what the sound was: mosquitoes, clouds of them. It was still daytime. The whine was continual, and at sunset it rose in a crescendo that possessed your skull. The best feature of the rest-house was a powerful shower, but even under this there was no escape from the mosquitoes, which had developed the ability to fly between the streams of water.

We were surprised to discover some other *nasrani* guests – a pair of Frenchmen. When they said they were entomologists we thought they were joking. In fact they were deadly serious – a glimpse inside their room revealed a row of killing-bottles and swathes of netting. They were also equipped with the latest footwear and rucksacks and, according to their Suqutri guide, ate nothing but pills.

Hadibu's main interest lies in its being a meeting place for all the elements that make up Suqutri society. There were traders with mainland ancestry, fishermen, and mountain *badw* with bare feet, knotty calves and shocks of hair; but no blue eyes. Many of the town's resident population are negroes descended from sultanic slaves, and one of these took us to the palace of the last ruler, Sultan Isa bin Ali.

'Palace' is a misnomer for such a modest building. All the same, its former inhabitants had a distinguished history. As long ago as the time of the *Periplus*, Suqutra was subject to the King of the Incense Land, an area which overlapped with much of the territory under the later Mahri Sultanate of Qishn and Suqutra. The sultanic family themselves, the Al Afrar, are of Himyari origin and had been prominent at least since medieval times. The family tree, however, was very nearly extirpated in the sixteenth century when the expansionist Hadrami ruler Badr Bu Tuwayraq murdered all the Al Afrar males but one, as yet unborn. The child's mother preserved some of his dead father's blood and, when he was old enough, showed it to him to instill the spirit of revenge. Grown to manhood, he took a vow of celibacy which he would only break if he defeated the Hadramis. He also refused to shave, and as a result became known as Abu Shawarib, Father of Moustaches. Eventually, the blood feud was successful and in celebration Abu Shawarib had his first shave at Friday prayers in the mosque of Qishn. His vow of celibacy he broke more privately, and his descendants ruled on the Mahri mainland and Suqutra for the next four hundred years.

The last sultan was – despite his martial ancestry – a mild and undistinguished-looking man. He bothered little about the more modern accoutrements of state. It is said that, in the absence of a sultanic seal, he stamped the scraps of paper which did for his subjects' passports with the bottom of a coffee cup. Photographs taken during a British administrator's visit in the early 1960s show him peering warily from beneath an enormous Saudi *iqal*, surrounded by a handful of courtiers and flunkeys. These included the executioner, a huge slave with severe scrotal elephantiasis. The Sultan's procreative powers were considerable: one of Naumkin's informants, a daughter of Sultan Isa who now works as a midwife, stated that she had one full brother and twenty-six half-siblings on the island alone, not counting those who had emigrated after 1967. The Al Afrar were making up for nearly getting wiped out.

As we neared the sea, the houses, built of coral stone, became more ramshackle and lost themselves among the palm groves. The palms, in turn, ran into the water in a maze of dead-ends and paths where we had to wade through little estuaries. Some of the houses had miniature gardens growing a few tobacco plants, carefully fenced off from the omnipresent goat. There was a perplexing lack of demarcation between land and sea, an amphibious mingling of humus and spume.

Back in the main street a crowd had gathered, and I squeezed in to see what had drawn them. A man was butchering an upturned turtle, slicing round the carapace as if opening a can. In deference to Islamic precepts he had cut its throat, but inexpertly, and every so often the turtle gulped and waved its flippers. There was a strong sea-smell, and I remembered the pale, graceful creatures gliding beneath the *sambuq* off Sitayruh. They would eat the meat; the shell, which in the days of the *Periplus* would have been exported to the cabinet-makers of Rome or Alexandria, was going to be the roof of a chicken coop.

★

The 'raggie mountains' beckoned, and next day we crossed the arena of the Hadibu Plain. At the foot of the great shattered grandstand that backed it the going got rougher; the Hajhir peaks, said to be one of the oldest bits of exposed land on Earth, are of granite, but with a limestone topping that has crumbled and fallen like icing from a badly cut wedding cake. Fragments as big as houses, riddled by erosion, were home to shaggy goats which sat eyeing us from their niches like dowagers in opera boxes.

We made for a gap far above. As we climbed, the vegetation grew denser, streams appeared in unexpected clefts, and now and again one of us would exclaim at some new discovery, a spider's web constructed on perfect Euclidean principles or a caterpillar in poster-paint colours. But it was the plants that fascinated us most. Whatever the Darwinian equations in force here, they had produced fantastical results. Nondescript bushes erupted into bunches of asparagus, trees turned into organ pipes then chimney-sweeps' brooms, begonia-like flowers sprang from pairs of enormous conjoined boxers' ears, whisky stills grew on the rocky crags. It was the botanical equivalent of Dictionary Land, the semantic jungle.

Sap, juice, resin and gum exude from branches and leaves so fleshy they often suggest the animal more than the vegetable. Several species are edible. There are tamarinds, grape-like berries, wild pomegranates and wild oranges. The last are a long way from their sweet mainland cousins: eating one is like biting into a battery. Frankincense and myrrh made Suqutra an important outpost of the thuriferous mainland regions in ancient times, and other species produce everything from incense-flavoured chewing gum to a kind of birdlime; Douglas Botting, leader of an Oxford University expedition to the island in the 1950s, noted that the juice of a certain euphorbia causes baldness, and was used to punish convicted prostitutes. Medicinal plants abound and the Suqutris use them regularly to treat scorpion stings, rashes and wounds. For over two millennia, one of the island's most famous products was the Suqutri aloe. Its sap gained popularity in seven-

teenth-century Europe with the rise of the East India trading companies; it was exported, packed in bladders, to the relief of many a costive Restoration bowel or itching pile.

Nearer the crest, the vegetation thinned. Limestone gave way to naked granite. Suddenly, above us and sharply outlined against a brilliant sky, there appeared what at first seemed to be a line of giant conical funnels, their narrow ends stuck in the skyline. The upturned cones resolved as we got closer into branches, topped with spiky leaves and bursting out of a central trunk like fan-vaulting in a chapter house. Even after all the other weird flora, the sight was startling: it is with good reason that this, the dragon's blood tree, has become Suqutra's unofficial emblem. Botanically, and by one of those evolutionary quirks that makes the rock hyrax a cousin of the elephant, *Dracaena cinnabari* is a member of the Lily family. The common name, according to Pliny, derives from blood shed during a fight between an elephant and a dragon, from which the trees sprang. The story seems to be drawn from Hindu mythology, which might explain the *Periplus's* reference to 'cinnabar, that called Indian which is collected in drops from trees'. Perhaps in the Arabic name, *dam al-akhawayn*, the blood of the two brothers, there is an echo of Castor and Pollux, the twin sons of Zeus whose epithet, Dioskurides, is by

coincidence the Classical geographers' name for Suqutra. The etymology, complex as it is, seems to bear out other evidence of the
island's early trade. Dragon's blood was formerly in great demand
as an ingredient of various dyes, including those used in violin
varnish and the palates of dentures; medieval European scribes
made ink from it, and Chinese cabinet-makers used it in the
famous cinnabar lacquer. Now, consumption is almost entirely
local – the Suqutris use it to decorate pots and as a remedy for eye
and skin diseases.

I climbed one of the larger trees, perhaps twenty feet tall to the
flat bristly top of its canopy. Its smooth bark was marked by scabs
where the resin had oozed out and coagulated. In one of the
highest branches I found a tiny lump that had been missed by the
harvesters. It was globular and brick-red, the outside matt, the
inner face glassy where it had been stuck to the tree. I turned it
over in my palm; then remembered the blood of the Arabian
dragon in my father's bureau.

★

On the far side of the col a valley opened out. We were at the head
of Wadi Ayhaft, which drains down to the north coast west of
Hadibu. The deep green of montane forest was framed by glittering granite. It was late afternoon, and we chose a campsite in a
grassy meadow near a spring. The first mosquitoes were biting,
and as I set up camp – by spreading an opened-out grain sack –
Kevin went off in search of dead wood. A fire, he said, would keep
the insects away. Half an hour later, he'd collected a good pile and
arranged it into kindling, twigs and larger branches.

'Where's your lighter?'

I looked in my pockets. It wasn't there. I hunted round the
campsite. 'I must have dropped it when I climbed the tree.' We
looked up to the ridge, disappearing in the failing light.

'Forget it,' Kevin said. He was silent for a long time.

The first thing I saw when I awoke at dawn, stiff with cold and
dew, was my lighter lying in the grass beside me. Strangely, we
were unbitten except for my left eyelid, which had swollen almost
shut. I tried unsuccessfully to prop it open with a twig. Visual
memories of that morning are therefore monocular, as if the

mountains had been flattened into a painted set. But reality became painfully three-dimensional as we tried to climb the far side of the valley, making for a plateau that lay above. There seemed to be no path, and in the end the gradient and dense undergrowth defeated us and we retraced our steps.

Further down the *wadi* we rested in a dappled clearing between silver-barked trees, where the air was scented with mint and aniseed and the river tumbled below. It had the intense clarity of a Pre-Raphaelite landscape. But on closer inspection, everything was wrong. Upward-pointing leaves became fingers, as though a fleeing nymph had been caught, supplicating, in mid-metamorphosis. Brush your hand against that plant and it stung like a wasp. It was Arcadia but, again, unknown and disturbing. A feral goat came and watched us through slitty irises.

The valley broadened into parkland, but with great gnarled tamarinds in place of oaks. It was strangely empty. Not yet the Suqutri winter, the herds were still up in their high pastures. In one tree someone had hung a dead wildcat, not much bigger than a fireside tom but with powerful kid-killing claws. Upside down, with its face desiccated into an eternal smirk, it was a horrible parody of the Cheshire Cat.

Although it has the advantage of being totally dogless,* Suqutra's mammalian wildlife falls short of its flora. The most interesting large mammal is the civet cat – not a cat but a member of the mongoose family. The Suqutri version is *Viverricula indica*, also known as the rasse. Civet, an ingredient of perfumes, is obtained in Suqutra by capturing the animal in a cage and then stimulating it until it produces a buttery secretion from a sac near its genitalia; it is then released to stagger off into the bush, exhausted but little wiser, as it will soon be caught again. We were curious to watch the operation, but civet production has declined in recent years and we drew a blank. Probably it was never as highly organized in Suqutra as elsewhere. A French physician, M. Poncet, mentions in

---

* Wellsted says that the dog they had on board the survey vessel *Palinurus* was often mistaken for a lion. The distinction of being the only dog to penetrate the Suqutri interior probably goes to Rappo, a huge black Newfoundland that accompanied Schweinfurth in 1881. The reaction of the Suqutris is, unfortunately, not recorded.

his *A Voyage to Aethiopia* of 1709 that the people of Emfras, in the Gondar region, kept civet catteries up to a hundred strong: 'once a week they scrape of [*sic*] an unctious matter which issues from the body with the sweat. 'Tis this excrement which they call civet, from the name of the beast.* They put it carefully into a beef's horn, which they keep well stopt.'

The parkland came to an abrupt end. The valley sides closed in again and the *wadi* was all but blocked by a boulder the size of a large house. This, we realized, was what it was: the hollow under-side was partly walled off and domestic objects – skins, a jerrycan, a mattress, blankets, clothes – hung at the entrance. We called but no one was at home. Inside, the ceiling was blackened by generations of cooking, and a battered tartan suitcase lay open on the floor. A side niche contained a padlocked green tin trunk. Some Suqutri herdsmen lead permanently troglodyte lives – the 1994 Yemeni census form included 'cave' under 'Type of Accommodation' – but this was a seasonal dwelling which would be occupied in the winter months only. Judging by the three criteria estate agents use to assess the value of a property – location, location and location – this one, situated above a waterfall with dwarf palms below, was truly desirable.

Kevin and I explored the theme of troglodytism as we skinny-dipped in a pool beneath the palms. We would move to Suqutra, find a cave, grow our hair, and live wild on goats, tamarinds and pomegranates. We fantasized about reviving the civet industry and installing little luxuries in our grotto: octophonic CD systems, tropical fish tanks, central vacuum cleaning, a Steinway grand. Alternatively, I would become a professional hermit; Kevin, as my agent, would tout for custom from the cruise ships, and tourists would part with hard cash to hear me spouting Delphic drivel out of a matted beard. With the right sort of PR and an appearance in *National Geographic* I would eventually be able to move to California, where grateful disciples would give me Cadillacs and clamour for phials of my used bathwater.

At the time, we were unaware of the flip-side of Suqutri rural

---

* In fact it is the other way round, 'civet' having entered the European languages from the Arabic *zabad*, itself from the root connected with butter.

life, the notorious *di-asar*, a fly which causes a potentially fatal infection by laying its eggs in the nose and throat at certain seasons. People protect themselves by wearing face-masks and amuletic beads, or by stuffing their beards into their mouths. No deaths have been recorded, so the prophylaxis must work.

We daydreamed the hot hours away until we realized that, with ten miles still to go back to Hadibu, we had to move fast. All the way down the *wadi* and along the coast Kevin, who had cave-dwelling on the brain, sang snatches of 'Wild Thing' by the Trogs.

For the coastal stretch we were following Hadibu's airport road, probably the worst airport road on Earth. Past Qadub, it fords inlets of the sea and climbs an appallingly steep pass up to the cliffs of Ra's Haybaq, the Suqutri Tarpeian Rock from which witches were hurled. More cliffs tower above, riddled with caves; and between them, the bottle trees and the sea, the unsurfaced track is hardly less narrow than when Wellsted came this way: 'A meeting of two camels on such a spot at night could scarcely fail to be fatal to one, or both.' When you finally descend to sea-level again, the air is full of spray from the breakers that boom and crash in the undercut shore.

It was night when we reached the rest-house. The French entomologists had buzzed off on the morning flight, to be replaced by a lugubrious one-man *wafd*, or delegation, from the Ministry of the Interior. He divided his time between moaning on his bed, playing patience, and visiting the Hadibu pharmacy to get remedies for nausea, malaria, liver dysfunction, and an abrasion on the knee caused, he said, 'by violent contact with a car door'. He was not enjoying his visit.

★

A few miles east of Hadibu, along a shore that crunches with a litter of shells and coral, lies the village of Suq, the island's original commercial centre. Proof that it was so in ancient times came from excavations carried out by a Yemeni-Soviet team of archaeologists, who discovered fragments of a Roman amphora and other, possibly Indian, imported wares. Suq was still Suqutra's capital when the Portuguese decided to occupy the island in 1507.

We had come to visit the fort of St Michael, which the

Portuguese captured from a Mahri garrison and rebuilt. It lies on a spur of Jabal Hawari, the eastern limit of Hadibu Bay. Most of the inhabitants of Suq seemed unaware of its existence, but eventually a boy showed us the way. A scramble up a rough track brought us to a flattish area filled with the remains of a cistern, bastions and walls with rough lime-plaster facing that reminded Kevin of Albuquerque's fort at Malacca. The ruins are unprepossessing but the view over Hadibu Plain is panoramic: below us, palms crowded round a lagoon where a *wadi* met the sea; eastwards stretched a broad bay backed by dunes, while in the opposite direction were the little gable-ended thatched houses of Suq and, in the distance, the palms and houses of Hadibu; to the south, a thick cloud blanket was pierced by the Hajhir spires; in front of us lay the ocean.

It seemed incredible that this was just one of an immensely long chain of coastal and island forts stretching from Mozambique via Muscat and the Malabar Coast all the way to the East Indies – that, for a few decades, the Indian Ocean had been a Portuguese lake. In the history of empires, this was one of the shortest-lived, an over-blown thing like the monastery of Belem, outside Lisbon, where sober Gothic suddenly burst out in a Manueline nautical panoply of prows, poops, hawsers, anchors and dolphins – a building that stands as an allegory of the strange mix of crusading Christianity and naked capitalist expansion which propelled Iberians across the Old and New Worlds.

In Suqutra, the Portuguese expected to find a ready-made outpost of Christendom – the Gospels are said to have been brought by St Thomas, *en route* for India, while a sixth-century visitor from Egypt, the monk Cosmos Indicopleustes, noted that the Suqutris were Nestorian Christians of Greek origin.* But after a thousand years of increasing isolation, what the Portuguese found was not a long-lost and innocent version of Christianity but a syncretic nightmare. In a report to Rome, written after his visit in 1542, Francis Xavier complained that the Suqutris practised circumcision and that their forms of service had decayed into

---

* Qalansiyah, where we first landed, probably gets its name – like San'a's al-Qalis – from the Greek *ecclesia*.

mumbo-jumbo incomprehensible even to their priests; in the following century, the Carmelite Padre Vincenzo commented that the islanders named all their women Maria, prayed to the moon for rain, and buttered their altars.

Moreover, the island was controlled by the Muslim 'Fartaquins' (Mahris – named after Ra's Fartak in Mahri territory), and the Suqutris, preferring the devil they knew, offered no assistance to their new would-be masters. For a few years a Portuguese garrison mouldered unprovisioned up on its redoubt, until Suqutra was given up as a bad job. St Michael reverted to the Fartaquins, and Our Lady of Victory, the church which the invaders had converted from a mosque, returned to the embrace of Islam. Its plaster floor and column bases, excavated in the 1960s, were visible down below.*

Following this abortive occupation Suqutra, on the whole, eluded the imperialist grasp – though never quite as spectacularly as when it vanished out of sight of the Ayyubid fleet. The Portuguese returned on and off but never stayed; the Omanis attacked half-heartedly in 1669; the British tried it out as a coaling station before deciding on Aden, but their garrison succumbed to fever; the British Secretary of State for India suggested in 1943 that it might become an 'adjunct' to the Jewish state in Palestine and was told by the Colonial Secretary, in as many words, not to be such a bloody ass. The Suqutris of the interior, meanwhile, went on as before, collecting dragon's blood and aloes, and milking their goats.

★

It was as if the Portuguese had been and gone and left nothing. Or had they? There were the blue-eyed people of Shilhal. Or could they be an even older genetic throwback, connected with the claim of Cosmos and later writers that the island had been colonized by Greeks? We hired another Salim, the owner of a battered

---

* The Englishman John Jourdain, who visited Yemen in the early seventeenth century, gives a vivid picture of Portuguese decline. In Ta'izz he passed his time with 'an old blind Portugall renegado witch', who was considered a saint by the local inhabitants and consequently was in demand for his blessings and pious incantations. In private, however, the Portuguese 'would burst out in laughing to me, sayinge . . . hee was noe other than a divell'.

green Landcruiser, to take us as far east as possible. We would finish the journey to Shilhal on foot.

There are no petrol stations on Suqutra – you just knock on a door and fill a jerrycan, if you're lucky. Petrol is in short supply because of the difficulty of importing it, and costs up to five times the official rate in San'a; the cost of hiring a car is correspondingly high. After a lengthy tour of downtown Hadibu, we had a full tank and had also picked up a Hadrami, an official of the Central Organization for Control and Auditing, who wanted to come for the ride. The Hadrami said that hard statistical facts were difficult to come by on the island, although when I asked him how many cars he thought there were he replied, without hesitation, 'Three hundred and one.' Considering vehicles had to be brought to Suqutra lashed to the decks of *sambuqs* and then rafted ashore, it seemed a lot. Whatever the true figure, most were laid up through lack of fuel and spare parts.

An hour out of Hadibu, we were up on the high rolling moors, heading east under low cloud. Occasionally the cloud parted to light up a distant peak or hamlet, but at the village of Ifsir the rain set in, thick and wet. Here lived Salim's sister, so there was another slaughter, another massive lunch of meat, rice and *rawbah*. Outside on the grassy roofs Egyptian vultures sat hunched against the rain; at every settlement here they sit and wait, ruffling their grubby plumage, patiently watching the houses until someone makes for the spot used as a public latrine. After he has defecated, the vultures gobble it up: a happy symbiosis but unnerving, for they encircle you as you squat, edging closer and closer.

From Ifsir to Kitab and Aryant the rain fell hard, turning the red road to mud and making the Landcruiser slip on the pass up to the higher plateau. But by the time we reached our destination, the village of Qadaminhuh, the rain had stopped. Kevin and I were dropped at a newly built house and wandered off into the sodden landscape while Salim went to find the owner.

Qadaminhuh is also known as Schools, from the big quadrangle of incongruous barrack-like buildings next to it. Here, a hundred or so weekly boarders live and study, boys from across this eastern region of Mumi. As we walked down the track towards the schools a fitful light broke through the cloud and a rainbow materialized.

240

The place seemed deserted, but then a figure appeared from a doorway and headed towards us. He was dark-skinned and tall, clearly not a Suqutri, and before we could greet him he spread his arms in a wide sweep that took in the plain, the low surrounding hills and the rainbow, and said in rich and unaccented English, 'Welcome to our . . . *humble* surroundings!'

Muhammad was an Adeni high-school graduate sent to do his obligatory teaching service on Suqutra. At first he had thought of it as a punishment posting. But up here in Mumi, he said, the scenery was so beautiful, the people so kind that you might imagine yourself in England. I agreed that even if the nearest country, in a direct line, was Somalia, you might be forgiven for thinking you were in northern Europe. 'But in England you couldn't just turn up on someone's doorstep and stay for the night.' Not in England, but perhaps further north. Again, I found myself remembering my months in the Outer Hebrides.

The rain – that at least could be English – came on again with sudden force. We shouted goodbye to Muhammad and ran for the house. Like the other houses of Mumi, this one was built of dry-stone and plastered on the inside with mud. Two columns supported a roof of irregular branches fitted together with great skill, and in the corners squinches were formed from wishbone-shaped boughs.

Sa'd, our host, expressed no surprise that two total strangers should be billeted on him. 'It's our custom,' he said simply. In spite of his protests, Salim and the auditor left to drive back to Hadibu in the dark. We asked Sa'd about the blue-eyed people of Shilhal; he, too, was sceptical, and spoke of the place – only a few miles away as the vulture flies – as if it might not have existed.

We turned in early and spent a night disturbed by fleas and bedbugs. They (or, from the insects' point of view, we) were only a taste of what was to come.

By seven the next morning we were high in the uplands under a lowering sky on the way to Shilhal. The going was hard, over sharp rocks dotted with tiny alpines. Kevin found a beetle with iridescent peacock-blue wing cases splotched orange and yellow, a furry orange head and bright green feet and feelers; as it was dead he put it in his shirt pocket. Every so often we had to cross low walls of misshapen lichen-covered stones that were clearly very old: some authorities have taken them to be the ancient boundaries of incense plantations, but in fact they marked out claims allotted by the Sultan for the harvesting of aloes. The Bents, who visited Suqutra in the 1890s and must have seen them under the same grey sky, commented that 'the miles of walls . . . give to the country somewhat the aspect of the Yorkshire wolds'. Once more, the sense of displacement was extraordinary.

We crossed a little dale, filled with basil and lemon-scented herbs, where we breakfasted on unripe tamarinds. Here, Kevin's beetle suddenly came back to life. He put it on a stone, where it stretched its legs and tottered about: against the grey rock, its acid-trip colour scheme made it look like an escapee from *Naked Lunch*.

The valley marked the beginning of cattle country, and up on the far top we passed a herd. Like their cousins in al-Mahrah and Dhofar, these were humpless beasts no bigger than a small donkey; one of them glared at us and pawed the ground. Progress was slow, for at each hamlet we passed we were invited in for *rawbah*, and at lunchtime we joined an apparently never-ending feast in honour of a villager just returned from the Emirates. He sat in a corner, glassy-eyed, Buddha-like, mopping his face with a towel that said 'Hawaii' in multicoloured capitals, while plate after plate was set in front of him. They had killed a calf and seemed determined to finish it at one sitting, however long it took. I thought it was the prodigious quantity of food that made the prodigal so silent, until someone whispered to me, 'He hasn't been back for twenty-five years.' It was, then, a severe case of culture shock. Or, maybe, time shock: over the last quarter-century, the Emirates had undergone as much change as Europe had over the last hundred years or more; in Mumi, almost nothing had altered. The man was like a long-term coma patient who comes round only to find that his dreams were more eventful than waking reality.

Groaning from a surfeit of *rawbah* and meat on top of green tamarinds, we set off again. Past the village of Ambali a wide, airy valley opened out. By now, the cloud had dispersed and the sun lit up lone clumps of bottle trees, megaliths with quiffs of foliage cut oblique by a sea wind. At the end of the valley the track climbed under a crag with walled caves at its base, then petered out. Before us, a few houses in a hollow, was the village of the blue-eyes: Shilhal. It looked no different from the other villages of Mumi. It felt like the end of the world.

★

'A year or two ago,' said Thani, in whose guest-house the clan of Shilhal were gathered, 'a foreign woman came here. She might have been French, or Russian. I don't know. Anyway, we were sitting round like this, talking about history, and she asked us: "Do you think your grandfathers were oranges?"'

There were tears of laughter at the memory. Thani got out of a leather pouch what looked like a clay cigar holder, then a fragment of tobacco leaf which he placed for a moment on the lamp before crumbling it and putting it in the holder. When his match refused to light I handed him my disposable lighter; he looked at it with curiosity then, shaking his head, handed it back.* A second match worked. He took a single long drag then went on. 'Then she said, "I mean the people, not the fruit." You see, "oranges" and "Portuguese" sound the same in Arabic.'

'So what do you think – have you got any Portuguese blood?' I asked. In build the people of Shilhal looked the same as the other mountain Suqutris we had met; but a few of them did have fairer skins, and there were undeniably striking eyes that ranged between green and light hazel. Striking enough, anyway, for reports of them to circulate and become embroidered.

A man who had so far been silent, a dashing figure, bare-chested and with a shawl thrown round his neck, replied. 'They say that we, the real Suqutris, have two ancestors. One lived here in Mumi and the other at the western end of the island. In time, people came in from outside and married with their descendants.'

I remembered the claim later, when reading Naumkin's analysis of Suqutri palm-prints and teeth. He was able to come to few firm conclusions about the islanders' origins, other than saying that they

---

* There can be few places left in the world where people are unacquainted with so ubiquitous an object. Watches appeared in the interior only recently; Wellsted, 160 years ago, had trouble persuading the Suqutris that his was not a live animal.

are a mixture. However, he goes on, the inhabitants of the western and eastern highlands are both 'mutually similar' and markedly different from other groups. Linguistically, he puts forward the hypothesis that Suqutri became isolated from the ancient South Arabian languages at some time between 1000 and 500 BC – well before Mahri and other related tongues. This suggests a rough date for the settlement of the island by groups from the mainland.

It is probably true to say, then, that here – in these isolated communities on an isolated chunk of land – are the people who are closest to the first sons of Qahtan: true ancient naturals, whom the genealogists digging for Qahtani roots had overlooked.

Schweinfurth went so far as to call them 'the last real South Arabians'. Recalling the similarity between the singing figurehead on the *sambuq* and the earliest Sabaean portraits, I wondered if he might not have been exaggerating.

As for Portuguese forebears – if there ever were any in Shilhal – time has obliterated all memory of them.

Talk was reverting to Suqutri. I was interested to hear some Suqutri poetry and asked the Shilhalis if they knew any. It was the bare-chested man who answered again. 'I have a little,' he said, and chanted a *haiku*-length verse. It was received with sighs, then silence.

I asked the man what the verse meant. He smiled. 'Ah, it's about love. But I only know the words, not the meaning. I'm not a *sha'ir*, a poet.'

Then I remembered the root sense of the word: *sha'ir* – not a reciter of verses or an arranger of words, but one who was endowed with insight, one who perceived. Suqutri poetry is a dense thicket of ellipsis and metaphor. It needed a perceiver to see the way through it. Perhaps it is the language of Dictionary Land, of the wilderness of idea within the wall of words.*

I had come to Yemen to learn a language and understand a people. In Suqutra, where they spoke with the purest of ancestral

---

* Naumkin quotes an example of love poetry from Abdulkuri:
>   The nose of the woman who gave birth to her first child
>   Who forgot-you the agony
>   The bush which covered-you-it
>   The stone bush so that-would-not-stir.

voices a language I did not understand, I was back at square one. And now there was this other language, that of the non-*sha'ir* and the singing figurehead. Looking round, it had clearly moved the Suqutris; yet they could not tell me what it meant.

The mood of the gathering had changed. More pipes were lit. I had a go with Thani's. The single puff seemed to contain as much nicotine as a whole cigarette; combined with the effects of yet another meal of meat, rice and *rawbah* it made me reel with queasiness. The diet was beginning to tell.

Kevin was staring at the sinuous beams in the ceiling. I followed his gaze and noticed a single sawn timber. Thani told us it came from an old wreck.

'The sea must be very close,' Kevin said.

'Oh, about four or five hours,' Thani replied.

I sat up and looked at Kevin. It seemed impossible – we should be almost at the eastern tip of the island, and were hoping to see the sea in the morning. We could only afford to spend tomorrow here, and as we were both in bad shape ten extra hours of hard walking would be too much. The gathering broke up and we went to bed, disappointed.

To bed, but not to sleep. *Klinophilos horrifer* saw to that. This aptly named bedbug was new to science when Ogilvie-Grant squashed the first specimen in the pages of *Vanity Fair*, around the turn of the century. 'It does not bite white men,' he says. The claim is strangely unscientific; if apartheid does exist in the insect world, then this was another species. But whatever it was, it was certainly no ordinary bedbug: it *hurt*.

The morning was bright and cloudless. Down in a large stone pen the goats of Shilhal were queuing to be milked. Thani dealt with them deftly, pinioning one of each goat's back hooves under his big toe and milking her into a spherical clay pot, which he placed on a small fire of sticks. We were given a pot and drank the sweet, foaming liquid, thankful for a change from *rawbah*.

'By the way,' Thani said, 'I'm sorry I didn't give you any blankets, but they've got a few fleas in them. They come off the goats. I hope you slept well anyway.'

We checked with him about the distance to the sea. He confirmed that it was half a day's walk to reach the shore, 'More for you. But if you just want to look at it, go up there,' he added, pointing to the hill behind the village.

We made our way slowly upwards over a cracked limestone pavement. Near the top of the hill, a breeze began to buffet our faces. Then the ground vanished. A 2,000-foot cliff fell sheer to white sand, white surf, blue sea where a single speck of black, a *hawri*, hung in motionless suspense between the elements. To the right was the great dome of al-Jumjumah, the Skull, then the long promontory of Ra's Mumi, a haunt of sirens, a wrecker of ships, a scimitar cutting the ocean. *The last place in Yemen.*

★

I remember sitting above the village that afternoon under a westering sun. Light raked across ruddy earth and bald limestone, across the grassy roofs and drystone walls of Shilhal. They were bringing in the goats. I remember remembering the gathering of the sheep on Harris.

Here they buried every second baby. Treatment for many illnesses was a brand with a red-hot iron. But they had the Arabian dream, a simple pastoral existence, rich in milk and meat. In most of Arabia, as in most of Europe, the pastoral life is dead, living only in the idealized memory of a shared ancient past. Virgil described the scene at Shilhal in the *Eclogues*:

> *Ite domum saturae, venit Hesperus, ite capellae.*
> Go, my full-uddered goats, go home, for the Evening
>   Star is rising.

And, in the *Georgics*, Suqutra itself appears as the incense land of Panchaea. Virgil inherited the name from the Pharaonic Egyptians, whose Pa-anch was a Utopian island ruled by the King of the Incense Land. The myth of the island paradise – from Pa-anch through Odysseus's land of the Phaeacians and Sindbad's fabulous isles, all the way to *South Pacific* – is one of the most enduring in the world. Here, perhaps, at the end of Yemen, was its beginning.

The early genealogists, confused by reports of Greek and Indian blood, hadn't thought of digging here for their Qahtani roots. Similarly, I hadn't expected to find – in an island nearer Africa than

Arabia – such a strong sense of the identity of Yemen. To put the identity into words was harder. I had come to Yemen to understand it via its language, but the experience of hearing that snatch of poetry had made me doubt whether such an understanding were possible. What was language, as Emerson said, but fossil poetry? And, like Samuel Johnson, even if I dreamed myself a poet I was doomed to wake a lexicographer, to a magpie round of collection and collation.

But then, even lexicographers have occasional flashes of insight. I had been given a glimpse of the prototype enchanted isle, older than Serendip, antediluvian – Dictionary Land revisited; and with the strange *déjà vu* of dragon's blood I had bumped, unexpectedly, into my own childhood.

9

Venus and Mars

'We are so made, that we can only derive intense enjoyment
from a contrast, and only very little from a state of things.'
Sigmund Freud, *Civilization and its Discontents*

WE REACHED SAN'A at the time when the *qat* is finished,
when the airy castles have evaporated, the time of regrets.
Relentless as an advancing oil slick, the city was lapping at Hizyaz,
where a cairn had once marked the place of Imam Yahya's murder.
At Dar Salm I used to go out with a tommy gun and shoot cans off
cacti; now the land was being gobbled up by an insatiable suburban
tapeworm. Then the traffic jams began. Men leaned on their horns
and cursed in a dialect that was harsh and brutal. The language I
thought I had learned, and the people I had come to understand
through their language, now seemed foreign. I might have been in
Babel. What would Thani have made of San'a, this city founded
after the Flood?

Al-Razi, who compiled his great *History of the City of San'a* in
the eleventh century, littered the work with grim predictions:
San'a will fill the space between its mountains and 'there will be
no pleasure in dwelling there'; San'a will be so crowded that its
very roofs will be sold for living space; and, concluding an
immense digression on the fate of Sodom, the historian warns that
'at the end of time, God will likewise cause San'a and Aden to be
swallowed up'. There were latter-day Cassandras, too, lamenting in
the press and on the airwaves the nosediving *riyal* and the Current

Political Crisis: for months Ali Salim al-Bid, son of the Hadrami *sayyid* charm-writer, pre-Unification leader of the Marxist People's Democratic Republic and now Vice-President, had been sulking incommunicado in Aden, embittered by the loss of absolute power; Unity was at stake; there would be war . . .

I knew I loved San'a. Why then, looking out of the taxi window, was it so alien? Like Odysseus returning to Ithaca – 'Alas! Whose country have I come to now?' – I seemed not to know the place that was my home. At Bab al-Yaman I shouldered my bag, said goodbye to Kevin, and sighed for Suqutra, for sailing over the turtled ocean to a land of herdsmen and heroic feasts.

Along the narrow way to the Great Mosque, houses leaned towards each other in parallax, shutting out the sky. Noise did not penetrate. Going into the dark silence was like being swallowed by a whale. My heart pounded in my neck.

A hiss cut into the silence – a man making tea on a paraffin burner, the sweet milky tea you drink after *qat*. I sat on a metal bench and a glass was placed in front of me. And, as I drank, my heartbeat slowed. The dislocation of homecoming, which for Odysseus was caused by a jealous goddess, had been for me the work of *qat*.

After a second glass of tea, the dark and the leaning houses ceased to threaten. The traffic jams outside now seemed a necessity: without them the long afternoons chewing would be empty. The Arabs are an ambivalent people for whom pleasure only comes after its absence – and no more so than in San'a, the city founded under the contradictory influences of Venus and Mars.

My mind went back to Suqutra. It was beginning to seem less like the land of the Phaeacians, more like those other islands of the *Odyssey* where amid all the voluptuousness there is always a catch. In Suqutra the snag was the lack of health facilities, essential foods and communications. The myth of the island paradise has bewitched us all. The Suqutris are the best enchanters in the world, but their island is even better. You have to turn your back on it and pinch yourself to see that cities and conflicts are the reality. Most of us – including the *qat*-chewers – live in Troy-town, not Lotus-land.

I left the maze of lanes and entered al-Zumur, the broad straight street where I live. Something was different or, rather, the same as it had always been: the street traders were back. San'a was refusing to be turned into a museum.

I shut the door of the house behind me. Even now, a smell of basil lingered on the seventy-eight stairs. (Strange, it never seems to be the same number; like the length of Hud's tomb.) Up in the belvedere on the roof, I sat and looked over the lights of the city. They licked the feet of Jabal Nuqum and Jabal Ayban. San'a was filling the space between its mountains, fulfilling its destiny.

★

At 8.10 p.m. on Wednesday, 4 May 1994, while I was in the room on the roof, the lights went out and stayed out. The night was abnormally quiet.

Since our return from Suqutra the Aden media, under Ali Salim al-Bid's direction, had been attacking the Socialists' partners in government. The two other members of the ruling coalition – the General People's Congress led by President Ali Abdullah Salih, and the Islah Party led by Shaykh Abdullah ibn Husayn al-Ahmar – had a very different background to that of al-Bid's Yemeni Socialist Party. Since the late 1960s, successive leaders of the YAR had performed a juggling act with the various elements of society – tribesmen and townsmen, progressives and conservatives. Politics had reflected this pluralist structure; rule was by consensus. In foreign relations, the YAR had taken a pragmatic and non-aligned stance: its armed forces, for example, were equipped with both US- and Soviet-supplied hardware. The PDRY, however, had thrown itself into the arms of the Eastern bloc; the hardliners who had come to power in the bloody events of 1986 in Aden ruled by coercion. Four years later, their Eastern European counterparts were toppling under popular pressure, and al-Bid's agreement to a merger of the two Yemens in 1990 had less to do with a desire for unity than with the need to save his own skin. By nature unable to participate in a democratic coalition, his apparent transformation from dictator to statesman was a sham.

Al-Bid did not have to wait long for an excuse to attack his coalition partners. Yemen's attempt to promote an Arab solution to the invasion of Kuwait by Iraq, only three months after

Unification, and the expulsion of Yemeni migrant workers from the Gulf States, led to a dramatic decline in national income. The YSP leader began to blame the resulting economic problems on 'reactionary northerners'. Then, in Yemen's first democratic general election of April 1993, the YSP came third; al-Bid, although he was allowed to retain the post of Vice-President, was incensed. Following a trip abroad, ostensibly for medical treatment, he arrived in Aden in August 1993. And there he stayed, refusing to participate in the business of government and ignoring all attempts at mediation. Chances of an agreement faded. Then, in a surprise meeting in Amman on 20 February 1994, Ali Abdullah Salih and Ali Salim al-Bid agreed to forget their differences. The unity of Yemen was back on track.

The Amman Accord was announced as people were breaking their Ramadan fast. In the *saltah* restaurant where I was having supper, the fast-breakers stopped eating when they heard the news; some, I noticed, had tears of joy in their eyes. The sense of relief was palpable. We all thanked God.

I arrived home elated, with a bunch of particularly good *qat* in celebration, and went to discuss the news with my neighbour the goldsmith. His face, however, was grave. 'Have you heard what's happened?' he asked.

Within minutes of the smiles and handshakes, units of the former PDRY army had opened fire on the Amaliqah Brigade of the old YAR, stationed in Abyan east of Aden. The assault was beaten off, but the Amman Accord lay in pieces. Two months later there was a repeat of the Abyan incident, when the former PDRY 3rd Armoured Brigade attacked their 1st Armoured Brigade comrades north of San'a, starting a twenty-hour tank battle in which seventy-nine were killed. Still, many Yemenis hoped against hope. The stupidity, the utter tragedy of the threatened break-up was too nightmarish to be real. About this time, trees in the region of San'a were struck by a disease that made them drop tears of sap; it was, some said, a warning – as if a warning were needed.

At dawn on 5 May the storm broke. I was awoken by an apocalyptic din and ran up to the roof: the earth was pumping out fire, the sky was a rash of tracers and explosions. On another roof nearby a lone figure was firing an assault rifle into the air. Below, dazed men were stumbling on to the street. I shouted at them over the parapet, 'What the fuck are you doing to yourselves?' No one heard.

Over the next week the air raids continued fitfully, but with no effect. It seemed that the ancient notion of San'a being a divinely protected city was true. I would sit in the room on the roof, watching the anti-aircraft fire. And then the Scuds came. The Scud missile is a weapon of terror, a monstrous airborne car bomb a stage or two up the evolutionary scale from the V2. One of them landed behind the Republican Hospital, killing or injuring 120. I visited the scene soon after. My diary reads:

> Four houses have disappeared into the ground. Others are missing entire sides. There are a lot of sightseers, all moving about in silence. A man is selling sweets from a barrow under a Rothmans umbrella. At the back of the Republican Hospital, all the windows are gone. Even the name of these missiles is terrifying: Scud – an amalgam of skim/scream/thud. Half-embedded in the dust is a woman's navy blue cardigan – like the scraps of indigo cloth sticking out of the dust at Baraqish.

But Baraqish had taken two thousand years to become a ruin. History happens more quickly now.

Kevin's house was not far from the place where the missile had landed. When the raids had started, he took his wife and children to the safety of Yorkshire. He had left the key with me, and I went to see if there was any damage. The windows and doors facing the blast had been blown in, and fallen plaster littered the courtyard. I peered into the rooms, then went down the steps into the kitchen. There, on the table, among the children's drawings and covered with a layer of dust and rat droppings, was the account of our journey to Suqutra. Before the war, I had left it with Kevin to comment on. I blew the dust off, started reading, and got as far as the second paragraph: 'It might as well have been a place in a dream.'

Now, it was not only Suqutra: the whole book seemed to be fading into unreality. I had been trying to write about the steady and ordered progress of history, and history had suddenly gone on the rampage, a beast escaped from the theme park. It was, in its way, grimly fascinating; but how would it all end? The pessimists were predicting months, maybe years, of conflict.

And then the Scuds stopped − miraculously, only two had caused casualties. Government forces were moving south, slicing through Abyan towards the coast. Resistance on the ground crumbled, although there was a heavy battering from the air. Both sides were fighting, they said, for Unity. On 20 May the President announced a unilateral three-day ceasefire to mark the Festival of Sacrifices. Al-Bid's response was to declare the secession of the southern part of Yemen and the restoration of the old border. 'The unity of Yemen', he added, paradoxically, 'remains the basic goal of the State.'

Some of Yemen's neighbours were delighted − not least the Kuwaitis, still smarting from Yemen's decision to call for an Arab solution to the 1990 invasion of their country.* The Saudi-backed MBC satellite channel, meanwhile, in what was either a flash of ghostly prescience or a ghastly PR blunder, had broadcast al-Bid reading the declaration of secession eighty minutes before the official announcement on Aden Radio.

No one, however, recognized the self-proclaimed state. In the south, such public support as al-Bid had enjoyed plummeted with the declaration to secede. Militarily, too, the rebels were losing ground. Brigade after brigade deserted; then came the fall of al-Anad, the massive Soviet-built base north of Aden. Al-Bid left for al-Mukalla and shut himself in his seaside house, blocking all incoming calls. By mid-June, communications between Aden and the outside were severed and by the end of the month the huge province of Hadramawt, where the rebels had been expected to make a last and bloody stand, had been taken. On 7 July Government forces moved without opposition into the heart of Aden. The war was over.

During the war I often recalled the old border post, out in the finger of desert beyond Marib, the place from which the early Yemenis set out to leave their names across the map. Now, those

---

* In 1993 a Kuwaiti newspaper, *Al-Siyasah*, said: 'We have lost ten billion dollars in the Gulf War, and we are ready to lose ten billion more to ensure the partition of Yemen.'

ugly cement-block buildings would, in time, disappear into the sand like Iram of the Columns, the city of Ad. Ever since the days of the incense caravans, traders and travellers, nomads, pilgrims and smugglers have passed through that barren short-cut. Even under partition, communication carried on. And if the secessionist gamble had paid off, if the border had been restored, the traffic would have continued behind the next range of dunes, or the one after. Yemenis do not abandon their ancestral routes.

★

Nearly two years on, history is back to a more regular rhythm. Down on my street, the processions come and go as San'anis bring in their brides and take out their dead. From time to time, the men from the Municipality chase off the pavement shopkeepers, who surge away, whooping, in a cohort of barrows, then skulk back with wheels squeaking. Rain also sees them off, and since the war the rain has been good. (During one heavy storm the street flowed red. Ripe tomatoes, thousands of them, were bobbing along in the flood. As I watched, a veiled woman jumped in and filled her skirts with them.) From the room on the roof, I can follow the slow climb of the outer suburbs up the mountains; nearer to hand is a roofscape of sprouting satellite dishes which contrive, now, to look like dragon's blood trees.

At night, sitting in my belvedere, I sometimes revisit that other Dictionary Land. There are still discoveries to be made there: *laqayt minhu banat awbar*, 'I have experienced many a disappointment from his part', literally, 'he has given me small and bad truffles', or, even more literally, 'I have received from him the daughters of a furry one'; *dabbab*, 'to feed another with butter and rob', cognate with *dabub*, 'to abound in lizards (land)' and *adabb*, 'to be misty (day), to be numerous, to remain silent, to speak, to scream'; *qarqar*, 'Grumbling loudly (camel). Be quiet! (said to a woman)'; *sinn*, 'Basket. Urine of the hyrax'. And Dictionary Land is, like the universe, continually expanding. I suppose I am responsible for a recent addition, a word that appears in neither the lexica nor the works on dialect: *bartan*, cognate with Britani, 'to speak about strange matters, to speak at length'.

And when I'm done exploring I close the dictionary, switch off the lights, and look out of the window. All around, marked by panels of coloured glass, late chewers sit in other belvederes, high above the noise of the street, hard by heaven like the lords of Ghumdan.

Glossary

abayah	A loose-fitting over-garment of flimsy material
Abbasids	Dynasty of caliphs whose ancestor, Abbas, was the Prophet Muhammad's paternal uncle. Their capital was Baghdad, where they ruled from 750 until 1258 when they were overthrown by Mongol invaders. Despite their claim as caliphs – *khalifahs*, or successors, of the Prophet – to be the leaders of the entire Muslim world, the Abbasids' authority began to wane almost from the start; from the ninth century onward local rulers in many Islamic lands, including Yemen, asserted their independence.
abu/abi	Father (of); possessor of, as in Abu Shawarib, '(the man) with the moustaches'. Often appears as a component of names
Ad	The prehistoric People of Ad, or Adites, are often mentioned in the Qur'an. They lived in al-Ahqaf, a region identified with the area around Wadi Hadramawt. The Adites – and their fabulously wealthy capital, Iram of the Columns – were destroyed by God when they refused to worship Him, as commanded by the Prophet Hud.
Adnanis	The name given by traditional genealogists to Arabs of northern origin. Their ancestor was Adnan, a descendant of Isma'il b. Ibrahim (Ishmael the son of Abraham).
Al	Family, clan, as in Al Afrar. Not to be confused with the definite article, *al–*
ali	'Mechanical'. The usual name for the AK47 assault rifle
ambar	Ambergris
asid	Porridge of sorghum flour, usually eaten with broth and clarified butter. A traditional food of the highlands
asr	Afternoon (prayers)
atlal	Traces of an abandoned dwelling or encampment. A frequent subject of amatory verse
Ayyubids	A medieval dynasty named after Ayyub, a Kurd originally from Armenia.

Glossary

In 1171/2, his son Salah al-Din (Saladin) ousted the Fatimid Caliphate in Egypt. A year later, Salah al-Din's brother Turanshah led an expedition to Yemen, probably for both political and commercial reasons. He occupied Tihamah, Aden and Ta'izz; San'a was taken by another brother, Tughtakin, in 1189/90. The Ayyubids were able to bring a degree of unity to Yemen, which at the time was split between a number of local powers; but their rule was precarious, and ended with the departure of the last Ayyubid sultan in 1228/9. The deputy to whom he entrusted the affairs of Yemen declared independence and founded the Rasulid dynasty.

Ba	A common component of Hadrami family names, like Ba Abbad
bab	Door, gateway
badw	Rural people, nomads, 'bedouin'
baghiyyah	A grade of honey, literally 'an object of desire'
baghlah	A large ocean-going sailing vessel of the Arabian Gulf. Literally 'a she-mule', the word probably derives from the Latin *vascellum* via Spanish-Portuguese *bajel*. It entered English as 'buggalow'.
banu/bani	Descendants (of). Used to denote a tribe or subsection of a tribe, a tribal territory, and occasionally a dynasty
bara'	A display of steps (not, strictly speaking, a dance), performed to the beating of drums
barakah	Blessing emanating from God, which may be transmitted through particularly pious individuals or places associated with them
bayt	House. Often used to mean 'family', and as a component of the names of villages, like Bayt Ma'din
bin	Son (of). See also *ibn*
dar	Large house, palace, as in Dar al-Hajar. Occasionally a component of the names of villages, like Dar Salm
da'wah	Call, summons, invitation. Also the announcement that one is standing as a candidate for the imamate
Dhu/Dhi	Possessor of, endowed with. Often appears in the names of pre-Islamic notables, like Sayf ibn Dhi Yazan; and sometimes in the names of tribes, like Dhu Muhammad
fils	A small coin (from the Greek *obolos*)
funduq	Hotel, inn (from the Greek *pandokheion*)
futah	A sewn waist-cloth, sarong
ghayl	A flowing stream; a man-made water channel, often partially subterranean
Hadramawt	The Kingdom of Hadramawt seems to have been an ally or vassal of Saba

until the fourth century BC, when it became independent. From its capital, Shabwah (known to Classical writers as Sabota), it controlled the production of frankincense; its wealth enabled it to become an expansionist military power. At the beginning of the third century AD it was defeated by the Sabaean army, and towards the end of the century was absorbed, like Saba itself, into the Kingdom of Himyar.

halal Permitted in religious law (the opposite of *haram*)

hani'an 'May you [have] enjoy[ed] it!' – in reference to food or drink. Often said when someone belches after a meal

harish Porridge of coarsely ground wheat, eaten with clarified butter and, on special occasions, honey

hawri A small boat of narrow beam, similar in shape to a canoe

hijrah Protected, inviolable place or person. Used for enclaves reserved for religious study and/or trade, and for persons who may not be attacked in a dispute. Any violation of a *hijrah* will incur the severest penalties. The Hijrah of the Prophet Muhammad was his migration from Mecca to al-Madinah.

Himyar Name of a people and of the last great power of pre-Islamic Yemen. The Himyaris descend, according to traditional genealogy, from Himyar b. Saba. Their power-base was in the southern highlands of Yemen; their capital was Zafar, near Yarim. The decline of overland trade in the last centuries before the Christian era, together with the rise in maritime commerce, prompted the Himyaris to develop ports along the Red Sea coast of Yemen. By the first century AD they had become a military power and were contesting the Sabaean royal title. At the end of the third century, they finally succeeded in overthrowing the Sabaeans and absorbed the Kingdom of Hadramawt. Later attempts to enlarge their domains are attested by a Himyari inscription of the early fifth century, found in Central Arabia. The dynasty effectively ended with the Ethiopian invasion a century later.

ibn Son (of). Often abbreviated to 'b.'. Appears as a component of personal names, like Ibn al-Mujawir. See also *bin*

Idrisis In 1909/10, Muhammad b. Ali al-Idrisi – a descendant of the Idrisi *sharifs* who had ruled in tenth-century Morocco – set himself up as an independent ruler in Asir. With the end of the First World War and the expulsion of the Ottomans from Yemen, he occupied part of Tihamah including the port of al-Hudaydah. In this the British supported him, but he was ousted by Imam Yahya when British backing was withdrawn in 1925.

ilb *Zizyphus spina-Christi*, the jujube tree. Valuable as a source of timber and fruit (the small berries are called *dawm*), and as a source of food for bees

Glossary

Imam   The title held by the leaders of various Shi'ah groups. Also a leader of prayers.

In Yemen, the imams of the Zaydi sect (the most moderate of all Shi'ah groups, named after a third-generation descendant of the Prophet Muhammad's daughter, Fatimah, and his cousin Ali b. Abi Talib) proved to be the most enduring power in Islamic times. The Zaydi imam was both spiritual and temporal ruler; although any suitably qualified descendant of Ali and Fatimah could make a bid for the title, in practice it often remained within one *sayyid* family for several generations. The imamate lasted from 897 until the Revolution of 1962, reaching its zenith under al-Mutawakkil Isma'il (ruled 1644–76): he controlled the whole of present-day Yemen, and his spiritual suzerainty was recognized as far away as Yanbu' in the northern Hijaz. For much of its history, however, the imamate was in conflict with other powers, both internal and external, and its real authority was often limited to the north-western part of Yemen. The capital of the imamate varied according to political events and to the whims of individual imams; later holders of the title usually resided in San'a.

iqal   A cord of camel hair used to keep the headscarf in place. Not worn by Yemenis

jabal   Mountain, mountain range

jambiyah   A curved dagger, literally a 'side-arm' but worn most often in the middle, over the stomach

jinn   The third group of rational beings, along with men and angels. The *jinn* (singular *jinni*) are invisible to mortals, but can affect their lives

Kathiris   A tribe originally prominent in Dhofar. In the sixteenth century, their leader Badr Bu Tuwayraq conquered extensive territories in Hadramawt and inaugurated the Kathiri Sultanate. Subsequently, much of their land was lost, particularly to the Qu'aytis in the nineteenth century, although the Kathiris retained Say'un as their capital. The last Kathiri ruler was deposed after the British withdrawal in 1967.

kidam   Leavened bread rolls of Turkish origin, made of a mixture of different types of grain

lukanda   A dormitory or doss-house (from the Italian *locanda*). The cheapest form of overnight accommodation

mafraj   A large room for entertaining guests, situated either at the top of a house or at ground level. In the latter case, the *mafraj* opens on to a pool with fountains.

Ma'in   A pre-Islamic state in Wadi al-Jawf. Once believed to be older than Saba, it is now thought that the Ma'inians (also known as Minaeans) broke away from the larger state towards the end of the fifth century BC and remained independent for some 250 years. Although Ma'in appears not to have been a military power, its commercial influence is evident from the existence of a trading colony set up by Ma'inians in the far north-west of Arabia, and from inscriptions found in Egypt and the Aegean.

Mamluks	The word, which means 'owned' or 'possessed', generally refers to slave-soldiers of European or Asian origin. Mamluk dynasties ruled in Egypt and the Levant from the mid-thirteenth century until 1517, when they were overthrown by the Ottomans. In 1516 a body of Mamluks, fleeing from the Ottoman advance, took control of the Yemeni island of Kamaran; from there they occupied Tihamah and many other parts of the country including, briefly, San'a. The success of their short-lived expedition, which effectively ended the power of the Tahirids, was largely due to their use of firearms.
mizmar	The double reed-pipe, the most common musical instrument in country regions
mutur	Motor cycle
nabi	Prophet
nakhudhah	A ship's captain (from the Persian *naw khuda*)
nasrani	Properly, a Christian, but often used in Yemen to mean 'a Western foreigner' (hence one may be asked if there are Jewish *nasranis*)
nawbah	A round tower
nurah	Lime plaster
Ottomans	Turkish dynasty taking its name from Uthman, a fourteenth-century leader of the Ghuzz Turks in Asia Minor. In 1538 the Ottomans occupied Aden and began taking over Lower Yemen and Tihamah. San'a, however, was not captured until 1547. Yemeni resistance to the Ottomans, under Imam al-Qasim and his son Imam al-Mu'ayyad, resulted in their expulsion in 1636. The mid-nineteenth century saw renewed Ottoman expansion in Arabia. At first, their presence in Yemen was limited to Tihamah, but reinforcements sent by way of the newly opened Suez Canal were able to take San'a in 1872. Some twenty years later, Yemeni resistance united under Imam Muhammad Hamid al-Din; it continued under his son Imam Yahya, with whom the Turks signed a power-sharing agreement in 1911. Following their defeat in the First World War the Ottomans left Yemen, although some Turkish officials stayed on to work in Imam Yahya's administration. During both occupations, Ottoman authority was largely limited to the cities.
PDRY	The People's Democratic Republic of Yemen (originally the People's Republic of South Yemen) came into being with the British withdrawal from Aden on 30 November 1967. It ceased to exist on 22 May 1990, when it merged with the YAR (Yemen Arab Republic) to form the unified Republic of Yemen.

Glossary

qa'	A plain. The word often occurs in toponyms, like Qa' Jahran
qabili	A tribesman
qadi	A judge. Often used as an honorific title for members of certain families known for their learning
Qahtanis	The name given by traditional genealogists to Arabs of southern origin. Their ancestor was Qahtan (biblical Joktan), the son of the Prophet Hud. (Some accounts make Qahtan, like Adnan, a descendant of Isma'il.)
Qataban	One of the lesser states of pre-Islamic Yemen, Qataban (or Qitban) probably became independent from Saba at the end of the fifth century BC. At its greatest extent, Qatabanian territory covered the area from south of Marib to the Gulf of Aden; the capital was Timna'/Tamna' in Wadi Bayhan. From the second century BC onwards, rival states began to encroach on Qatabanian domains, and the name finally disappeared from inscriptions in the second century AD.
qatal	Leaves or sprigs of *qat*, plucked usually from the lower branches of the tree
qishr	The husks of the coffee bean, or the drink made from them (often flavoured with ginger)
Qu'aytis	The Qu'ayti Sultanate of Hadramawt was founded in 1858 by Umar b. Awad al-Qu'ayti, a member of a Yafi'i tribe who had enriched himself in the service of the Nizam of Hyderabad. From their capital in al-Mukalla, the Qu'aytis expanded their territory at the expense of the Kathiris, becoming the principal power in Hadramawt. The last Qu'ayti Sultan was deposed following the British withdrawal in 1967.
ramlah/-t	A stretch of sandy ground, a component of names like Ramlat al-Sab'atayn
ra's	Head; headland, as in Ra's Fartak
Rasulids	A medieval dynasty in Yemen named after Muhammad b. Harun al-Rasul, who earned his surname by acting as an envoy (*rasul*) for the Abbasid Caliph. According to Rasulid historians, the family descended from the Yemeni tribe of Ghassan, who had migrated northwards in the pre-Islamic period and had subsequently intermarried with Turkoman tribes. In 1228/9 Muhammad b. Harun's grandson Umar was appointed to govern Yemen by the last Ayyubid sultan of the country; he soon declared independence. Over the next few decades, the Rasulids gained control of the whole of Yemen, and at times their rule extended to Dhofar and even Mecca. The Rasulid sultans both promoted and actively participated in many branches of the arts and sciences; their capitals, Ta'izz and Zabid, became centres of learning. Later Rasulid history was marked by a decline in power and by internecine disputes, and in 1454 the Tahirids took over what remained of their territory.
rawbah	Soured milk from which the fat has been removed to make butter

Glossary

riyal
The currency of Yemen. Also the large Maria Theresa *thaler*, the principal coinage of pre-Republican Yemen and of many neighbouring countries (from the Spanish *real*)

Saba
(Also Sheba, Sabaeans.) The name of a people and of the most prominent state in pre-Islamic Yemen. According to traditional genealogy, it originates with Saba b. Yashjub b. Ya'rub b. Qahtan. The earliest mention of Saba seems to be the biblical account of the Queen of Sheba's visit to the Prophet Solomon in the tenth century BC; names of Sabaean kings appear in Assyrian inscriptions of the eighth and seventh centuries BC. Sabaean rule extended from the capital, Marib, over much the same area as present-day Yemen. In the late fifth century BC various parts of the kingdom began to break away from central authority, but Saba remained a formidable power. From the first century AD onwards the Himyaris claimed the title 'Kings of Saba', and at the end of the third century succeeded in unifying Yemen under their control.

saltah
A stew based on broth and vegetables, topped with fenugreek flour whipped to a froth with water (from a verb meaning 'to dip bread into food')

sambuq
A medium-sized boat

sayl
A flash flood

sayyid
A title given to a male descendant of the Prophet Muhammad. Whether to use *sayyid* or the alternative *sharif* seems, today at least, to be a matter of regional usage

sha'ir
A poet (from the verb meaning 'to sense, to perceive'). Infrequently, according to Lane's *Lexicon*, 'a liar' . . . 'because of the many lies in poetry'

shamlah
A striped blanket or rug of wool

shari'ah
Islamic law, based on the Qur'an and on the Tradition of the Prophet Muhammad

sharif
A title given to a male descendant of the Prophet Muhammad. See also *sayyid*.

sharifah
A title given to a female descendant of the Prophet Muhammad

sharshaf
A women's black outer garment consisting of three pieces – skirt, cape and veil. Introduced in the more recent Ottoman occupation

shaykh
The root meaning is 'an old man'. In general, 'a leader' – from the headman of a small village to the chief of a large tribe; also, occasionally, the head of a traditional trade organization. Some prominent Islamic scholars are also given the title. In Hadramawt, the term is used for descendants of families who had enjoyed high religious status in pre-Islamic times.

shilin
Shilling. A unit of currency in the former South Yemen

Glossary

sitarah	A large multicoloured cotton cloak worn by women
Sufi	Loose term denoting a devotee of various (more or less) mystical brands of Islam
Tahirids	A dynasty named after Tahir b. Ma'udah, the father of its founders. Members of the family had been prominent as governors under the Rasulids, and with that dynasty's final collapse in 1454 the Tahirids assumed power in Lower Yemen and Tihamah, also occupying San'a for limited periods. They suffered heavy defeats at the hands of the Mamluks in 1516, but a Tahirid was still in control of Aden in 1538, when the Ottomans captured the port and began their first take-over of Yemen.
tahish	A monster encountered in lonely places
Umayyads	Dynasty of caliphs who ruled the Muslim world from Damascus, 661–749. Their ancestor was Umayyah, a first cousin of the Prophet Muhammad's grandfather. They were overthrown by the Abbasids, but a cadet branch survived as rulers in Andalucia.
wabr	*Hyrax syriaca*, the biblical coney
wadi	A valley; a (seasonal) river bed
wali	A holy man
waliyyah	A holy woman
wallah	'By God!' An oath asserting the truth of a statement
YAR	The Yemen Arab Republic began life on 26 September 1962, when a republican revolution in San'a overthrew the last Zaydi Imam, al-Badr. The YAR ceased to exist on 22 May 1990, when it merged with the PDRY (People's Democratic Republic of Yemen) to form the unified Republic of Yemen.
zabj	Playful (and at times apparently insulting) banter, often exchanged at the beginning of a *qat* session. Possibly connected to the Classical Arabic *zamaj*, 'to sow discord among others'
zannah	An ankle-length shirt, fitting closely around the torso. Usually white, but other colours become briefly fashionable
ziyarah	A visit. Often used of a visit to the tomb of a holy man or prophet

Bibliography

As this is not an academic book, I have not tried to give a complete list of sources. However, the following list is reasonably full. The intention is threefold: to include titles mentioned in the text, to provide guidelines for further reading, and to list sources which may have escaped the attention of specialists. For the benefit of the Arabists, I have rendered Arabic names and titles in the most commonly accepted form of transliteration, that used in *Arabian Studies*. The arrangement by section is to some extent arbitrary; for example, the Bents' book *Southern Arabia* might as well appear under 'Suquṭrā' as 'Ḥaḍramawt'.

What is and what is not compulsory reading is, of course, a matter of taste. While anything by al-Hamdānī is of prime importance for the earlier period, readers of Arabic might start with al-Qāḍī 'Abdullāh al-Shamāhī's *Al-yaman*, a clear and concise guide to Yemeni history up to the 1960s; the gazetteers of al-Ḥajarī and al-Maqḥafī are both invaluable as works of reference; and the annals of al-Washalī are a fascinating personal record written in an age of change. In English, the books on Ḥaḍramawt by Freya Stark and the Ingramses are – like many of the South Arabian titles published by John Murray – classics; Doreen and Leila Ingrams's *Records of Yemen*, a vast collection of documents on the country, includes some early and hard-to-find accounts by outsiders but has the disadvantage of being neither portable nor affordable. Paul Dresch's *Tribes, History and Government* is scholarly, wide-ranging *and* well-written; Francine Stone's Tihāmah book is both informative and beautiful. Personally, should I ever find myself marooned on Suquṭrā during the season of storms, there are three books I would hope to have with me: Ibn al-Mujāwir's *Tārīkh al-mustabṣir*, a work of sometimes dubious reliability but packed with *sūq* gossip; Serjeant and Lewcock's wonderful book on Ṣan'ā'; and, of course, Hava's *Dictionary*.

General Background

'Abdullāh b. 'Abd al-Wahhāb al-Mujāhid al-Shamāhī, al-Qāḍī, *Al-yaman: al-insān wa 'l-haḍārah*, Beirut, 1406/1985
Aḥmad Jābir 'Afif *et al.* (eds.), *Al-mawsū'ah al-yamaniyyah*, Ṣan'ā', 1412/1992
Bidwell, R.L., *The Two Yemens*, Harlow, 1983
Bradley, Chris, *Discovery Guide to Yemen*, London, 1995
Daum, Werner (ed.), *Yemen: 3000 Years of Art and Civilisation in Arabia Felix*, Innsbruck–Frankfurt/Main [*c.* 1988]

Bibliography

Dresch, Paul, *Tribes, Government and History in Yemen*, Oxford, 1989

al-Ḥajarī *see* Muḥammad b. Aḥmad

al-Hamdānī *see* al-Ḥasan

al-Ḥasan b. Aḥmad al-Hamdānī, *Ṣifat jazīrat al-ʿarab*, ed. Muḥammad b. ʿAlī al-Akwaʿ, Ṣanʿāʾ, 1403/1983

Hava, Revd J.G., *Al-farāʾid al-durriyyah: Arabic-English Dictionary*, Beirut, 1915

Ibn al-Mujāwir *see* Yūsuf

Ibrāhīm Aḥmad al-Maqḥafī, *Muʿjam al-buldān wa 'l-qabāʾil al-yamaniyyah*, Ṣanʿāʾ, 1988

Ingrams, Doreen and Leila (eds.), *Records of Yemen*, 16 vols., Neuchâtel, 1993

Ingrams, Harold, *The Yemen: Imams, Rulers and Revolutions*, London, 1963

Muḥammad b. ʿAbd al-Malik al-Marwānī, *Al-thanāʾ al-ḥasan ʿalā ahl al-yaman*, Beirut, 1411/1990

Muḥammad b. Aḥmad al-Ḥajarī, al-Qāḍī, *Majmūʿ buldān al-yaman wa qabāʾilihā*, 2 vols., ed. Ismāʿīl b. ʿAlī al-Akwaʿ, Ṣanʿāʾ, 1404/1984

Nashwān b. Saʿīd al-Ḥimyarī, *Muntakhabāt fī akhbār al-yaman min kitāb shams al-ʿulūm*, ed. ʿAẓīm al-Dīn Aḥmad, Leiden, 1916, reprinted Ṣanʿāʾ, 1401/1981

Niebuhr, Carsten, *Travels through Arabia*, trans. and abr. R. Heron, Edinburgh, 1792

Serjeant, R.B., and Bidwell, R.L. (eds.), *Arabian Studies*, Cambridge–London, 1974–85

al-Shamāḥī *see* ʿAbdullāh b. ʿAbd al-Wahhāb

Smith, G. Rex, *The Yemens* (World Bibliographical Series), Oxford, 1984

Wilson, Robert T.O., *Gazetteer of Historical North-West Yemen*, Hildesheim, 1989

Yāqūt b. ʿAbdullāh al-Ḥamawī, *Al-buldān al-yamāniyyah ʿind yāqūt al-ḥamawī*, ed. al-Qāḍī Ismāʿīl b. ʿAlī al-Akwaʿ, Beirut–Ṣanʿāʾ, 1408/1988

[Yemeni Centre for Research and Studies], *Dirāsāt yamaniyyah*, Ṣanʿāʾ, 1978–

Yūsuf b. Yaʿqūb Ibn al-Mujāwir, *Ṣifat bilād al-yaman (tārīkh al-mustabṣir)*, ed. O. Löfgren, Leiden, 1951–4, reprinted Beirut, 1407/1986

Pre-Islamic and Early Islamic Yemen

ʿAbdullāh b. ʿAbd al-Wahhāb al-Mujāhid al-Shamāḥī, al-Qāḍī, *Al-hijrāt al-yamaniyyah*, Cairo–Ṣanʿāʾ, 1396/1976

Anon., *The Periplus of the Erythraean Sea*, trans. and ed. G.W.B. Huntingford, London, 1980

Beeston, A.F.L., *A Descriptive Grammar of Epigraphic South Arabian*, London, 1962

——et al. (eds.), *Sabaic Dictionary*, Beirut–Louvain-la-Neuve, 1982

Bidwell, R.L., and Smith, G. Rex (eds.), *Arabian and Islamic Studies* (festschrift for R.B. Serjeant), London, 1982

Doe, Brian, *Southern Arabia*, London, 1971

al-Ḥasan b. Aḥmad al-Hamdānī, *Kitāb al-iklīl*, VIII, ed. Nabīh Amīn Fāris, Princeton, 1940, reprinted Beirut–Ṣanʿāʾ, n.d.

Ḥusayn Aḥmad al-Sayāghī, al-Qāḍī, *Maʿālim al-āthār al-yamaniyyah*, Ṣanʿāʾ, 1980

Ismāʿīl b. ʿAlī al-Akwaʿ, al-Qāḍī, *Barāqish fī kutub al-muʾarrikhīn* (unpublished typescript), Ṣanʿāʾ, 1407/1986

Muḥammad ʿAbd al-Qādir Bā Faqīh, *Fi 'l-ʿarabiyyah al-saʿīdah*, Ṣanʿāʾ, 1408/1987

Muḥammad b. ʿAlī al-Akwaʿ, *Al-yaman al-khaḍrāʾ mahd al-lḥaḍārah*, Ṣanʿāʾ, 1402/1982

Muṭahhar ʿAlī al-Iryānī, *Nuqūsh musnadiyyah*, Ṣanʿāʾ, 1990

Bibliography

Nashwān b. Saʿīd al-Ḥimyarī, *Mulūk ḥimyar wa aqyāl al-yaman*, ed. Ismāʿīl b. Aḥmad al-Jirāfī and ʿAlī b. Ismāʿīl al-Muʾayyad, Beirut, 1978

Pirenne, J., 'Les Sud-Arabes à travers leur Art' (and other articles), *Les Dossiers de l'Archéologie*, no. 35, Dijon, March–April 1979

Pyotrovsky, M., *Malḥamah ʿan al-malik al-ḥimyarī asʿad al-kāmil*, trans. Shāhir Jamāl Āghā, Ṣanʿāʾ, 1404/1984

——*Al-yaman qabl al-islām*, trans. Muḥammad al-Shuʿaybī, Beirut, 1987

Robin, Christian, 'Le Haut Plateau' (and other articles), *Les Dossiers de l'Archéologie*, no. 35, Dijon, March–April 1979

——*Les Hautes-Terres du Nord-Yémen avant l'Islam*, 2 vols., Istanbul, 1982,

——'Les plantes aromatiques que brûlaient les Sabéens', *Saba*, no. 1, n.p., 1994

Serjeant, R.B., *South Arabian Hunt*, London, 1976

Wahb b. Munabbih al-Yamānī, *Kitāb al-tījān fī mulūk ḥimyar*, Hyderabad, 1347/1928, reprinted Ṣanʿāʾ, 1979

Yūsuf Muḥammad ʿAbdullāh, *Awrāq fī tārīkh al-yaman wa āthārihi*, Beirut, 1411/1990

Later Yemen

Aḥmad b. ʿAlwān, al-Shaykh, *Al-futūḥ*, ed. ʿAbd al-ʿAzīz Sulṭān Ṭāhir al-Manṣūb, Ṣanʿāʾ, 1412/1992

ʿAlī b. al-Ḥusayn b. ʿAlī al-Masʿūdī, *Murūj al-dhahab wa maʿādin al-jawhar*, 4 vols., ed. Muḥammad Muḥyī al-Dīn ʿAbd al-Ḥamīd, Beirut, n.d.

ʿAlī b. Muḥammad b. ʿUbaydullāh al-ʿAbbāsī al-ʿAlawī, *Sīrat al-hādī ila 'l-ḥaqq yaḥyā ibn al-ḥusayn*, ed. Suhayl Zakkār, Beirut, 1401/1981

Anon., *Tārīkh al-dawlah al-rasūliyyah fī 'l-yaman*, ed. ʿAbdullāh Muḥammad al-Ḥibshī, Damascus, 1405/1984

Ḥabshūsh *see* Ḥayīm

Harris, Walter, *A Journey through the Yemen*, Edinburgh, 1893, reprinted London, 1985

Ḥayīm b. Yaḥyā b. Sālim al-Futayḥī Ḥabshūsh, 'Ruʾya 'l-yaman', *Ruʾyat al-yaman bayn ḥabshūsh wa halévy*, ed. Sāmiyah Naʿīm Ṣanbar, Ṣanʿāʾ, 1412/1992; the French translation by Samia Naïm-Sanbar [Sāmiyah Naʿīm Ṣanbar], *Yémen*, Arles, 1995

Ḥusayn b. ʿAbdullāh al-ʿAmrī, *The Yemen in the 18th and 19th Centuries: A Political and Intellectual History*, London, 1985

Muḥammad b. Aḥmad al-Nahrawālī al-Makkī, Quṭb al-Dīn, *Al-barq al-yamānī fī 'l-fatḥ al-ʿuthmānī*, ed. Ḥamad al-Jāsir, Beirut, 1407/1986

Muḥammad b. Muḥammad Zabārah, *Nashr al-ʿarf*, Ṣanʿāʾ-Beirut, n.d. (vol. I), 1405/1985 (vols. II and III)

al-Muqaddasī *see* Shams al-Dīn

Playfair, R.L., *History of Arabia Felix*, Bombay, 1859, reprinted St Leonards–Amsterdam, 1970

Pridham, B.R. (ed.), *Contemporary Yemen: Politics and Historical Background*, Beckenham, 1984

Salwā Saʿd Sulaymān al-Ghālibī, *Al-imām al-mutawakkil ʿala 'llāh ismāʿīl ibn al-qāsim*, n.p., 1411/1991

Shams al-Dīn al-Muqaddasī/al-Maqdisī, *Aḥsan al-taqāsīm fī maʿrifat al-aqālīm*, ed. M.J. de Goeje, Leiden, 1967

Bibliography

Varthema, Ludovico di, *Travels*, ed. G.P. Badger, London, 1863

Yaḥyā b. al-Ḥusayn b. al-Qāsim, *Ghāyat al-amānī fī akhbār al-quṭr al-yamānī*, ed. Saʿīd ʿAbd al-Fattāḥ ʿĀshūr, Cairo, 1968

The Twentieth Century

ʿAbdullāh al-Sallāl et al., *Thawrat al-yaman al-dustūriyyah*, Ṣanʿāʾ–Beirut, 1405/1985

ʿAbd al-Wāsiʿ b. Yaḥyā al-Wāsiʿī al-Yamānī, al-Shaykh, *Tārīkh al-yaman (farjat al-humūm wa 'l-ḥazan fī ḥawādith wa tārīkh al-yaman)*, Ṣanʿāʾ, 1990–1

Aḥmad ʿAbd al-Raḥmān al-Muʿallamī, *Kitābah ʿalā ṣarḥ al-waḥdah al-yamaniyyah* [Ṣanʿāʾ, 1994]

Aḥmad Shabrīn al-Qardaʿī and Muqbil Aḥmad al-ʿUmarī/al-ʿAmrī, *Al-shahīd al-shaykh ʿalī nāṣir al-qardaʿī*, Ṣanʿāʾ, 1993

Aḥmad Waṣfī Zakariyyā, *Riḥlatī ila 'l-yaman*, Damascus, 1406/1986

Ameen Rihani [Amīn al-Rayḥānī], *Arabian Peak and Desert*, London, 1930

Fayein, Claudie, *A French Doctor in the Yemen*, London, 1957

Holden, David, *Farewell to Arabia*, London, 1966

Ḥusayn b. Aḥmad al-ʿArashī, al-Qāḍī, *Bulūgh al-marām fī sharḥ misk al-khitām*, ed. and continued by Fr. Anastase-Marie al-Kirmilī, Cairo, 1358/1939, reprinted Beirut, n.d.

Ismāʿīl b. Muḥammad al-Washalī al-Tihāmī al-Ḥasanī, *(Dhayl) nashr al-thanāʾ al-ḥasan*, ed. Muḥammad b. Muḥammad al-Shuʿaybī, Ṣanʿāʾ, 1402/1982

Luce, Margaret, *From Aden to the Gulf*, Salisbury, 1987

Muḥammad b. ʿAlī al-Akwaʿ al-Ḥuwālī, *Ṣafḥah min tārīkh al-yaman wa qiṣṣat ḥayātī*, Damascus, n.d. (pt. I), [Aden], n.d. (pt. II), n.p., 1414/1993 (pt. III)

Muḥammad Ḥasan, *Qalb al-yaman*, Baghdad, 1948

Nazīh Muʾayyad al-ʿAzm, *Riḥlah fī 'l-ʿarabiyyah al-saʿīdah*, Beirut, 1407/1986

Scott, Hugh, *In the High Yemen*, London, 1942

Smiley, David, *Arabian Assignment*, London, 1975

al-Washalī *see* Ismāʿīl

Yaḥyā al-Sudumī, *Suqūṭ al-muʾāmarah*, [Ṣanʿāʾ], 1994–5

Ṣanʿāʾ

ʿAbd al-Raḥmān Yaḥyā al-Ḥaddād, *Ṣanʿāʾ al-qadīmah*, Ṣanʿāʾ, 1992

ʿAbd al-Wāsiʿ b. Yaḥyā al-Wāsiʿī, al-Shaykh, *Al-badr al-muzīl li 'l-ḥazan fī faḍl al-yaman wa maḥāsin ṣanʿāʾ dhāt al-minan*, Cairo, 1345/1927

Aḥmad b. ʿAbdullāh al-Rāzī, *Tārīkh madīnat ṣanʿāʾ*, ed. Ḥusayn b. ʿAbdullāh al-ʿAmrī and ʿAbd al-Jabbār Zakkār, Damascus, 1394/1974

ʿAlī b. ʿAbdullāh b. al-Qāsim b. al-Muʾayyad bi 'llāh, al-Sayyid Jamāl al-Dīn, *Waṣf ṣanʿāʾ*, ed. ʿAbdullāh Muḥammad al-Ḥibshī, Ṣanʿāʾ, 1993, and English translation by Tim Mackintosh-Smith, *City of Divine and Earthly Joys* (forthcoming)

Anon., *Ṣafaḥāt majhūlah min tārīkh al-yaman*, ed. al-Qāḍī Ḥusayn b. Aḥmad al-Sayāghī, Ṣanʿāʾ, 1404/1984

Isḥāq b. Yaḥyā b. Jarīr al-Ṭabarī al-Ṣanʿānī, *Tārīkh ṣanʿāʾ*, ed. ʿAbdullāh Muḥammad al-Ḥibshī, Ṣanʿāʾ, n.d.

Bibliography

Muḥammad b. ʿAbd al-Malik al-Marwanī, *Al-wajīz fī tārīkh bināyat masājid ṣanʿāʾ*, Ṣanʿāʾ, 1408/1988

Muḥammad ʿAbduh Ghānim, *Shiʿr al-ghināʾ al-ṣanʿānī*, Beirut, 1987

Muḥammad b. Aḥmad al-Ḥajarī, al-Ḥājj, *Masājid ṣanʿāʾ*, Ṣanʿāʾ, 1361/1942, reprinted Ṣanʿāʾ–Beirut, 1397/1977

al-Rāzī *see* Aḥmad

Serjeant, R.B., and Lewcock, Ronald, *Ṣanʿāʾ: An Arabian Islamic City*, London, 1983

al-Wāsiʿī *see* ʿAbd al-Wāsiʿ

Watson, Janet C.E., *A Syntax of Ṣanʿānī Arabic*, Wiesbaden, 1993

Zayd b. ʿAlī ʿInān, *Al-lahjah al-yamāniyyah fī ʾl-nukat wa ʾl-amthāl al-ṣanʿāniyyah*, [Cairo?], 1400/1980

Qāt

ʿAbd al-Malik ʿAlwān al-Maqramī, *Al-qāt bayn al-siyāsah wa ʿilm al-ijtimāʿ*, Beirut-Ṣanʿāʾ, 1407/1987

Aḥmad b. Muḥammad al-Muʿallamī, ʿTarwīḥ al-awqāt fī ʾl-munāẓarah bayn al-qahwah wa ʾl-qāt', in Aḥmad ʿAbd al-Raḥmān al-Muʿallamī, *Al-qāt fī ʾl-adab al-yamanī wa ʾl-fiqh al-islāmī*, Beirut, 1988

Kennedy, John G., *The Flower of Paradise*, Dordrecht, 1987

Weir, Shelagh, *Qat in Yemen*, London, 1985

[Yemeni Centre for Research and Studies], *Al-qāt fī ḥayāt al-yaman wa ʾl-yamāniyyīn*, Ṣanʿāʾ–Beirut, 1981–2

Aden

ʿAbdullāh al-Ṭayyib b. ʿAbdullāh b. Aḥmad Abī Makhramah [Bā Makhramah], *Tārīkh thaghr ʿadan*, ed. Oscar Löfgren, Uppsala–Leiden, 1950, reprinted Beirut, 1407/1986

[Aden Port Trust], *Port of Aden Annual*, Aden, 1960–1, 1961–2, 1963–4 (and other dates)

Allen, Charles, *The Savage Wars of Peace: Soldiers' Voices, 1945–89*, London, 1990

Bā Makhramah *see* ʿAbdullāh

Belhaven, The Master of [Hamilton, R.A.B.], *The Kingdom of Melchior*, London, 1949

Foster, Donald, *Landscape with Arabs*, Brighton–London, 1969

Gavin, R.J., *Aden under British Rule, 1839–1967*, London, 1975

[Guides and Handbooks of Africa Publishing Company], *Welcome to Aden: A Comprehensive Guidebook*, Nairobi, 1963

Halliday, Fred, *Revolution and Foreign Policy: The Case of South Yemen, 1967–1987*, Cambridge, 1990

Ḥasan Ṣāliḥ Shihāb, *ʿAdan furḍat al-yaman*, Ṣanʿāʾ, 1410/1990

Hunter, F.M., *Account of the British Settlement of Aden in Arabia*, London, 1877, reprinted London, 1968

Johnston, Charles, *The View from Steamer Point*, London, 1964

Knox-Mawer, June, *The Sultans Came to Tea*, London, 1961

Kour, Z.H., *The History of Aden 1839–72*, London, 1981

Bibliography

Ledger, David, *Shifting Sands: The British in South Arabia*, London, 1983
Lunt, James, *The Barren Rocks of Aden*, London, 1966
Morris, James [Jan], *Farewell the Trumpets*, London, 1978
[PDRY Ministry of Culture], *Aden's Bloody Monday*, Aden, 1986
Stookey, Robert, *South Yemen: A Marxist Republic in Arabia*, Boulder, 1982
Trevaskis, Kennedy, *Shades of Amber*, London, 1968
Waterfield, Gordon, *Sultans of Aden*, London, 1968

Ḥaḍramawt

Abdalla ['Abdullāh] S. Bujra, *The Politics of Stratification*, Oxford, 1971
'Abd al-Qādir Muḥammad al-Ṣabbān, *Ziyārāt wa 'ādāt* (duplicated typescript issued by the Say'ūn Department of Culture and Tourism), Say'ūn, n.d.
Allfree, P.S., *Hawks of the Hadhramaut*, London, 1967
Bent, Theodore [and Mabel], *Southern Arabia*, London, 1900
Bujra *see* Abdalla
Bulliet, Richard W., *The Camel and the Wheel*, New York, 1980
Hoek, Eva, *Doctor Amongst the Bedouins*, trans. Mervyn Savill, London, 1962
Ingrams, Doreen, *A Time in Arabia*, London, 1970
Ingrams, Harold, *Arabia and the Isles*, London, 1966
Johnstone, T.M., 'Knots and Curses', *Arabian Studies*, III, Cambridge–London, 1976
Lewcock, Ronald, *Wādī Ḥaḍramawt and the Walled City of Shibām*, Paris, 1986
Meulen, Daniel van der, *Aden to the Hadhramaut*, London, 1947
al-Ṣabbān *see* 'Abd al-Qādir
Saqqāf 'Alī al-Kāff, *Ḥaḍramawt 'ibr arba'at 'ashar qarn*, Beirut, 1410/1990
Serjeant, R. B., *The Portuguese off the South Arabian Coast*, Oxford, 1963, reprinted Beirut, 1974
——*Studies in Arabian History and Civilisation*, London, 1981
Stark, Freya, *The Southern Gates of Arabia*, London, 1936
——*A Winter in Arabia*, London, 1941
[Yemeni-Soviet Archaeological Mission], *Natā'ij a'māl al-ba'thah li 'ām 1984*, trans. 'Abd al-'Azīz Ja'far Bin 'Aqīl and Muḥammad Aḥmad Bā Makhramah, Say'ūn, 1984

Suquṭrā

Beckingham, C.F., 'Some Notes on the History of Socotra', *Arabian and Islamic Studies* (festschrift for R.B. Serjeant), ed. R.L. Bidwell and G. Rex Smith, London, 1982
Botting, Douglas, *The Island of Dragon's Blood*, London, 1958
Doe, Brian, *Socotra: Island of Tranquillity*, London, 1992
Ḥamzah 'Alī Luqmān, *Tārīkh al-juzur al-yamaniyyah*, Beirut, 1972
Naumkin, Vitaly V., *Island of the Phoenix: An Ethnographic Study of the People of Socotra*, Reading, 1993
Ogilvie-Grant, W.R., *The Natural History of Sokotra and Abd al-Kuri*, Liverpool, 1903
Schweinfurth, G., 'Recollections of a Voyage to Socotra by George Schweinfurth, 1881', trans. E.A.F. Redl, Bombay, 1897, reprinted in *Records of Yemen*, vol. IV, ed. D. and L. Ingrams, Neuchâtel, 1993

Simeone-Senelle, Marie-Claude, 'Suquṭrā: Parfums, Sucs et Résines', *Saba*, no. 2, n.p., 1994

[University of Aden Research Programme, Faculty of Education], *Socotra Island* (in English and Arabic), Aden, 1982

Wellsted, J.R., 'Survey of Socotra' (India Office Records MS), facsimile in *Records of Yemen*, vol. I, ed. D. and L. Ingrams, Neuchâtel, 1993

Miscellaneous

ʿAbdullāh al-Baraddūnī, *Al-thaqāfah al-shaʿbiyyah: tajārib wa aqāwīl yamaniyyah*, Cairo, 1988

———*Funūn al-adab al-shaʿbī fi 'l-yaman*, Damascus, 1995

ʿAbdullāh Muḥammad al-Ḥibshī, *Al-ṣūfiyyah wa 'l-fuqahāʾ fi 'l-yaman*, Ṣanʿāʾ, 1396/1976

———(ed.) *Majmūʿ al-maqāmāt al-yamaniyyah*, Ṣanʿāʾ, 1407/1987

[Admiralty Office, Naval Intelligence Department], *A Handbook of Arabia*, 2 vols., London, 1916–17

Adra *see* Najwa

Ahmed al-Hubaishi [Aḥmad al-Ḥubayshī] and Müller-Hohenstein, Klaus, *An Introduction to the Vegetation of Yemen*, Eschborn, 1984

ʿAlī b. Zāyid, *Aḥkām ʿalī b. zāyid*, compiled by Anatoly Agarichev, Beirut–Ṣanʿāʾ, 1986

al-Baraddūnī *see* ʿAbdullāh al-Baraddūnī

Caton, Steven C., *'Peaks of Yemen I Summon': Poetry as Cultural Practice in a North Yemeni Tribe*, Berkeley–Los Angeles–London, 1990

Costa, Paolo, *Yemen Land of Builders*, London, 1977

Ḥamzah ʿAlī Luqmān, *Asāṭīr min tārīkh al-yaman*, Beirut–Ṣanʿāʾ, n.d.

Hansen, Eric, *Motoring with Mohammed: Journeys to Yemen and the Red Sea*, Boston, 1991

Ḥasan Ṣāliḥ Shihāb, *Aḍwāʾ ʿalā tārīkh al-yaman al-baḥrī*, Beirut, 1981

al-Hubaishi *see* Ahmed

Ismāʿīl b. ʿAlī al-Akwaʿ, al-Qāḍī, *Al-amthāl al-yamāniyyah*, 2 vols., Beirut–Ṣanʿāʾ, 1984

Makhlouf, Carla, *Changing Veils: Women and Modernisation in North Yemen*, London, 1979

Muḥammad Sharaf al-Dīn, *Islam and Romantic Orientalism*, London, 1994

Najwa Adra, *Qabyalah: The Tribal Concept in the Central Highlands of the Y.A.R.* (unpublished Ph.D. thesis), Philadelphia, 1982

Qāʾid Nuʿmān al-Sharjabī, *Al-sharāʾiḥ al-ijtimāʿiyyah al-taqlīdiyyah fi 'l-mujtamaʿ al-yamanī*, Beirut–Ṣanʿāʾ, 1986

Stone, Francine (ed.), *Studies on the Tihāmah*, Harlow, 1985

Varanda, Fernando, *Art of Building in Yemen*, London, 1981

Varisco, Daniel, 'Dirāsah fi 'l-taqwīm al-zirāʿī al-yamanī', *Al-maʾthūrāt al-shaʿbiyyah*, no. 16, al-Dawḥah, 1989

Index

Index

Index